A hard book to put down.
Phil Parshall, SIM missionary to the Sons of Ishmael

This book can help build our faith and give us a spirit of expectation for the future.
Dr George Verwer, Founder and former International Director, Operation Mobilisation

Through the life and example of Greg and his wife Sally, we get a real opportunity to see how to face these challenges head on, trusting that no Godly obedience will fail to bring about Godly results.
And so, I highly commend this book to you. It's an incredible story…
As you read this book, rejoice with us that God is at work through his people in the Muslim world. And may you be open to how the Lord is calling you to respond.
Tim Lewis, International Director, Frontiers

Greg Livingstone's life is a demonstration of what God will do with a person who revels in His word, His love, believes His promises and is surrendered to anything God wants regardless of the price to be paid. He is a giant in the field of missions…
This autobiography is a treasure trove of God at work and should be required reading for any prospective missionary. It's an honor to stand up and call him blessed and my beloved friend in Christ.
Nate Mirza, International Student Ministry Senior Staff, The Navigators

God has a sense of humor. He used Greg Livingstone against all odds to impact the world for Christ. Read this book and you'll get a sense of how God can use you too.
Bob Sjogren, President, UnveilinGLORY, Virginia, USA

I've "blurbed" hundreds of books over the years, but I don't think I've enjoyed any of them as much as this one. I just couldn't put it down… What an adventure God led Greg and Sally through! Here it is superbly written… This book… made me praise God for the great evidences of His working today.
Dr John Frame, Professor of Systematic Theology and Philosophy, Reformed Theological Seminary, Orlando, Florida, USA

The indomitable journey from disadvantaged, but radical, young follower of Jesus to his rightful place as an iconic pioneer in global missions… one of missions' most challenging and engaging life stories.
Paul McKaughan, Ambassador at Large, Missio Nexus

Greg Livingstone, as a mission recruiter without parallel, recruited two of our children to missions. My wife and I are ever grateful that God used this man of God to open great doors of ministry to them – ministries that are still evolving.
Dr Don McCurry, Founder and Former Director, Zwemer Institute of Muslim Studies and Author of *Healing the Broken Family of Abraham: New Life for Muslims*

Greg Livingstone is a modern-day, globetrotting apostle… His passion for unreached and unengaged peoples is infectious… Read his story and let God expand your heart and fill you with fresh gospel courage.

Jay Childs, Senior Pastor, The Evangelical Free Church, Crystal Lake, Illinois, USA

Greg Livingstone lets us see his hopes and choices – even his prayers – evoking shock and incredulity from certain peers. Frankly, Greg invites us all to risk that same gamut of emotion. The end result is a bracing encounter with an utterly real, high-impact, sham-free life story that a mere book can barely contain!

Don Richardson, Missiologist and Author of *Peace Child*, *Eternity in Their Hearts*, *Heaven Wins*, and other books

With deep humility and honest transparency Dr Livingstone takes us on a journey covering over seven decades of his life. It is a record of God's faithfulness to him… This book is hard to put down for its captivating style and highly informative content. It is a must-read for everyone engaged in Muslim work.

Georges Houssney, President, Horizons International

Greg's telling of his life story is transparent, humorous, and always focused on the remarkable favour of the God who picked him up and chose to use him. I found the story so absorbing that I had to read it from cover to cover without stopping – and I hope that you will do the same.

Gordon Dalzell, Trainer, Living Leadership UK and Former Senior Pastor at Rock Baptist Church, Cambridge, UK

In his famously irrepressible and slightly irreverent way, Greg reveals the heart of a mission leader sold out to God's purposes.

David Lundy, Development Director, Dalit Freedom Network Canada

You've Got Libya is a witty, funny, challenging, and inspiring read… I couldn't put it down. I encourage you to pick it up.

Steve Moore, President, Missio Nexus

This compelling account reminds us that God takes broken lives and uses them in extraordinary ways for his purposes… May his story inspire many more to give up small ambitions, and cause faith to rise for the task yet to complete.

Phil Goodchild, British Director, Frontiers

You've Got Libya is a must-read for anyone following the way of Jesus into the Muslim world. Greg is my friend and in many ways my mentor – I recommend him as much as the book!

Carl Medearis, Author of *Muslims, Christians and Jesus* and *Speaking of Jesus*

You've Got Libya *is a riveting read. Mission biographies are often challenging but Greg and Sally Livingstone's story is irresistible. The superb writing sparkles with warmth and humour… despite setbacks and disappointments, you get the feeling here that it would have been fun to be on the Livingstone team. These deeply personal pages reveal Greg's pioneering passion for sharing God's heartbeat in today's complex Muslim world… biography at its very best!*
Peter Conlan, OM World Partner

There is something awe-inspiring about the way God selects and anoints his servants for world-changing assignments… Greg's personal story and the ripple effect of his radical faith continue to challenge and stir the global church.
Steve Richardson, President, Pioneers-USA

From a castaway child from birth living in five foster homes until becoming a Christian at age sixteen, this account is an "open book" into the life of Greg Livingstone, who became the founder and leader of Frontiers… Greg's autobiography reveals his humility and dependence on Jesus Christ, and it is laced with humor.
John E. Kyle, Wycliffe Bible Translators

This is the story of a man with true grit. The dire obstacles Greg endured while growing up brought me to tears. Was ever success less likely, was ever a jar more earthen, or the power of God more displayed than in Greg Livingstone's life? Was ever a man assigned a more far-fetched dream – "You've got Libya!" – than Greg at the age of 20? Did ever a romantic fall more in love with a young woman than when Greg met Sally? And did ever a band of nobodies believe so daringly that nothing is impossible with God?
Bob Blincoe, PhD, US Director, Frontiers

Living up to his missionary namesake, Livingstone reveals what it means to be sold out to Jesus and His mandate to "go where the church isn't." Read this book to see what God has done with Greg and Sally, who risked it all for the kingdom.
George Carey, Director of Evangelical Presbyterian Church/World Outreach, USA

Writting in a conversational style, in You've Got Libya *Greg is open and honest about his strengths and especially his weaknesses. This is an enjoyable, challenging, and inspiring read.*
Jeffrey Jeremiah, Stated Clerk, Evangelical Presbyterian Church

The story of a leader and inspirer… Greg's story will continue to inspire and produce new leaders who will see the success of the gospel for which Greg longs. This book is fast-moving, funny, challenging and a great read.
Bryan Knell, Founding Leader, Christian Responses to Islam in Britain

Greg Livingstone is a born writer with a wealth of vital life experience worth writing about. This book is a racy read that grabs you by the throat and pulls you along on an exhilarating ride into the missionary heart of God.

Steve Bell, Author, Trainer, and National Director of Interserve in England & Wales

A wonderfully inspiring read of God's grace unfolding through the years.

David Milligan, Regional Leader, Pioneers

It was not a promising start – a Jewish father (Greg never met) and a bar-room girl for a mother – followed by many foster homes… The accounts include a Who's Who of mission leaders, and what was happening behind the scenes – warts and all – told in a way that leaves the reader switching between bending over in laughter and bending over in prayer.

J. Dudley Woodberry, Dean Emeritus and Senior Professor of Islamic Studies, School of Intercultural Studies, Fuller Theological Seminary, Pasadena, California, USA

This is a down-to-earth book of disarmingly honest (warts and all), funny, and riveting stories of a radical, single-minded couple, following Jesus, with a passion for the Muslim world.

Jim Green, Senior Associate Production and Strategy, Executive Director Emeritus, The JESUS Film Project

This deeply inspiring narrative of Greg's lifelong call to Muslim peoples will challenge you, beckon you, and make you laugh. With wry wit, he points us toward his Holy Spirit-inspired heartbeat: Go to Muslim peoples who have never heard the story of Jesus.

Dr Mark Hausfeld, International Director, Global Initiative: Reaching Muslim Peoples, Assemblies of God World Missions

Written in a highly readable style, with plenty of humour and devastating honesty about mistakes and failures, You've Got Libya is an inside story told by someone who was involved first in the birthing of Operation Mobilisation, then in the leadership of the North Africa Mission and later in the formation of Frontiers… It provides a unique insight into the ways that evangelical approaches to mission among Muslims have developed in the last forty years… And this account of his life in his own words is sure to be an inspiration and a wake-up call to many.

Colin Chapman, Formerly Lecturer in Islamic Studies, Near East School of Theology, Beirut, Lebanon; Author of *Cross and Crescent: Responding to the Challenges of Islam* and *Whose Promised Land?*

You've Got Libya

A life serving the Muslim world

Greg Livingstone

Kregel
Publications

Original edition published in English under the title You've Got Libya by Lion
Hudson IP Ltd, Oxford, England.

This edition copyright © 2014 Lion Hudson IP Ltd

Published by Kregel Publications
2450 Oak Industrial Dr. NE
Grand Rapids, MI 49505
www.kregel.com

ISBN 978-0-8254-4612-2

First edition 2014

Acknowledgments
Scripture quotations taken from the Holy Bible, New International Version,
copyright © 1973, 1978, 1984 International Bible Society. Used by permission of
Hodder & Stoughton, a member of the Hodder Headline Group. All rights reserved.
"NIV" is a trademark of International Bible Society. UK trademark number 1448790.
Scripture quotations marked "NASB" are taken from the New American Standard
Bible®, Copyright © 1960, 1962, 1963, 1968, 1971, 1972, 1973, 1975, 1977, 1995 by
The Lockman Foundation. Used by permission.
Scripture quotations marked "NET" used by permission. Quotations designated
(NET) are from the NET Bible® copyright ©1996-2006 by Biblical Studies Press,
L.L.C. http://bible.org All rights reserved.
Scripture quotations marked "RSV" are from The Revised Standard Version of the
Bible copyright © 1346, 1952 and 1971 by the Division of Christian Education of the
National Council of Churches in the USA. Used by permission. All Rights Reserved.
p. 314: Extract from "Never Once". Words & Music by Tim Wanstall, Matt Redman
& Jason Ingram © Copyright 2011 Chrysalis Music Limited – a BMG Chrysalis
Company. All Rights Reserved. International Copyright Secured. Used by permission
of Music Sales Limited, Intergrity Music and Sony/ATV Music Publishing.

A catalogue record for this book is available from the British Library

Printed in the United States

Although it may be assumed that dedicating a book to one's wife is simply the thing to do, there is, in fact, no human on earth or in heaven who has meant more to me. She kept me from drifting to the left or to the right. She hung in with me when others would have quit.

She patiently set up home twenty-seven times!... from Pasadena to Kuala Lumpur, Beirut to Toronto, Uttar Pradesh to Brussels, Philadelphia to Buckinghamshire... and more. My feminine pioneer never stopped believing in me.

I'll be thanking you, Sally, through all eternity!

Contents

Foreword

by Phil Parshall
SIM missionary to the Sons of Ishmael

One of my early remembrances of Greg is in the 1970s when we were at a conference on Islam together. We were standing apart from the crowd and I was holding forth, criticizing one of the leaders of the consultation. Suddenly Greg looked over my shoulder, saw the person who was the object of my slander, and said, "Oh, Bob, come join us. Phil has something he wants to share with you." Needless to say, I was greatly embarrassed.

That was vintage Greg. Transparency and forthrightness are his hallmark. How does a missionary statesman get away with such a lifestyle of calling it like he sees it? Firstly, he is harder on himself than on others; secondly, he surrounds his criticism with a warm, concerned, caring personality; and thirdly, he does it with a smile.

I was one of Greg's detractors in the early 1980s. In reality, why did Greg want to start a *new* mission? Did I see evidence of pride in his insistence that mission to Muslims be done the Livingstonian way? Did evangelicalism need another group competing for the small pool of candidates willing to enter one of the most dangerous, difficult, and least rewarding ministries on the planet? And then there was the issue of stick-to-itiveness. Greg seemed to be a high-powered man always on the move. I observed no real gift of administration in him.

Fortunately for the Muslim world, Greg recognized his limitations and from the start sought to surround himself with Aarons who could cover for his deficiencies. In this he has been eminently successful. Thus Greg was the ever-moving *force* that swept over the landscape challenging, cajoling, and shaming people into giving their body and soul for the cause of seeing Muslims enter the kingdom. Following closely behind was the army of consolidators, the people without whom Greg would have been an abysmal failure in pioneering a new Frontier for Christ.

For me, godly character is the all-important issue for Christian leadership. Too often executives are seduced by power, sex, and financial gain. In Greg and Sally I have observed models of absolute commitment to engage in the battle to overcome temptations in these three areas.

Their journey has been long and arduous – always a new mountain to climb or another dark valley to traverse. For decades the battle of Sally's depression has sought to bring total defeat into the lives of this wonderful, yet vulnerable, couple. I could only stand amazed at how Greg would travel two and a half hours a day on California freeways to visit and comfort his beloved in the hospital. And that, after hours of struggling with the hassles of launching and shepherding a newborn mission.

Greg and Sally... I salute you both as humble, gracious, God-seeking servants of the Lamb. All who read this memoir will definitely concur! In places you will read with moistened eyes; in other paragraphs your heart will swell with praise and thanksgiving at all God has accomplished through his two obedient children. It's a hard book to put down.

Foreword

by Dr George Verwer
Founder and former International Director,
Operation Mobilisation

As I write this foreword, I am in the midst of a conference near Atlanta where the whole focus is the Muslim world. Of course Greg has been mentioned. With Sally, his name is a household term among those who have this vision and passion. Before he helped found Frontiers (and what a fantastic ministry that is), he worked with us in OM – and that amazing bit of history will be found in this book.

The Muslim world and places like Libya represent by far the largest bloc of peoples unreached with the gospel message. Everyone who believes the Bible should be involved in doing something about this. Compared with when I first got involved with Muslims with Greg in India in 1964, we have seen some major breakthroughs in the Muslim world. There are now dozens of people groups like the Berbers of Algeria where Muslims in good numbers are turning to Jesus. This is because of people like Greg and Sally. They helped set the pace and began to change the course of history, but it's our prayer that this book will help get more people involved.

That is one of the reasons I would urge you to read this book with an open heart and mind. I would urge you to get more than one copy so that you can pass it on to someone else. I am planning to buy many hundreds to give to friends and Christian leaders.

This book can help build our faith and give us a spirit of expectation for the future. Today, people like Greg are often aborted before birth, which must be one of the greatest crimes in the history of humanity. I pray this book will be used to turn people away from abortion and to look for other alternatives like adoption. Then we might get a few more Greg Livingstones coming our way.

In their senior years, Greg and Sally seem as committed and active as ever – an example for all of us. God bless them and God bless this book.

Foreword

by Tim Lewis
International Director, Frontiers

Greg and I have served alongside one another over the last three decades. We've faced many challenges together, some of which you'll read about in this book. Through it all, Greg has consistently loved me, challenged me, inspired me, prayed for me, and pointed me toward Jesus. He's also often made me laugh. I hope that in turn I've been able to do that for him.

One thing we have regularly discussed is how humbling it has been for us to see many hundreds of "ordinary" men and women – from many nations and many organizations – sacrificing their all for the call of God in some of the hardest places on earth. In so many ways, this is their story too. Not all of this makes for easy reading. But then, God never said obedience would be easy. In fact he tells us to expect challenges. Through the life and example of Greg and his wife Sally, we get a real opportunity to see how to face these challenges head on, trusting that no Godly obedience will fail to bring about Godly results.

And so, I highly commend this book to you. It's an incredible story, even though it's not a story that Greg was eager to write. What motivates Greg is not having people know about him, or look up to him. Rather what motivates him is the Great Commission. At an age when many have already retired, Greg is still giving his all to see the church of Jesus love Muslims the way Jesus does.

More Muslims have come to faith in Jesus during our lifetime than in the rest of history combined. Greg's story is a significant part of that bigger picture. As you read this book, rejoice with us that God is at work through his people in the Muslim world. And may you be open to how the Lord is calling you to respond.

Preface

"Butterflies" in my stomach hardly describes the way I felt as I was about to go on stage in front of 17,000 university students at the mission conference in Urbana in 1984. I was the youngest of four speakers on a panel – and the most scared. My fellow panelists – Ralph Winter, Sam Wilson, and Warren Webster – were all mission icons.

What could I say that wouldn't turn off the students? Hoping that my handshake with Billy Graham a few minutes earlier had transferred some anointing, all I could say was what I've told countless other audiences since then: "I was once a normal person."

Well, I was normal in the sense that my world was comprised of whatever was on my own agenda. I did what I had to do to stay out of trouble. Like many, I was focused on how to make friends and influence people in the direction of accomplishing whatever was on my plate at the time. Not a bad chap, really. Just, well… normal.

I assumed that the thing to do was to get the educational badges, meet the right people, pursue a career, have a wife and children, and live in a pleasant suburb in America with friendly neighbors.

Some people desire to travel and see the world. That hadn't occurred to me. For one thing, spicy food isn't a friend of my palate.

Generally, I didn't like people very much. My mother had taught me: "Get them before they get you." "Haughty" would have described me well. I had no experience of the kind of friends the Bible alludes to – people who were devoted, lay-down-their-lives-for-others, band-of-brothers types. I could hardly imagine that such persons existed outside of novels.

Having never lived with a father, uncle, or brothers, I wasn't very practical. I knew I needed to find a career that utilized my talking, not my hands. To be like Perry Mason, the television lawyer of my childhood, was my dream. The plan was to manipulate my way into Princeton University and then into an equally prestigious law school.

My driving force was to be Somebody, to gain respect from significant others – maybe even to get my face on the cover of *Time* magazine. Even years later, after I switched my allegiance from my own will to God's (at least as much as I knew how), my quest for recognition didn't lessen all that much. I simply switched my aspiration from being on the cover of *Time* to the cover of *Christianity Today*.

But that comes later in the story...

It's embarrassing to admit the more idiotic aspects of my pilgrimage. Over the years, our gracious Father revealed some of the hidden faults that unknowingly ruled over me (as described in Psalm 19:7–14). I've tried not to hide those faults in the pages that follow. I hope that my story offers hope that, in spite of our massive immaturity, God uses weak, self-absorbed people who strive to please him.

No one knew my off-putting, inconsistent manners more clearly than my fifth foster mother, Ruth Ringle. After hearing me speak to 2,500 people, she blurted out, "My, oh my! If the Lord can use Greg, he can use anybody." A more true word was never spoken.

Today, I feel so privileged. My heavenly Father is so hugely magnificent that he could even use me, a kid from a terribly dysfunctional non-family, with all the unenviable accompanying idiosyncrasies and emotional damage.

In case I was ever tempted to think I am a big deal, the Lord once sent me a humbling dream. I was on a stage in heaven, standing shoulder to shoulder with many others. We were looking out at the multitude that no man could number. I realized the Lord himself was speaking about me! He was talking about some of the things described in this book. I was feeling great!

Then I turned to a man next to me, who was a head shorter than me and evidently from another era. I asked him, "What happened to you, brother?"

"Oh," he replied, rather nonchalantly, "I was burned at the stake."

Three truths

I'm convinced of three truths:

- Roughly 90 percent of God's people settle for less than what he wants to do through their lives.

- God is looking for availability and perseverance as Elisabeth Elliot (quoting Nietzsche) called "a long obedience in the same direction."

- It surely puts a smile on God's face when we take his promises at face value and act on them. Sooner or later, we realize that he uses weak people who hunger and thirst to be used by him – usually when we keep ourselves accountable to wise, godly overseers. No matter where you come from, no matter how damaged and scarred you are, he will use you – if you want to be used and if you don't take your hand off the plow.

Disclaimer

Between my lost memory and my lost journals, I've lost a few pieces of my story. The chronology is far from exact. (Is it true that at my age, ten thousand brain cells die daily?) Besides, how long can a guy prattle on about himself? I'd prefer to write more about the people God has engineered into my life, but the names of many who have been a very significant part of my story are omitted. That's partly because of my failing memory, and it's partly because some of them don't want to be identified. Many of our closest colleagues are still proclaiming the message of Jesus in places where they would prefer to be expelled because of their *own* mistakes (or no one's) – not for being named in a book. Still, I regret I can't honor them by name. If you're one of those colleagues, or if you are one of our Father's servants who was an instrument of healing in my life, may you be greatly honored in heaven.

Greg Livingstone

I want to know Christ and the power of his resurrection and the fellowship of sharing in his sufferings, becoming like him in his death, and so, somehow, to attain to the resurrection from the dead.

Philippians 3:10–11

CHAPTER 1

Inauspicious Beginning

Perhaps my father, Forrest Theodore Foss, was feeling rebellious toward his over-controlling Jewish mother in Boston, back in September 1939. A year out of Harvard, he might have found that his job as a social researcher for the city didn't hold any excitement. It had been fun organizing Harvard students into various social clubs, but now what?

I'm guessing that my grandfather Foss had come to America with the thousands of other *Fiddler on the Roof*-type Jewish peasants escaping the tsar. Our family name might have originally been Fostoyevsky. It wouldn't be unlikely that their name got the typical abbreviation, chopped at Ellis Island to a good old 'merican length: Foss.

In 1939, Forrest heard stories escaping from Hitler's Germany that his fellow Jews were being persecuted once again. Should he join the Army? President Roosevelt insisted it wasn't America's war. It wasn't as if Forrest was a save-the-world type anyway.

Still, a Harvard graduate was supposed to *be* somebody, not simply go to an office every day and come home to his mother in the evenings. Okay, she wouldn't approve of his nightclubbing, especially since he had no siblings to keep an eye out for him in those dens of iniquity. Yet I suppose there was enough man in Foss to find an acceptable excuse to meet some sexy girls.

He was fascinated with Laura. How could this tiny, pretty, four-foot-ten-inch thing be so witty? She was confident, fun-loving, and seductive, not to mention the fact that her clothes revealed a good deal of her legs and well-endowed bosom. She never let it come up in their banter that she had barely gotten through high school. Her idea of study was reading the horoscope and the entertainment section of the *Boston Herald*.

Of course, there was no doubt that his mother, Natalie, would choose an appropriate Jewish girl for Forrest. Naomi Stevenson seemed suitable; after all, her brother was a professor at Boston University. So when Forrest meekly revealed to his mother that Laura, the Gentile showgirl, was pregnant, the conversation was over! Never mind that she was the daughter of a Swedish engineer who worked for the inventor Thomas Edison and his son Charles. To Natalie Foss, Laura Berge was nothing but a slut.

No one wanted the baby. Not the mother. Not the father. Not either set of grandparents. Well, actually, there was One who wanted the baby. That One declared: "Before I formed you in the womb I knew you, before you were born I set you apart; I appointed you as a prophet to the nations" (Jeremiah 1:5).

Abortions were not easily accessible in 1939, especially in Catholic-dominated Boston. In any case, Laura was not going to risk one of those back-alley operations. There was no choice but to have the baby.

Not one to easily let an adversary off the hook, Laura let Forrest know in no uncertain terms that if he didn't arrange for her to deliver at the Richardson House in Brookline (where the Roosevelt babies were born), she would be most happy to let the world know whose baby she was carrying.

The extortion technique worked. Not only did Laura get the best hospital with all the bills paid, she likely got some extra money to help her leave town.

The baby – Gregory Martindale Foss – was born on 3 May 1940, just a few days before Hitler unleashed his blitz on Europe. (There is no connection as far as I'm aware!)

Why my mother named me Gregory, I'll never know. It was too early to be after Gregory Peck, and she certainly wouldn't have honored any of the sixteen popes named Gregory, even if she had known church history. But I've looked it up in the Greek: Gregory means either "warrior" or "watchman." I'd like to think that Jeremiah 1:5 ("before you were born I set you apart") refers even to our naming.

Martindale was my mother's middle name as well as the maiden name of her mother. It was passed on to me. Laura liked to claim that her mother was a "Daughter of the American Revolution." She was perfectly convinced of the truth of the statement, but that claim was as fictitious as the story that her mother's mother was the Scarlett O'Hara-like wife of a wealthy Southern plantation owner. She also claimed that I was a descendant of "Lighthorse" Harry Lee, an early American patriot, and thus related to Robert E.

Lee. Disappointingly, our Harry Lee was probably only a blacksmith.

Never a slave to truth, my mother managed to convince the hospital that she was married and that I was the legitimate son of Forrest Foss from Harvard. She even signed his name to the application for my birth certificate, thereby giving me his last name!

Probably at his mother's insistence, Forrest married Naomi Stevenson. I wonder why he quickly joined the Army. As a "ninety-day wonder" trained in the get-them-to-the-war-in-a-hurry Officer Candidate School, he was commissioned as a Second Lieutenant in the 349th Regiment of the 88th Infantry Division. Four years later, in June 1944, he was killed in Italy and posthumously awarded the Purple Heart medal.

In 1969, at the American cemetery in Florence, I stood at his grave. Here was the father I never knew and who never saw me. It has always puzzled me that his Star of David grave marker was engraved with the same rank he started with four years before he died – Second Lieutenant. Most officers rose in rank quickly during wartime. I wonder if he got busted, was denied promotion because he was Jewish, or simply (like me) didn't fit well in a hierarchical organization.

Doesn't everyone want to know what his father was like? What was a man who graduated from Harvard with academic honors doing in the infantry anyway? Was he the nerd of his Harvard records who merely organized social events, or was he the party boy himself?

In God's providence, it would seem that I was bequeathed Foss's critical faculties. I like to imagine my heavenly Father and Creator looking down on earth in 1939, musing, "The missionaries are getting a bit bland and stereotypical. I think I'll combine a Jewish scholar with a feisty chorus-girl comedienne."

Many years later, I got introduced to the Myers-Briggs Type Indicator, a personality inventory. It helped me realize that many of the things we do and the ways we do them are neither meritorious nor sinful. Each of us is an original whom our Father God, the ultimate artist, put together. I laughed with embarrassment when I read that my personality type (ENTP) was the least likely to be in church – unless he was on the platform!

Since I had no training to be practical with my hands, I thank God that I could entertain like my mother, but I could do it with some depth of thought because of some critical faculties donated by my biological father.

CHAPTER 2

Fostered

Giving Gregory away for adoption didn't seem to occur to Laura Berge. Maybe it was her lifetime hatred for paperwork. Maybe it was just too complicated. In any case, with the baby under her arm, she boarded the train in Boston headed for San Diego to get a job entertaining the troops. For this purpose, she adopted her mother's first name, giving herself the show-business name Laura LaVanche.

As we stopped to change trains in Chicago, three of her aunts met us at the station. The aunts offered to take baby Gregory. Doubtless, they perceived that Laura was more interested in being a nightclub singer than a mother. Perhaps she didn't want to admit she had made a mistake. Inexplicably, she insisted on keeping the baby. That insistence faded as soon as she got a singing job in San Diego. Then it was only practical to find a foster home for little Gregory.

Though she was not motherly, she did occasionally visit. Once, she found me in a playpen outside my foster home in the rain, with no guardians anywhere to be found. So she picked me up and went back to the Yellow Pages to search for foster home number two.

I don't know why number two didn't work out, but number three was my emotional jackpot. Fred Blauvelt was a World War I veteran who was left with shrapnel in his leg and a bronchial condition from being gassed in the trenches of France. By 1941, he was a fixture as a janitor at San Diego High School. His favorite stories were about Ted Williams, a San Diego boy who broke into baseball's major leagues with the Boston Red Sox. Fred remembered when the younger Ted used to walk around the school swinging a sawn-off bat to strengthen his wrists! (Since I was born in Boston and raised in San Diego, in the shadow of Ted Williams, is it any wonder that I've been a fervent Red Sox fan since I was seven years old?)

If I have any emotional stability, I owe it to God's engineering. He placed me into the Blauvelts' humble home in San Diego. Momma Helen was a large woman who could wrap a little boy up in a bosom that felt safer than Fort Knox. I was their pride. Fred and Helen were my joy.

I still have a couple of scrapbooks that give evidence of elaborate birthday parties with all the neighborhood kids. I smile at the photos of Dad Fred attempting to teach a five-year-old how to use a hammer and saw or to water the garden with a hose. Not all the lessons were that fun. One day when I refused to obey, Dad Fred took a small twig from the pepper tree in front of the house and gave me a swat! I was shocked by my first spanking.

It seems the Blauvelts occasionally took me with them to church. My scrapbook boasts a Sunday school certificate presented to me as a six-year-old from the Christian Church, the denomination that the Blauvelts must have attended at least periodically. I vaguely remember being fascinated that the church met in a theatre and used a movie short as a prelude!

What I recall more clearly is that ten years later, at sixteen, when I finally stepped through the door of another movie theater into a church service in Aspen, Colorado, the figures sticking to the flannelgraph looked somehow familiar. Might I have heard stories of the Lord Jesus when I was five years old? Were those stories the seeds that caused me to be more favorably disposed to the message of the cross as a teenager?

Occasionally, my mother would come to the Blauvelts to take me to a show where she was singing. I'd sit with the latest of her Marine boyfriends. While World War II was still raging in the Pacific, I found myself in an auditorium packed full of Marines and sailors. Suddenly a woman's leg, clad in French fishnet stockings, wiggled through the curtain. The men went wild, screaming and throwing their hats in the air! I can still feel the mixed emotions I experienced that day. Pride: "Wow, that's my mother!" Then anxiety: "How are they going to find their own hats again? All those hats look alike!"

My encounters with my mother during my first seven years were brief. Only a few were memorable, but one rare outing stands out. When I was about four, she took me to downtown San Diego, promising we would go to a soda fountain for a milkshake. I grasped my nickel as if it were a treasure. Mom plopped me on a high stool at the soda fountain and told me to "sit right there" while she went to another shop to buy cigarettes.

The soda jerk looked down at me and asked, "Whatcha want, kid?" I couldn't answer, but I knew what a milkshake was, and I was dearly anticipating it. He saw the nickel in my hand, took it, and delivered an ice cream cone, which was not at all what I wanted. Stunned and tearful, I got off the stool and wandered out the door, looking for my mom to set this injustice right, absent-mindedly holding the ice cream cone but not eating it because I wanted a milkshake. Seeing my mom across the street, I hurried to meet her, ignoring the traffic. My mother tackled me, the ice cream fell to the pavement, and before I could report the misunderstanding, I was shocked by getting a spanking right on the spot! It was my first encounter with injustice.

That incident was a mini-picture of our entire relationship. We never really connected. I never knew what she was thinking, and she didn't bother to ask me what I might be thinking.

Happiness with the Blauvelts in San Diego was not to last. Before my seventh birthday, Dad Fred put his arms around me, crying uncontrollably. Momma Helen was gone. I'd had no realization that she was dying of cancer. To me, she just "went away." Perhaps I assumed Momma Helen's family would take care of us. After all, her father owned a Chevrolet dealership in town. But their loyalty was only to Helen, not to me or even to Dad Fred, whom they had never considered to be on their social level.

Dad Fred certainly didn't know what to say to this once-more-abandoned seven-year-old. Neither could he imagine how to raise me alone. He had to go to work, so he called my mother.

CHAPTER 3

Damage

Being sent back to my mother was not a happy reunion for either of us. By then, Laura was an alcoholic who had lost her singing voice. But like me, she had strong reactions to her weaknesses, so throughout her life she never stopped working. By 1947, she had a job as a cocktail waitress at Morrie's Bar & Grill in La Jolla, California.

Twelve miles north of San Diego, La Jolla is another beautiful place for the well-off. The palm trees and cacti are surrounded on three sides by ocean bluffs and beaches. Not that I noticed at the time. I never became a surfer or any kind of beach boy. Looking back, I wonder why I so seldom went to the beach. In later life, walking a deserted beach became my favorite retreat with the Creator. (I still longingly look at yachts, but I figure I'll need to wait until after the Lord returns!)

In no shape or mood to return to mothering, Laura phoned her divorced but childless older sister, Charlotte, and asked her to leave her job as a hotel receptionist in Manhattan and come to California.

Aunt Charlotte was as different from my mother as any two sisters born eighteen months apart could be. Charlotte was compassion in a dress. She could give Hitler and Stalin the benefit of the doubt: "They probably meant well." It must have been her compassion that motivated this woman, who had never been west of Chicago, to move to Southern California.

Eternity will show how our Father was once again showing his care by providing me with Aunt Charlotte. She was there with me at home while Mom worked at Morrie's Bar & Grill into the early hours of the morning.

Occasionally, Aunt Charlotte would need to work late at the *San Diego Times*, so Mom would take me to Morrie's after school. The customers, mostly men, would buy me Cokes and peanuts. I longed for attention from men; gaining their attention was the closest I came to having uncles. I thought nothing of the fact that the smoke was so thick that it was difficult to see across the room. To this day, I feel more relaxed in a bar than in many churches!

My mother used to tell the story of how I tried to convince her not to come to the only Parent Teacher Association meeting she did decide to attend. When she insisted on knowing why, I sheepishly admitted that I was embarrassed because she was so little!

In 1949, Aunt Charlotte returned to New York City, and Mom put me on a prop plane to fly to New Jersey, unaccompanied by an adult. (I was only nine. It was all very avant-garde, really.) Grandpa and Grandma Berge didn't smile much. I never felt welcomed or wanted. Maybe they felt their irresponsible daughter had dumped me on them?

They clearly thought it was their duty to instill in me the discipline and habits that my mother apparently could not. At one meal, when I failed to take the bowl of potatoes that he was passing, Grandpa dropped it! I suppose the shattered dish was meant to provide some kind of lesson.

It wasn't all bad there. At least I wasn't alone! Grandpa Berge was still commuting to Edison's factory in Long Island. He took me along a couple of times for a history lesson. He received royalties until his death for developing a better spark plug for cars. Hungry as I was for his affection, I wanted to call him "Grandpal," but he didn't get it.

In addition to Charlotte, my mother's siblings were Martindale (Mart), Bob, and Jim. As often as they could, my grandparents pressured Uncle Jim to let me tag along while he courted soon-to-be Aunt Beth. Years later, we both still remembered his bribing me with ice cream money if I would play a hundred yards away from the bench where they were courting in the park!

At the end of the summer of 1949, I returned to La Jolla. What a surprise to learn that my mother had married Bob Livingston! Bob's humble job as a cook on a tuna fishing boat didn't reflect his fairly renowned parents. His father Jack had played opposite Tom Mix in the silent movies as the bad guy with the black hat riding the black horse. His mother, known as Madame Delorié, had invented the Lov-é bra for the May Company.

As a nine-year-old, if I was hoping for a real dad in Bob Livingston, those hopes were quickly dashed. Again! Bob and my mom argued vehemently at the top of their voices. I recall that I often ran out the back door and climbed a huge eucalyptus tree, and waited there for an hour until their fury died down.

Laura and Bob clearly perceived me as an extra, unwanted chore, so I was often packed off to stay with Grandma Livingston at her ranch in Valley Center, California, near Escondido. Far from any shops or entertainment, I amused myself with the interesting, but lonely, pastime of wandering through the bushes in her huge aviary full of pheasants and peacocks. Other than that, I suffered great embarrassment when she took me around the May Company stores while she provided ladies with personal fittings of her exclusive brassieres!

During one visit to the ranch, Bob tried to "make a man outta me" by putting me on an uncooperative horse. It seemed as though I was twenty feet off the ground. That was the beginning of my lifetime aversion to horses.

Although we always knew we were not related by blood, Grandma Livingston was very kind, perhaps because I was the closest thing to a grandchild she had. Years later, when I was twenty, I still had enough connection with Grandma Livingston to ask her if she would loan me $500 to buy a station wagon to drive to Honduras as a summer missionary. I promised to pay it back before the year was over. She did, and I did.

One of the sad mysteries of my life is that I failed to stay well connected to the major figures of my childhood. I didn't remain closely connected to Grandma Livingston, Grandmother Foss, my mother's aunts, or anyone I knew in

La Jolla. And only barely with Fred Blauvelt. I simply had no concept of how a family worked. It didn't help that I had no siblings and no real connections with my nine cousins, seven of whom I never saw until I was over thirty years old.

My mother, Bob Livingston, and I shared a one-bedroom house in La Jolla for two miserable years. So I suppose I had mixed emotions the night Bob came to my bed on the outdoor porch and whispered that he was "leaving for a while." When I asked where he was going, he said he was going to search for emeralds. When he came back, he promised, we would be rich.

I only met him one other time, many years later, when he pointed a shotgun into my face. Eager to make some sort of family connection, I had plucked up my courage to visit Grandma Livingston's ranch to look for Bob. The entrance to the ranch was signposted: "Warning: Trespassers will be shot"! As promised, at the end of the long driveway I found a man with a full beard and shaggy hair… and a gun. As fast as I could blurt it out, I introduced myself as the son of Laura Livingston – the boy whose home he had shared for two years. Without softening his glare, Bob swore, "Because of your ***** mother, I ended up on skid row." Without lowering his gun, he demanded my departure.

After Bob left us, life seemed more peaceful – or maybe it was merely lonely. My mother and I were seldom at home at the same time. I basically lived alone. Either that bothered my mother or she needed more money, so she rented our only bedroom to a newly married young couple. That didn't work for long, so she kicked them out.

"What the hell," she shrugged. "You're old enough to take care of yourself." To her credit, despite her carelessness, she always left out enough quarters from her tips for my school lunch. I would claim them when I woke up in the morning and got ready to ride my bicycle three miles to fifth grade. I appreciate that she saw to it that I had clothes as nice as any of the other kids; I think that was a real point of pride for her. To this day, I feel loyal to the JCPenney department store!

That Christmas, my mother's latest Marine boyfriend took us to an event for kids at Camp Pendleton. Santa Claus came down in a helicopter and gave out presents, calling out by name to each of the very excited kids. I waited with intense concentration, but my name was never called. Every kid got a present but me. Even though I'm in my seventies, that story still resurrects sadness in me.

Seeing the tears running down my cheeks, my mother scolded me for crying. "You're too old to get presents from Santa Claus." Still, maybe it was her compensation that I was treated to a horseback ride. Unfortunately, the saddle wasn't cinched well enough, so it slid sideways. As I went under the horse, it kicked me unconscious! I woke up in a hospital.

The worst thing about being left at home alone so much was that I had no siblings, and no friends came to the house. Maybe that's when I learned that if you want companionship you have to go out and get it. I used to ride my bike to the home of Ralph Dam. His was the only home where I felt tolerated, if not profusely welcomed. I knew enough to realize that if I sounded polite, his mother wouldn't send me home.

In the sixth grade at La Jolla Elementary School, I made two new and exciting discoveries: girls and leadership!

I couldn't decide between the blonde twins Marilyn and Marsha. Or maybe the little brunette Dorothy? By saving up my mother's waitressing tips, I was able to treat all three of them to a five-cent cherry Coke at the local soda fountain.

Even more exciting than thinking about girls was attending dance classes. There, I could *touch* girls! At twelve, being invited to hold a girl's hand and put my arm on her back became the brightest moment of my life. Because my mother had been a singer and dancer, she was willing to pay for dancing lessons. Finally, I had found something that I was good at!

Sports were a different thing. When we played kickball at recess, how humiliating that a girl was usually chosen before I was! It didn't help that by this time I was significantly overweight. Instead of running, all I could manage was to waddle like a duck.

The moment of crisis had come into my sixth-grade life. Would I drop out of society, seething with resentment? Or would I find a positive way to get what I wanted?

One day when the recess bell rang, I ran out the door first and unflinchingly declared with authority, "Bobby and I are the team captains. I choose Joey." To my amazement, my surge into leadership found acceptance. I concluded that if you act like a leader and put yourself in charge, it just might work.

My next leadership challenge was the election for La Jolla Elementary School president. I decided to run and found myself pitted against Barbara, the daughter of a wealthy family. She was bribing our classmates with free bubble gum. Undaunted, I gathered the boys and pointed out how shameful it would be if a girl was elected president. My plan was for each of them to stuff the ballot box with extra votes. I won. The abandoned fat boy decided to take over the world.

But I still didn't belong.

Near our house was the Little League baseball field. I went to join a team, but it was clear that I wasn't an athlete. Rejected and sent home, I was devastated. With overwhelming sadness, I remember feeling utterly alone, angrily crying my heart out. For hours, I threw a tennis ball against the steps of the house, driven by an inner rage. The prince of darkness was conceiving an embryo of anger and hatred in me against what seemed to be a very unfair world.

Some years later, a University of Texas student ensconced himself in a tower above a crowded campus plaza and shot as many students as he could. I identified with him; I remembered also wanting to shoot people! However, while he was evidently ready to die, I wasn't.

My rigged election, that first step into crime, soon led to another. Bobby Morrison taught me how to shoplift candy bars. One of us would distract the clerk while the other stuffed his pockets with Hershey Bars, Snickers, and Mars Bars. If I had stayed in La Jolla as Bobby's friend, I wonder whether I would have ended up in the penitentiary, as I heard he did. Perhaps stealing was a step toward my aspiration to exact revenge on a hostile world.

Thankfully, the One who knew me before I was created had other plans.

The next year, I found myself at La Jolla High School, which included seventh to twelfth grades. I was a nobody again. From being at the top, I'd fallen back to the bottom of the pile.

With little else to do, I decided to join the band. I must have shown up late, because I had no guidance or introductions. Totally baffled by the other instruments, I chose the drums.

Joining the band demanded that I get myself ready and ride my bike almost three miles to arrive at school in time for our 7:00 a.m. practice. Still, being at school early beat being alone. Strangely, I can't remember having even one friend during that first year in the new school. Looking back, I'm quite grateful this was an era before kids were using recreational drugs. I'm sure I would have turned to them in a quest to be accepted by the in-crowd.

On Palm Sunday 1952, when I was twelve, something inexplicable happened. My mother decided we would go to church! All dressed up, we found the local Episcopal church. As we came out after the service, my mother, looking somewhat triumphant, declared, "We shall go to church from now on!" I have no idea what was going on in her mind.

Of course, the next Sunday was Easter. The Episcopal church was so crowded that we were turned away. "No matter," Mom shrugged. "All churches are the same." Undaunted, we trotted off to the Presbyterian church.

"Sorry, we're full," they told us. So we went to the nearby Roman Catholic church. No room there either!

Incensed, my mother loudly shouted to the world, "Bunch of hypocrites, going to church only on Easter Sunday!" She never darkened the door of a church again, except (to my amazement) to attend my wedding ten years later.

When I finished the seventh grade, I was once again sent back to Grandfather Berge in Sea Girt, New Jersey. I spent that summer doing chores for Grandpa and playing baseball on the airfield where the Hindenburg dirigible had blown up years before. Even more interesting was meeting my first girlfriend, who liked kissing.

This time, Uncle Bob was the family member assigned to look after me. He was going through a divorce from Aunt Lynn and living in New York City. He and my Aunt Charlotte taught me how to get food out of Manhattan's trendy new vending machine, the Automat. Uncle Bob also helped me make a model airplane, but before I could admire it, he covered it with rubber cement, lit it on fire, and threw it out the third-story window to portray a World War II disaster. I pretended to enjoy the spectacle, but I was tight-lipped and upset that he ignored what I might have wanted to do with my new airplane.

Although Uncle Bob was an alcoholic and reportedly irresponsible, I must admit that he was my most fun and affectionate uncle. I last saw him when he visited us to borrow some money from my mother a few years later. I heard that he died on skid row in Los Angeles. I hope it wasn't true.

I feel sad thinking about my mother and her four siblings; I don't think any of them found what they had hoped for in their lives.

CHAPTER 4

On the Road Again

At the end of my summer with relatives in New Jersey and New York, I expected to return to California. Instead, I was informed that I should take the train from New York to Colorado. That summer back at Morrie's Bar & Grill, my mother had met Colonel Dutton. He had offered her a job as a cocktail waitress at a hotel in Aspen, where he was the new manager. I have always wondered uncomfortably about the nature of their relationship.

Because she had no tolerance for banks or paperwork, my mother had just walked away from her house in La Jolla, even though her divorce settlement from Bob Livingston had given her ownership of it. So we had no money to rent a decent house in Aspen.

Known today as a glamorous, glitzy ski resort for the rich and famous, in the autumn of 1953 Aspen, Colorado, had a single rickety chairlift up one mountain. In decline from its silver-mining heyday in the 1880s, it was a ghost town with a population of only 1,250.

Still, it had magnificence. The valley floor is 8,900 feet above sea level, and the peaks surrounding Aspen soar to

14,000 feet. At nearby Independence Pass on the Continental Divide, if you stand in the rain with your feet spread, the water falling on one foot will find its way to the Pacific Ocean and the water dripping on the other will eventually drain into the Atlantic via the Gulf of Mexico. The Roaring Fork River, which runs through Aspen, empties into the Colorado River, which journeys through the Grand Canyon and eventually waters Los Angeles.

Employee housing in the Hotel Jerome was minimalist. My so-called bedroom was at the end of a twenty-by-eight-foot space that also served as a kitchen and living room. My mom slept on a sofa bed at the other end. With increasing anger, I winced and gritted my teeth in the mornings as I walked past my mother's bed on my way to school. I purposely avoided recognizing whatever new man was under the covers with her.

My mother expected me to hold down a job, so she got me hired as an evening and weekend busboy in the hotel's dining room. My favorite part of the job was when I cleared a table with a barely touched steak, ignored by some little rich kid, and carried it into a corner of the kitchen where I could slice off an edge and feast! To my unforgettable embarrassment, I once tried to pick up a very large tray of dishes to impress the on-looking Colonel Dutton. I lifted it too quickly, so it continued to flow over my shoulder, sending the china crashing to pieces across the elegant dining-room carpets. Perhaps that reinforced my determination to get a white-collar job.

Moving into that mountain village at age thirteen, without explanation or preparation, left me unnerved, bitter, resentful, stunned. With my cool city-slicker duck-tail haircut, shuffling along in my penny loafers, I saw myself as "the Fonz" before "the Fonz" even existed. Yet now I had been thrust into a small cow-town with unpaved streets. To me, the other kids – the children of ranchers and small-shop owners – were… well, they were hillbillies.

Keith Patterson, a rancher's kid, took a dislike to me right away. "Whaddaya say we have us a fist fight, if you ain't a chicken?" he challenged me.

Sensing I would get the worse of the match, I relied on my developing verbal skills. "Okay, so let's say you bash me. Will that make you feel like a hero? And anyway, do you really want to spend your life picking fights? You don't have any higher goals than that?" It worked! Shamed, he walked off. Some months later, after I helped him with some homework, we actually became friends, though I never liked visiting his dad's ranch. I have an aversion not only to horses, but also to cows.

When I wasn't bussing tables, I spent a lot of time at Gene Mason's sports shop. He didn't have any kids, and I didn't have brothers or a dad. He used to give me copies of *Sports Illustrated* magazine. I think Gene really cared for me, though he never said anything remotely close to that.

My mother was the "mother of manipulation" – a skill, I fear, that I learned from her. Intimidated by no one, she found ways to get what she wanted. Once in the Hotel Jerome Bar, she was serving FBI Director J. Edgar Hoover. "Why would they hire someone as little as you, girlie?" he sneered.

Quick as a flash, my mother retorted, "To serve people like you when you're under the table."

Never one to stay in one place for long, my mother announced the next year that she and the Norwegian bartender, Carl Fagerstrom, were going to leave Aspen. "You don't want to come along, do you?" she asked me.

"No, not really," I replied. To be honest, I was fairly relieved.

With one of her typical quick fixes, Mom arranged for me to work in a local restaurant. At fourteen, I earned my room (in the attic) and board by clearing tables and washing dishes every evening. They granted me time off to go to high school football practice at an old field in the middle of the town. Since the soil was full of tin mine tailings, we tried to avoid hitting the ground as much as possible.

One aspect of Colorado life differed radically from California school life: skiing was part of the curriculum! On winter-time Wednesday afternoons, nearly every kid headed for the mountains. Due to my late start in the sport, I realized with consternation that I was one of the worst skiers on the slopes. Every time I attempted one of the four-mile runs, I felt I was risking my life! I was also a wobbly skater, a slow runner, and had never played football or basketball. In that mountain town, there was no space large enough to play my favorite sport, baseball. But whenever I could, I would throw around a baseball with my classmate and best friend Jim Glidden.

Jim's father was a renowned author of cowboy novels, writing under the *nom de plume* Luke Short. Jim and I dreamed together of going to Princeton University, both determined to become lawyers. My ambition was to provide legal counsel for the Mafia, since I supposed they had the most money. I was operating on one of the few values passed on to me by my mother: "Get them before they get you."

Though I was living on my own, the ninth grade went along okay. I liked learning, so I liked school. I wanted to be there as much as possible. After all, that was where the people were! Algebra seemed pointless, but literature, history, and other social studies fascinated me. I was determined to make some sense out of how the world worked. Why were people the way I'd experienced them?

By saving my earnings from my restaurant job, I somehow managed to buy a round-trip bus ticket from Aspen to Los Angeles to spend some of the summer of 1954 with Uncle Martindale and my cousins Dennis and Jo. Aunt Charlotte, my only link to my mother's family, had connected us. They didn't invite me to stay on with them in Los Angeles, so I returned to Aspen in time to begin tenth grade.

I was stunned to discover that the restaurant was locked up and empty. The proprietors, unable to pay their bills, had left in the middle of the night with all their belongings – and mine as well! I was abandoned again.

I could think of only one thing to do: walk to the home of Ralph and Marion Bohrson, who taught English and home economics at Aspen High School. They somehow managed to get in contact with my mother by phone. She promised, of course, to send them money for room and board if they would take me in. They did. She didn't. With no children of their own, they kept me anyway.

Bohrson thought he recognized some intellectual potential in me. In what now seems to me like a male version of *My Fair Lady*, he decided to develop me as an intellectual who would be somebody important. Rightly, and no doubt also wrongly, Bohrson infused in me the ambition to be Somebody and taught me to abhor the word "average." His tutelage fired up my desire to be someone others would notice. Maybe I could even become a US senator! I figured I would start climbing the ladder by getting the highest student position in Aspen High School.

CHAPTER 5

Finally, a Father

At sixteen, I fell in love with Judy Ringle, daughter of the editor of *The Aspen Times*. To my disappointment, the attraction was only from my side. Nevertheless, I summoned up the courage to ask her for a date to the movies. "Would you like to go with me to the Isis Theater on Saturday night?"

I was encouraged that her answer wasn't an unequivocal negative. She said, "I'm not available Saturday night, but if you want, you can take me to the theater on Sunday morning."

I wasn't aware that they showed movies at the Isis on Sunday mornings, but she challenged me: "Well? Do you want to take me or not?"

Grasping at any opportunity, I readily agreed. On Sunday I picked her up, and we walked to the movie theater. But I was totally puzzled when we got inside. I saw none of my schoolmates, only families with children running around. There was no evidence that a movie would be shown. I quietly followed her lead to sit down and wait. To my utter surprise, a young cowboy, dressed in his boots and vest, walked to the front carrying a podium and a big black book. Then he began to talk about God!

In the back of my mind, I supposed there was a God. If I thought about it, I imagined he was probably a decent sort of chap, so there would be no reason why he wouldn't like me (or at least tolerate me). Basically, I assumed he was minding his business, and I was minding mine.

However, twenty-three-year-old Dan Raley talked about God like he had some inside information. I slumped down into my seat. I wasn't prepared for this! Dan told the story of God visiting earth. That sounded like pretty cool space travel, like I'd seen in the Buck Rogers films. But this cowboy preacher seemed to believe that God turned himself into a man. If that wasn't weird enough, this God-man was tortured and nailed on a cross with spikes! I lowered my eyebrows in a frown, totally skeptical. How could anybody kill God? Wouldn't he be tougher than Superman, with bullets bouncing off his chest?

Dan was God's vessel to tell me the good news for the first time. He explained that the Creator freely volunteered to lay down his life as a sacrifice – for me! Suddenly, my eyes got very big. I wondered nervously what kind of crazy people surrounded me in this theater. How did *I* get into this story about God?

Still, I couldn't throw off the thought: "How could it be? How could the head honcho of the universe do anything like that for me?" From my perspective, nobody had ever done anything significant for me.

Could there really be a God who was interested in me and my welfare? Somehow (thank you, dear Holy Spirit!) I was fascinated enough to decide that I needed to find out what this was all about. Could it possibly be true?

The church service came to an end. While I was trying to figure out my next move with Judy, her parents, Verlin and Ruth, showed up with an appealing offer: "Would you be interested in coming home with us for dinner? We're having roast chicken."

I didn't have to think for long. *Hmmm. A home-cooked meal and an opportunity to be with Judy?*

"You betcha!" I quickly answered.

At the dinner table, Mr. Ringle asked me if I considered myself an educated person. I nodded. "Then surely you have read the Bible?" I shook my head. "Well, all educated people have read the Bible," he insisted.

"I don't even have a Bible," I confessed. In fact, I was somewhat confused about what the Bible even was.

He gave me a Gospel of John, along with a challenge: "You read this," commanded Mr. Ringle, "and pray. Ask God to show you whether it is true."

"But Mr. Ringle," I protested, "I've never prayed in my life. I don't even know any prayers!"

"Just talk to God as you would talk to any other important person," he insisted, without any further explanation.

Back in my room at the Bohrsons' house, I decided the experiment was logical enough. So for the next six weeks, off and on, I read bits of the Gospel of John in the Elizabethan English of the King James Version. Then I looked at the ceiling and prayed, "God, I don't know if I am talking to the light bulb or if there is somebody out there, but if this is true, show me."

Inexplicably, I kept going to that little church meeting at the Isis Theater. After about six weeks, I began to wonder with alarm what was happening to me. A feeling had come over me with which I was totally unacquainted. It felt like weakness, as though I were losing my macho. I was afraid I was becoming vulnerable, dropping my guard, and losing my protective defiant stance toward the world.

Sometime later, I realized that I had been invaded. Jesus Christ, the man from Galilee, was still alive and had taken up residence in me. As we often say: I had been "born again." I came to understand that this feeling of weakness was actually not weakness at all. It was simply something I'd never known before – a desire to help people! My mother's parental script ("Step on people before they step on you!") began to dissipate.

I think it would be accurate to say that into this new life, I was born running. It never occurred to me to bargain with God. It didn't cross my mind that disobeying commands from God was an option. I've never been able to comprehend people who say they believe the Bible is authentic communication from God himself, yet calculate the minimum they can do and still make it into heaven! I quickly seemed to understand that the fear of the Lord is the beginning of wisdom. I had begun to discover that bowing the knee to Jesus as Lord opened the door to understanding history, current events – even my own existence.

One day the next summer, I was mowing the Ringles' lawn and found myself *literally* leaping and praising God, like the crippled man Jesus healed. (Thankfully, their very loud gas-powered mower drowned out my singing.) I don't know if I was experiencing the baptism of the Holy Spirit or simply meeting God and basking in his love. But I do know that I had been lost, and Jesus found me. I had finally been adopted by a Father who would stick with me.

Before September 1956, if you had asked me who Jesus was, I would have hesitated, pondered, and then weakly suggested, "I think he lived a long time ago, wore a white robe, and carried a sheep around." Now I had become one of the privileged among the world's population, to whom the Father had revealed that Jesus is the Christ, the Son of the living God, the Savior, the Creator, the returning King of kings!

Then, of course, the test began.

The Aspen High School band bussed to the big city of Grand Junction for a band tournament. We competed with about thirty other high schools from the western slope of the Colorado Rockies. That evening, after drumming our band through our marching drills, one of my buddies and I picked up a couple of girls from another high school. We found an unlocked car where we indulged in some enthusiastic kissing. Suddenly, I was struck like a lightning bolt with the conviction that this was wrong!

I realized I was only using this girl. To her shock, and to the confusion of the other couple, I blurted out, "I'm sorry. I'm sorry. This is wrong!" I jumped out of the car and fled. The fear of God is *indeed* the beginning of wisdom.

As incredible as it sounds, I can testify honestly that from that incident in 1956 to this very day, I have consciously sought to be obedient to the commands of God as I understood them. Of course, much of what I thought to be God's commands turned out to be just traditions of men.

Even then, I'm pretty sure my heavenly Father saw that my heart was seeking to obey.

Young Dan Raley had to leave town hurriedly, due to unpaid bills. I so loved the man who had introduced me to the Savior that I emptied my bank account of its $250 and insisted that he take it. He paid it back as soon as he could.

The next chapter of my life at Aspen High School didn't go well. Dan's replacement at the Baptist church in the Isis Theater was the Revd. Roy Tubbs. The responsibility fell to him to disciple this young man who was completely new to faith in Jesus. Roy and his dear wife Fern were extremely conservative. She wore long skirts and shapeless blouses; later in life, when I met Muslim women in burkas, I thought of Mrs. Tubbs. Pastor Tubbs taught me all the morally conservative values that had been passed along to him:

- Billy Graham was a liberal compromiser because he invited Roman Catholics onto the platform of his crusades.

- Denver Seminary was on a theological "slippery slope" because they didn't condemn Billy Graham, who shared his platform with Catholic priests.

- A true Christian could only believe that God created the world in six literal, twenty-four-hour days.

- Bob Jones University might be the only God-approved institution of higher learning in the country.

- Smoking, drinking alcohol, and playing cards of any type were most definitely inherently sinful activities.

- And (most devastating of all to me) Christians don't dance!

"What?" I thought. "Tell me Christians don't play sports or don't study, but don't tell me that Christians don't dance. That's the only thing I'm truly good at!"

At this time, although I was slowly becoming "a new creation in Christ Jesus," my ambition to be Somebody had not lessened. As a mere junior, I had politicked my way into the position of student body president at Aspen High School. But this was nothing next to my greatest claim to fame: I was the best dancer in the school. My favorite partner was Sylvia, the daughter of Aspen's mayor. We were so good at jitterbugging that sometimes the rest of the kids would stop dancing to watch us. We had actually thought about competing in dance contests. With typical teenage confidence, we were certain that Bill Haley and the Comets surpassed Beethoven and Tchaikovsky in musical excellence!

Imagine how completely crestfallen I was at the news that God didn't like dancing. This was a test right up there with Abraham being asked to sacrifice Isaac!

To make matters worse, as student body president I was expected to be the master of ceremonies at the school dances. At the first dance after Pastor Tubbs had given me the devastating news that dancing was sinful, I decided I would just stay behind the microphone all night. But Sylvia and a couple of other girls sidled up to me, trying to coax me onto the dance floor. Cornered and panicked, I blurted out over the microphone, "Christians don't dance!"

Suddenly, the dance hall was pin-drop quiet.

"Why is that?" someone demanded.

"I have no idea. They just don't," I replied weakly.

Assuming I was just being cranky, my lady suitors walked away. So did I. I left the building feeling very sad and lonely, wondering why Christians didn't dance.

I wasn't totally lonely that school year. After all, Judy Ringle was a Christian. But she was also in love with King Fisher, so she didn't have much time for me. I discovered one other high school student was a Christian, as was the football coach, Earl Burrows. But we weren't very well oriented to the concept of fellowship in Christ. I don't remember that we ever even prayed with or for each other. We were members of the Baptist church, and that was pretty much it. I was taught that we were the lucky ones – the only ones, in fact, who had got it right. Though the group was exclusive, at least for the first time in my life I belonged to a group. I wonder whether I would have been able to keep Christ-minded without the assurance that I was not the only believer in Aspen.

Today I ask myself: How can the lonely Muslim background believer in Libya, Eritrea, or Afghanistan stay faithfully obedient to the Lord Jesus? If Christian workers don't establish *fellowships* of believers in a Muslim country before we leave, then we are stopping short of what God has in mind.

Judy invited me to be baptized with her at a Baptist church forty miles away in Glenwood Springs. The Revd. Jim Warnock baptized us. Fifty-four years later Pastor Jim tracked me down. He wrote that he had been praying for his "son in the faith" all those years. I have often wondered how many people God has used to pray for me – without my even knowing!

Judy and I invited my friend Jim Glidden to church. He was also attracted to Judy (another thing we had in common), but he scoffed at God. After a couple of visits to church, he stopped coming. At the time, I couldn't understand why our friendship wasn't the same as it had been. I felt deeply sad that my best friend was abandoning me as well as turning his back on Christ.

Judy and Monte were a year ahead of me in high school. Judy went off to a place called Wheaton College near Chicago. Monte moved to Arizona. Coach Burrows left Aspen as well, and the new coach was a Mormon. Dear Pastor Tubbs seemed to be from another planet. The only other high school student in the tiny church was Sharon, a freshman who had a cleft palate. I felt like God's Lone Ranger.

Why did obeying Jesus result in my being alone again? No one could help me figure out how to keep both Jim and the Lord Jesus as my friends. Even with Jesus, I felt like I was having one-way conversations.

Even though I'd managed to grab nearly all the important non-sporty roles at Aspen High, no one was now attracted to this weird, legalistic, arrogant, hell-and-damnation-proclaiming kid.

It got worse. When I announced my new faith to Ralph Bohrson, my guide, teacher, patron, and generous host, he counter-announced, "If you insist on being a Christian, you can live somewhere else!" I was dumbfounded. He had been grooming me, but apparently my becoming a Christian had ruined his experiment.

In shock, I silently walked out of his door and wandered over to the Ringles' home. When I told them about Bohrson's ultimatum, they invited me to move in with their family. Bolstered by the Ringles' offer, I let the Bohrsons know that I couldn't abandon my newly found Savior. "I have decided to follow Jesus. No turning back," I told them, quoting a favorite hymn of the day. I packed my suitcase, and he showed me to the door. Abandoned again.

I felt a bit like Peter. When the crowds were deserting Jesus, Peter feared it might be a lost cause to follow him. So did I. But also like Peter, I was given the insight to realize that the alternatives were worse: "Lord, to whom shall we go? You have the words of eternal life" (John 6:68). I had decided to follow Jesus, and that was that. To hell with the rest of the world!

The Ringles took me into the first Christian family I'd known since I was a toddler with the Blauvelts in San Diego. Dad Ringle quickly informed me that as long as my feet were under his dining-room table, I would obey his rules. Strangely enough, I loved it! Most teenagers long to be free from someone else's control, rules, and authority. But for me, freedom had simply provided a lifelong sense that "No one gives a damn." Parameters provided security; total freedom had provided loneliness.

Judy Ringle, my foster sister, later wrote about my coming into their home:

> It amazes me that a homeless kid showed up at
> our house. You were born anew, called to radical
> discipleship, and then sent out with a lasting connection
> to our family.

Our folks prayed for you each day as they
watched your itinerary going over all the earth. Mom
occasionally was awakened from sleep to pray for you,
knowing that obedience, for you, was crucial. I know
your ministry was truly a result of the prayers of many
faithful people, but there was no one who loved you
more than our parents.

My dad was sometimes frustrated with your lost
coats, your generosity to a fault (in his eyes), and your
needing to learn basic responsibilities, but they saw that
as their investment into your life. They were proud of
you, and often said so.

It was now my senior year, the final year of high school. The whole school had only seventy-five students – only nineteen in the senior class. In order to build teams, each of the guys was expected to try out for all the sports. To have something in common with the other guys, I did my part.

Football went all right, although my teammates still have not forgotten that I tackled and broke the leg of one of our own players. Another time, I picked up a fumble and headed toward the goal line to score my first and only touchdown, only to trip over my own feet five yards short of the goal! We didn't score.

In basketball, I was a senior with a beard who played alongside the fourteen-year-olds on the junior high team.

Then there was track. Once I was asked to run the 400-meter race. We were in a meet competing against five other high schools. Each school was required to enter three athletes in each event. Aspen had two good runners for the 400. I was asked simply to start the race in order to provide our team's required third runner. No one conceived of my actually finishing it. Feeling insulted, I decided I would win! Most likely, I jumped the gun, and then I ran like my life depended on it. At the halfway point I was leading the pack when I heard the coach exclaim, "My God! That's Livingston!"

Well, my two teammates finished first and second, and in the last ten yards, Mickey from New Castle edged me out. Still, I came fourth out of eighteen, and I still have the yellow award ribbon to prove it! But I paid a price for running to win. For the next several hours, I couldn't stop vomiting. My only consolation was that my sickness gave me an escape from my class president duties to host the prom that evening.

The apostle Paul commands us "run to win" (1 Corinthians 9:24, NET). Because of that one effort in the 400 race, I understand what he meant. To this day, it has been my *modus operandi* to run 110 percent for God's kingdom. Paul said he had worked "harder than all of them" (1 Corinthians 15:10). I am challenged by the scriptural commands that commend hard work. Following the Lord Jesus is a marathon.

At Aspen High School, I began to realize that preaching hellfire was counterproductive. Nor was my mediocre skill as an athlete ever going to win me any awards. So I rediscovered more suitable ways to be Somebody. I wrote a column for the *Aspen Times* about school events. I became editor of both the school newspaper and the annual yearbook during my junior and senior years. I was also politically astute enough to get re-elected as student council president in my senior year. I was still the devious politician who had commandeered the kickball team in the sixth grade.

Fleeta Rowland and I were both honored with the senior "all around student" award. I tried to kiss her once, but her glasses got in the way! We were out of touch for fifty years, but when I attended my high school reunion, I learned that Fleeta is now paralyzed from a horrible automobile accident. I also discovered that she is now a beautifully mature sister in Christ.

Although I slowly realized that telling my fellow students they were going to hell was counterproductive, I remained truly worried for them. Somehow, even then, even with minimal teaching, I knew I had been recruited by God for his rescue operation! I challenged the Mormon coach in front of the other team members. I argued with my only other baseball-playing friend, a Roman Catholic, because he had ash on his forehead on Ash Wednesday. That didn't seem to be what saved people would do.

In 1974, seventeen years after our high school graduation, I returned to Aspen from India as pastor of the same little church where I had become a Christian. I invited my old classmates to come and hear me preach. "We've heard you!" was the typical response. Thankfully, over the years, I've been able to reconnect in small ways with those classmates whom I offended as a new Christian.

As the autumn progressed, I began to feel almost adopted in my fifth foster home. God had provided me with the wonderful gift of the Ringle family. Theirs was a truly Christian home, yet it took a long time before I could relax. I kept thinking it wouldn't last; something would surely go wrong. Surely they would give up on me.

My after-school job at the Aspen laundry provided a stark contrast to the warmth of the Ringle home. In nearly every other sentence, my boss would exclaim, "Well, I'll be God-damned!"

Having not yet learned to witness winsomely, I often muttered in reply, "Probably!"

I had planned to work just long enough to get enough money to buy Christmas presents for the Ringles. When I announced that I was quitting my job at the laundry, Dad Ringle said, "You just march right back there and get your job back." I did so without protest.

Dad Ringle not only taught me a work ethic, but he also taught me that "A man's word is his honor" and to "Say what you mean, and mean what you say." He also taught me to check out what the Bible actually teaches, no matter what anyone else says.

CHAPTER 6

Choices

Desperate for Christian friends, I hung on Judy's every word when she came home from college for Christmas. With a twinkle in her eye, she encouraged me to apply to attend Wheaton College – where a thousand Christian women went to school!

Tempted as I was by her invitation, I struggled. Who had ever heard of Wheaton College? I still thought my future was in the courtroom. After bowing the knee to the living Christ, I had switched to his side. Now, instead of planning to work for the Mafia, I assumed I would defend the defenseless as an altruistic hero. Still, I was sure my career as a lawyer would be much more successful if I went to Princeton University.

However, by this time, the grace of God was stirring in me a greater ambition. Obeying God was becoming more important than seeking status. I wasn't yet able to think about pleasing God, just obeying. I didn't yet know him as the magnificently affectionate Father God he actually is. But there was no question about who was *boss*! After all, we are commanded to start with obedience:

- "Make disciples of all… teaching them to *obey* everything I have commanded you" (Matthew 28:19–20).

- "Through him we received grace and apostleship to call all the Gentiles to the *obedience* that comes from faith for his name's sake" (Romans 1:5).

Pastor Tubbs gave me a copy of the June edition of *Moody Monthly*, which advertised Christian colleges (whatever *those* were). In that mindset of obedience, I spent hours poring over the college advertisements, trying to imagine what it would be like at Bemidji Bible College in Minnesota or Omaha Bible College (student population: 120). Somehow I knew I needed to die to my ambition to graduate from a highly esteemed university. I eliminated all the evangelical colleges except the two with the largest student populations: Wheaton College and Bob Jones University.

Pastor Tubbs insisted that Wheaton was too liberal. Dad Ringle disagreed. Knowing nothing of Christian politics, denominations, or theological differences, I was put off by both colleges. As an urbanite, I feared that Wheaton must be in a wheat field out in the country with cows. I was also skeptical after reading that Bob Jones called his school "the world's most unusual university." Neither particularly appealed.

I thought, "Who wants to go to the world's most unusual university? Mr. Jones must have quite an ego to name the university after himself." Then I noticed that Bob Jones University only played intramural sports. "What?! No competition with other colleges! What's their problem?"

Wheaton had a football team, and they played soccer and wrestled against Notre Dame! What topped it off was that Wheaton had a more spiritual-sounding motto: "For Christ and His Kingdom."

Trying to prove that I was a man's man, I had convinced myself that I actually enjoyed hitting and being hit in American football. Being a little guy (at 5 feet, 7 inches and only 140 pounds), I had been the kicker for Aspen High School's team. So in my application to Wheaton College, I mentioned that I had kicked for extra points. To my amazement, I got a telephone call from Wheaton's head football coach, Harve Chrouser, inviting me to football camp in August 1958.

That did it. The coach was inviting me to join the football team and there were a thousand Christian girls. Wheaton College, here I come!

Of course, there was the question of money. I had none! To my surprise, I was offered a scholarship from the Order of the Eastern Star, a part of the Freemasons' fraternal organization. Pastor Tubbs warned me that they were an evil secret society. When I looked to Dad Ringle for wisdom, he told me a story about the evangelist D. L. Moody. When visiting a bar in Chicago, Moody grabbed a five-dollar bill offered by a drunk, declaring, "The devil has had this long enough!"

"Take the scholarship money from Eastern Star and run," advised Verlin Ringle, with a grin. He also labored to acquire my university tuition from the Army's war orphan fund. With those funds and the money I earned driving a public school bus during my years at Wheaton, I graduated from university owing merely nine dollars in library fines. My strong reluctance to spend money on myself also helped me keep my budget in balance.

During that last year of high school, the fact that I stayed loyal to Christ is most likely a credit to Mom and Dad Ringle. I can only imagine how difficult it must have been for them. I had never before submitted to any real parental authority. My anger and bitterness didn't disappear in the first month (or even in the first years) after I repented. What does it say about the Ringles that I could trust them? I trusted virtually no one else. Everyone else in my life had been a traitor or ripped me off or eventually abandoned me.

They insisted I get a job after high school graduation to accumulate some money for college. The US Forest Service offered me a job clearing rocks from hiking trails in the mountains surrounding Aspen. I earned $1.67 an hour. As I was working one day at 12,000 feet, I looked up from the trail to find myself eyeball to eyeball with a bald eagle four feet away. We both froze, immobilized, for perhaps ten seconds before he (or she – it's difficult to tell!) jumped off the cliff, flapping from a free fall into a graceful glide.

My prayer life definitely intensified one night that summer when I was alone in a mountain cabin during a howling snow storm. My colleague Jim had gone into Aspen for supplies, and the only book I had for company in the cabin was a collection of spooky stories by Edgar Allan Poe! I did *not* have pleasant dreams.

Jim and I were provided with a stubborn old ex-Army mule to carry our supplies. I felt no love for this animal, because every time we tried to pack him up, he would stomp on my foot (which provided one more reason to hate horses). One day while we were stopped to eat lunch, something startled the mule. He broke the branch where he was tied. Running out of control, he stumbled in the rocky terrain, fell, rolled, crushed our packs, shattered our fishing poles, and broke his leg. Did you ever try to bury a mule in the Rocky Mountains? Our first mistake was to shoot him before we dug the hole. By the time we had created a hole big enough for him (or so we thought), rigor mortis had set in, and the mule's stomach was hugely bloated. Jim and I had to puncture his abdomen and endure the unbelievably awful smell that emanated as we chopped off the legs in order to fit the beast into the hole.

At the end of that summer, the day finally arrived for me to head to university! I boarded the train for Chicago in Glenwood Springs, where I had disembarked five years earlier.

At the first stop in Denver, a kid my age sat down next to me in his reserved seat. Sherod Miller was the son of a well-known Denver pastor. To my amazement, he was also a freshman en route to Wheaton College! While I was headed to football camp, Sherod was arriving early for soccer camp. Finally, here was someone with whom I shared Christian brotherhood. Sherod, my first college classmate, is still today one of our faithful financial supporters.

At Wheaton, I soon found myself in a football uniform "committing suicide" by running laps at the mercy of our always-yelling Coach Chrouser. He put me into the middle of the field and told me to kick a fifty-yard field goal. I could hardly see the goalposts. I failed.

I could kick a post-touchdown extra point fairly well. But our football league had decided, just that year, that a team could earn *two* points after a touchdown by passing or running the ball across the goal line instead of kicking it for one point. As far as Coach Chrouser was concerned, extra-point kickers were out of a job.

Enjoined to try a new position, I practiced with the running backs. In the sprints, I was so far behind the other backs that Coach Chrouser bent over laughing. He renamed me "The Aspen Flash." So I switched to guard. Twice my size, the other linemen went into hysterics as I tried to knock them down! I could no more move a defensive lineman in a block than move a stone wall.

The guest speaker at football camp was Olympic decathlete Rafer Johnson. His maxim was one I've not forgotten: "A Christian is somebody who takes Jesus Christ with him everywhere he goes." Though I didn't perform well enough to get into the games very often, I was hugely encouraged by being around those really big guys who loved Jesus as much as I did. Maybe Jesus wasn't just for little weak people?

In 1958, the Wheaton team had its first undefeated season in history. Unfortunately, I was not much involved in the championship season. Neither was Gary Taylor. We set foot onto the field for exactly two plays – against the Wheaton alumni team. As defensive linebackers, Gary tackled the runner and then I jumped on the pile! For the rest of the season, I supported the championship by warming the end of the bench with my buddy Gary. By December, the season was over and so was my football career.

Twenty-five years later, I was invited to speak at Wheaton's chapel service about my experience as a missionary to Muslims. To the amusement of this non-jock, the only faculty members who came to shake my hand afterwards were the four football coaches!

In 2008, Gary and I returned to Wheaton for our team's fiftieth reunion. During a homecoming game, we were paraded out onto the football field as the heroes. Given that the fans in the stadium had no idea about our two-play career fifty years earlier, Gary and I doffed our caps as if we had been star players in 1958. I think I caught God winking at us!

When I entered the college, Wheaton had a "big brother/sister" program. An older student would "adopt" a first-year student. My big brother David Scholer (who went on to teach at Fuller Theological Seminary) initiated our relationship by asking, "Are you *pre-mill* or *a-mill*?" Having no idea that he was referring to theological positions about the end times, I just stared at him, puzzled.

Still planning to go to law school, I majored in history. Sadly, I got bogged down attempting to memorize the kings and queens of England. I must confess that instead of learning about George, James, and Henry, I was much more interested in learning the names of the twenty girls I had selected from the photos in the first-year students' booklet. Halfway through our first year at Wheaton, number nineteen fell for me! To be more accurate, she fell in front of me.

During the semester break, a number of our class members went skiing on a small man-made slope in Illinois. I was the only person who knew how to ski. (The ski dud in Aspen became the ski champ in Illinois!) I spent my time on the little hill picking up the girls. Literally! Sarah Coltman was enamored as I helped her up, mistakenly concluding I was gallant. I learned that Sarah, who was also called Sally, was preparing for medical school so that she could become a missionary doctor to Muslim ladies in Pakistan or Egypt. I inwardly rolled my eyes, thinking, "Good luck with that!"

During that first year, one thing was perhaps more interesting to me than studying history – or even *girls*! That was learning how to share my faith, since I was wholly unsuccessful at it in Aspen. Like a kid in a candy store, I joined nearly every Christian service activity the college community offered. I was fascinated by all the things that Christians ought to do, all the ways we ought to reach out to others. (The one thing I wasn't at all considering was overseas mission!)

In one of my first experiences of cross-cultural outreach, I got involved every week in "Colored Sunday School". At the time the word "Colored" was considered more appropriate than "Negro". Once a week, we would take the bus to Chicago's South Side and knock on doors, offering to hold Bible studies. I was amazed that quite a few people actually invited us into their homes to teach their children. I wrote in my journal:

Very encouraged to realize that Robert Emory's prayer

*for salvation is showing to be real. He is asking good
questions. He is happy to go around the building with
me as we talk to other folks. With one single mother
who is barely literate, I decided to read from the Phillips
translation. She listened attentively, then commented:
"Tha's all right, but tha's not our Bible... we got the
Holy Bible!" Back to the King James!*

At Wheaton, I met for the first time real Christians who
weren't Baptists. I initially confused Plymouth Brethren
with Jehovah's Witnesses, because they used different church
vocabulary than I'd known. But I figured that since Wheaton
grad Jim Elliot, who had been killed two years earlier as a
missionary in Ecuador, had been Plymouth Brethren, they
couldn't be that bad. Even more riveting to me was my
discovery of Bible-believing Presbyterians. They seemed to
love God with their *minds*!

Unlike me, most of the other students at Wheaton
came from evangelical families. They'd heard it all before
– sometimes *ad nauseam*. Far too many students were at
Wheaton at the insistence of their families, who feared secular
universities. Wes Craven, a suitemate during my freshman
year, later became a director of horror films in Hollywood,
despite spending his first twenty-two years imbibing sound
biblical teaching.

I sought out the spiritual guys, the Bible bashers. Gary
Taylor, my fellow football bench-warmer, was more at home
with the "party" kids who joined the Young Life group.
I kidded with him that I had joined the Pharisees, and he

had joined the Sadducees! My second-year roommate Bill Kenny and I fell into one-upmanship as we competed to see who could stay in our walk-in prayer closet and read the Bible the longest!

In my quest to hang out with the spiritual guys, I got acquainted with an unknown Wheaton graduate, Bill Gothard, who was organizing Bible clubs in high schools. He asked me to oversee a group in Roselle, near Wheaton. Later, I became his assistant as he developed a new ministry. He would often use clever chalk illustrations to explain biblical concepts. Lugging his chalk board from church to church, we visited pastors to explain the principles that were later incorporated into his Institute of Basic Youth Conflicts. Gothard's ministry was helpful to many young people.

By the 1970s, his week-long seminars were drawing audiences as large as 10,000 in city after city. Back from India during that period, I contacted him for complimentary tickets to a seminar being held in a Philadelphia basketball stadium. From the vantage point of the "nosebleed" seats at the top of the stadium, I needed a telescope to see my one-time boss below. Opening my large red program/notebook, I saw that the lesson that night included something like, "Twenty-two things a divorced person must do before you can serve God." Perhaps because we were so close to heaven in those seats at the top, I thought I sensed God looking over my shoulder at the program and whispering, "I didn't know that! I thought I had simply commanded, 'Go and sin no more!'"

Being involved with the Chicago South Side Bible studies and Bill Gothard's ministry still was not sufficient ministry for me. Perhaps my true field of study at Wheaton was "extracurricular activity." In 1959, Pete Gillquist of Campus Crusade for Christ came to Wheaton College to train a number of us and recruit us to witness about Jesus on secular campuses nearby. We realized we had finally met someone who would help us to share our faith more effectively with non-Christians. Arming us with a short booklet to give away, Pete led the members of our group to the prestigious University of Chicago. To our surprise, we discovered we could get students to consider the claims of Christ by asking a question based on the booklet: "Have you heard of the four spiritual laws?"

Pete did more than help me share my faith; he helped me understand God's total forgiveness. In his book *Love is Now*, Pete illustrated the heart of our heavenly Father. He wrote of a guy who continually failed to stop sinning in a certain area. Still, he was a deeply repentant young believer, so each time he cried out to God, "Lord, I did it again." The forgiving Father God replied, "Did what?" (Gillquist, 1970, p. 36).

Up to that point, I had pictured God much like Coach Chrouser. When I failed to run the play correctly, I supposed God would throw down his clipboard in disgust. What a joy it was to me when the reality of God's promises really sunk into my innermost being: "He will remember my sin no more" (Hebrews 8:12, my paraphrase). "He has removed my sins from me as far as the east is from the west" (Psalm 103:12, my paraphrase). "There is now no condemnation for those who are in Christ Jesus" (Romans 8:1). "If God is for us [and he is!], who can be against us?" (Romans 8:31). "He remembers that we are dust" (Psalm 103:14). "His mercies are new every morning" (Lamentations 3:22–23, my paraphrase).

In my immaturity and short-sightedness, I concluded that studying the history of kings and queens and wars had little to do with serving God. As soon as I failed my British history exam, I switched my major to English literature. (Maybe I thought I might write books.) However, I was once again disillusioned when my Shakespeare prof gave me the impression that she loved Shakespeare more than the Lord Jesus! In any case, I was much too immature and impatient to appreciate Elizabethan poetry.

As Christmas 1958 approached, I realized that I needed to do something if I wanted to take Christmas presents to Aspen to my new family, the Ringles. I took a job on the graveyard shift with the Chicago Post Office. In those days, the post was sorted by hand. From midnight until 8:00 in the morning, I stood in front of a big wall covered with small boxes, one for each city of Washington State. At one point, the supervisor caught me asleep standing up. I was sticking all the envelopes into the slot for Walla Walla! But at least I made some money. I didn't have to go home to my adopted family empty-handed.

In contrast, later that summer, my relationships with my natural family suffered another blow. Dad Ringle had tracked down my paternal grandmother, Natalie Foss. He encouraged me to go see her at the beginning of the summer. He had assured Mrs. Foss that I would make no claims on her. Perhaps because she had no other grandchildren, she agreed for me to visit her in Boston. So off I went to meet a woman who, until recently, had not known whether I was alive. A person I'd never met, never corresponded with. The mother of a man who had never seen me, who just happened to be my father. As I walked toward her apartment in an upscale neighborhood, I wondered how much the genes from my father influenced who I was. What a shock it was to me when my grandmother opened her door, and I realized for the first time that I was half Jewish!

As most kids do, I had unquestioningly taken on the prejudices of my mother. Though I didn't personally know any African-Americans or Latinos, I didn't feel superior to them. But I was very prejudiced against Jewish people. Suddenly, while I was trying to ponder the implications of my Jewish heritage, Mrs. Foss gave me a cup of tea and an ultimatum. Either I would cut off all relationship with my mother, "the slut," and never speak to her again, or I would choose not to have any further contact with her, my paternal grandmother.

My esteem for my mother's life choices was not much higher than hers. However, my grandmother's demand felt like the epitome of arrogance, especially since we had known each other for only fifteen minutes!

I stammered in response, "I'm not at all sure I can do that!"

Mrs. Foss stood up, walked me to the door, said, "It's been nice to meet you," and ushered me out.

Abandoned again! I have often wished I'd had the poise and the counsel to know how to retrieve that relationship, but I never did. I sorrow that we never spoke or wrote again.

From Boston, I returned to my Aspen job with the US Forest Service. This time, being a people person, I opted to drive a pickup around the campgrounds to greet the campers and collect trash. Before that got boring, a forest fire broke out. I was excited at this opportunity to be a hero and save the forest. However, the ranger decided that since I was a little guy, my job would be to strap a five-gallon water tank on my back and walk through the hot ashes after the fire had passed, squirting water on the smoldering stumps! Though the flames had been extinguished, the heat was still so intense that sweat flowed out of every pore in my body. I wondered whether hell was like that.

My experiences at Wheaton College were certainly formative and preparatory for the rest of my life. Daily, we sat in chapel listening to some of the greatest Bible expositors of the time. I was stunned when the British pastor Alan Redpath spoke on Jesus' parable of the wheat and the tares. I worried that I might be chaff – that I wasn't really born again. I ran back to my room, dropped to my knees, and prayed, "Lord, if I am not really converted, if I am not really yours, I submit to you right now as my Lord and Savior." I've never had to bring up the question again.

In those years, every male student at Wheaton was required to do two years' training with the US Army's Reserved Officer Training Corp (ROTC). Those who continued for an additional two years would graduate with a commission as a Second Lieutenant in the Army. My first sense of calling into ministry was in that context. I had decided by then that helping people obtain eternal life was more important than winning a court case as a lawyer. As I considered how vulnerable eighteen-year-old Army recruits must be, I wondered who would win those kids to the Lord. Burdened for their salvation, I decided I was going to enlist as an Army chaplain. In order to qualify, I signed up for extra military training with the Pershing Rifles. But only a few weeks later, I discovered a different kind of "army."

CHAPTER 7

The Call

In October 1959, I was walking across Wheaton's campus, wondering what was most important to God, when a graduate student, Dale Rhoton, stopped me. "Hey, Greg, how would you like to come to an all-night prayer meeting at Moody Bible Institute?" He might as well have asked, "How would you like to become a monk?"

"What have you got to pray about that takes all night?" I asked.

At my little Baptist church in Aspen, I had attended what we called a prayer meeting. In reality, it was the Wednesday-night-Bible-study-with-the-weekly-health-report-tacked-on-the-end. After completing our study, the pastor would close his Bible and ask, "Are there any prayer requests?"

Someone would usually say, "I have an unspoken." Perhaps people were shy, or perhaps they thought their personal needs weren't worthy of our intercession. But "unspoken" was quite a popular request. Occasionally someone would make a specific prayer request: Susie would ask for prayer for her grandfather's hip pain. Or Joe would say he had an exam coming up, so he was nauseous. On the whole, our tepid intercession resembled what some Buddhists do. They write their prayers and tack them onto a windmill. As the wind twists them around, they hope for the best. I'd never heard the word "expectancy" in my little church. We prayed only "if it be thy will" prayers. But if God had ever dramatically answered on the spot, with Susie's grandfather jumping up after prayer to announce that he was healed, I'm afraid he might have been put under discipline for having Pentecostal ideas! So on that fateful day at Wheaton, I was honestly bewildered when I asked Dale: "What have you got to pray about that takes all night?"

"The Muslim world!" he replied, in a tone that seemed to infer that was how every good Christian spent Friday evening.

In 1959, none of our group knew anything about Muslims. We'd never even met one! Very few Americans knew anything about Islam. They were not the enemy – the Soviet Union was! This was the Cold War era, and we were sure that the Russians were out to annihilate us. Nuclear attack was considered so likely that Christians debated whether or not we should build bomb shelters.

Intrigued, I couldn't resist Dale's challenge. Full of pride, I figured I could pray as long as he could. Besides, I had wanted to visit Moody Bible Institute in the center of Chicago. I accepted his invitation, expecting to meet some nice girls and enjoy some coffee and doughnuts.

Arriving in the prayer room, I quickly noted that there were no girls, no coffee, and no doughnuts – only some guys kneeling on a hard wooden floor over maps of various

Muslim countries. The leader of the group was twenty-year-old George Verwer. I reached out to shake his hand, thinking he'd welcome me. Instead, leaving my hand dangling, he pointed his finger into my face with the challenge: "What country are you claiming, brother?"

I was momentarily speechless. I wasn't sure I knew what he meant by "claiming." But street kids like me are quick on our feet, so I pretended I was tracking with him and shot back, "What's left?"

"Libya. You've got Libya."

Semi-stunned, I wandered toward one of the prayer circles, trying to think of where Libya was. "It's probably one of those islands off of Florida!" I told myself.

That night I found out where Libya was – and a lot more! Never before had I realized that there were millions of people out there who had no access to a church in their language, and no Christian friends who could tell them the Christmas and Easter stories. Those facts bothered me more and more as the night went on. Verwer was not unlike the leader of a rebel band planning a coup. I took seriously his exhortation that night to obey our Lord's commands in Matthew 9:36–38:

- Lift up your eyes. (Look beyond where your feet are standing.)

- See the multitudes in trouble, like scattered sheep without a shepherd.

- Be moved with compassion.

- Pray for workers to take up residence among them and give them the good news.

Our roomful of guys spent the hours of that night pleading with God to send workers to Libya, Pakistan, Saudi Arabia, and Turkey. Though I didn't realize it at the time, that night was my life's turning point.

Initially, my only intention was to pray that *others* would go where the church didn't yet exist. Before that evening, I had never imagined myself as a missionary overseas. I liked America. I liked being a normal Christian. Until recently, I had been sure that becoming a good lawyer would be the best fit for the way God had made me, though I was already toying with the idea of forsaking a law career to become an Army chaplain. But becoming a missionary in a country where they didn't speak English? That option was definitely not on the table. I didn't long to travel outside the United States. And there was no way I was going to live in a hut with snakes and spiders!

However, it wasn't long until, somewhere in the process of God turning my ship in a new direction, I encountered this intriguing question: What if you met nine guys struggling down a path, carrying a heavy log, with eight of them carrying one end and one poor guy desperately trying to carry the other end? Whom would you help?

Well, I'm no intellectual, but I could figure that one out. The point: Why not serve God where the workers were fewest?

I still couldn't see God using me as a pioneer missionary, learning Arabic, Urdu, or Turkish. But I gradually began to realize that my ambitions were too small. As I began to see God as a big God who chooses and uses people who are weak, I began to realize that he could make *anyone* effective and fruitful.

After spending that night in prayer at Moody, I went back to my Wheaton dorm room newly aware of my destiny. Today, I'd call it being chosen to be an apostle to the Muslim peoples of the earth.

Each of us needs to have those moments when we pause and ask, "What is life all about?" And specifically, "What is *my* life all about? Why does God have me on this earth?"

It helps me to review what I know from the truths of God's Word:

- The fool has said, "There is no God."

- The Creator created us for his purposes.

- The Creator has communicated over the centuries through his chosen, validated vessels. We have the essence of what he wants us to know in the collection of their messages known as the Bible.

- In his time, the Creator visited the earth to bring us into his family.

- But we need more than information about God; we also need him to give us the desire and ability to obey him. So, though we were hostages in the kingdom of darkness, he redeemed us, adopted us into his family, and released us from our inability to live the God-purposed life.

- He did this because he loves us. Within the context of that love, he invites us to join him in accomplishing his purposes.

- His primary purpose for his sons and daughters is to demonstrate the difference that Christ makes in us, as individuals and as covenanted communities, so that other people may realize how wonderful God is.

- To do that, we need to be filled with his Holy Spirit, who enlightens us and empowers us to use his gifts. One of the purposes of those gifts is that we will execute our role in obeying his command to make disciples of Jesus Christ among all ethnic groups on the earth.

- As Christ's disciples, we are to follow him by laying down our lives on behalf of the people of our generation, in acts of compassion, while calling all to join us in bowing the knee to the King of kings.

In September 1956, that King had caught my attention, looked at me, and commanded, "Come, follow me." I awoke to the reality that being a follower of the Lord Jesus Christ meant full-time commitment to him and his purposes, no matter what I might do to put food on the table.

In October 1959, that night at Moody Bible Institute, my King smiled at me while I was hovering over the map of North Africa. He invited me to be his co-worker to proclaim the unsearchable riches of Christ in parts of the world where he was not yet loved and worshipped, where the church didn't yet exist. That was my calling to the apostolic mission.

Paul described it this way in Romans 15:20: "It has always been my ambition to preach the gospel where Christ was not known…" I can say with Paul that "I was not disobedient to the vision from heaven" (Acts 26:19). In Paul's day and today, the Lord Jesus commissions some people to be his apostles – a cadre of people in every generation who are called out of ordinary life to do nothing but labor night and day to see communities of obedient Christ-followers established among all the peoples who still don't have adequate access to the Christians who know, communicate, and demonstrate the good news.

In October 1959, I realized that God was so big, he was able to use even the likes of *me* in his apostolic mission. He would enable me to follow Jesus' command to love my neighbor as myself.

My previous career plans evaporated.

I was unbothered by losing my career. I was blithely unconcerned about opposition from Muslims. But one thing did trouble me. Where would I find a wife who was pretty, actually liked me, would stick with me, and was also willing to lay down her life for Muslims?

In my second year at Wheaton, I had met Grace from New York. She was sophisticated, funny, and fun. Plus, our ambitions matched: we both intended to be lawyers. But like most of our fellow students, Grace thought that by linking up with Verwer and his cohorts, I had joined the off-the-wall ranks of monastic, self-torturing, unbalanced fanatics. In any case, she never felt anything romantic toward me. "Muslim world? No thanks," said Grace, smiling.

Koral, a violinist from my home state of Colorado, was willing to go to the mission field. And she would even consider doing it with me! But I figured she was too fragile to take the rigors of pioneer missions.

Then that little redhead Sally came to mind. She was the one I'd picked up on the ski hill. Wasn't she preparing to be a doctor to Muslim ladies in Egypt or Pakistan? I found Sally in the library studying organic chemistry.

"Hi! Remember me?… Greg Livingston? How would you like to go with me to the Muslim world?"

In silence, she looked up at me, then turned her attention back to her molecular models.

"Good," I thought with a smile. "She'll be a challenge!"

Once I realized that God wanted me to proclaim the gospel night and day, I figured that I'd better learn more about the Bible. When I had arrived at Wheaton, I was so ignorant of Scripture that I thought Job might be the Bible's classified ad section. I thought Corinthians were pillars in Greek temples. However, switching my major to Bible and Theology was no small thing, especially since three years of Greek study were required. I found myself unable to get motivated to learn Greek. Before long, I decided: "I'll never be able to serve the Lord because I'm failing Greek."

I discussed my dilemma with my professor. He reassured me that he would arrange a tutor. He told me to show up at a certain time and place, where my tutor would meet me. To my amazement, when I showed up as instructed, there was Sally. He had asked the cute little redhead to tutor me in Greek. I never really got the Greek, but I (eventually) got the tutor!

Actually, with Sally's help, I learned just enough Greek to pass the course. In addition to the Greek and her own science classes, she joined me in systematic theology classes. Most of our dates revolved around studying together. Her scholarship so rubbed off on me that in our final semester at Wheaton, my grades qualified me for the honor roll!

CHAPTER 8

First Big Journey

In light of my new "exotic" calling, it seemed logical to me that I ought to find out what being a foreign missionary actually entailed. So I applied to join the Wheaton College Student Missionary Project in the summer of 1960. I was assigned to go to Honduras with Central America Mission. After I agreed, I found out that the guys I had been praying with on Friday nights at Moody were also brewing up a project to distribute New Testaments that summer. As the kid who wanted desperately to belong, I was tempted to stick around with Verwer, Dale Rhoton, and a new zealot, Roger Malstead.

Roger had caused uproar at Wheaton by resigning from his office as class president as an act of protest. Along with others of us, he was incensed that his fellow students chose to spend their funds on something frivolous like Wheaton College class jackets. He couldn't understand why the college was wasting money on building a new chapel rather than using it to spread the Word of God worldwide.

Those guys' fervor for the Lord attracted me, but I felt responsible to keep my promise to go to Honduras. "If you made a commitment, keep it." Dad Ringle had often drilled this sage advice into me, so I felt I should go ahead with the Wheaton project. Besides, my assignment with Central America Mission was to help a recently widowed missionary, Charlotte Marcy. I couldn't let her down.

On my way south to Honduras, I stopped at home in Aspen. Picking up a copy of the *Aspen Times*, I was stunned to see two photographs on the front page. One was captioned: "Greg Livingston, summer missionary to Honduras." The other was captioned: "Jim Glidden drowned in Princeton swimming pool."

I stared at the two pictures, pondering, "Why not the other way around? Why did God have mercy and open my eyes and not my best friend Jim's? Why wasn't I the one drowned in the Princeton pool?" Still today, I marvel at the indescribable, mysterious privilege of being chosen.

Once I arrived in Honduras, I teamed up with Paul Marcy from Moody Bible Institute to join his widowed mother. Charlotte showed me my room in a small house in the village of Guinope. Before closing the door, she said, "If there is anything you need, just let us know, and we'll tell you how to get along without it!"

My roommate was a young Guatemalan preacher, José Maria Sandoval. He snored very loudly with his mouth open, so I decided to surprise him by pouring some drops from his canteen into his snoring mouth. He woke with a start, yelling, "Gas! Gas!" The canteen didn't hold water; it was kerosene! Not an auspicious beginning for my bonding with the Honduran people.

In her conservative church, Charlotte was not allowed to preach because she was a woman. As she visited villages in the area, she took me along, ostensibly to do the preaching, which she would interpret. I soon realized that her "interpretation" was actually her own sermon, not what I was saying. Realizing that she knew what her adopted people needed much better than I did, I played the game, enabling her to pour out her heart to the people with whom she eventually spent more than sixty years! Charlotte Marcy was my first role model of a missionary who ran a lifetime marathon on the field – a truly great lady.

Even though I could only speak beginner-level Spanish, I attempted to lead everything that moved to accept Jesús Cristo as their personal Savior. My journal illustrates both naïveté and a compulsive obedience to what I assumed God expected.

From that summer onward, Charlotte appointed herself as my missionary mom. I can attest that Jesus' promise in Matthew 19:29 is true: "everyone who has left houses or brothers or sisters or father or mother or wife or children or fields for my sake will receive a hundred times as much and will inherit eternal life." Our heavenly Father not only provides a substitute for an earthly father, but also a mother.

In 2009, when she was ninety years old, my missionary mom flew from Honduras to Chicago to be present when Wheaton College honored Sally and me with the award for Distinguished Service to Humanity. It meant so much to me that Charlotte was able to be there that day.

As I was moving toward graduation from Wheaton, I assumed that a missionary should be an ordained minister. Part of my heritage from my mother was her injunction to climb to the top of the ladder and get all the badges you can, so I felt it was important to become "the Reverend Livingston." The Ringles had moved to Tulsa, where Tulsa Baptist Temple was their new church. Their pastor, Clifford Clark, took me under his wing like yet another father. He was one of those persons God engineered into my life; when I remember him, it simply makes me smile. Because of him, the Bible Baptist denomination agreed to ordain me.

After the summer in Honduras, I was more determined than ever to follow through on my new commitment to lay down my life for those who had never been confronted with the claims of Christ. Hungry for like-minded colleagues, I joined George Verwer's gang of thirteen guys who would spend our Christmas break in Oaxaca, Mexico.

The trip to Oaxaca involved an insane drive in an eleven-year-old Dodge truck from Chicago almost to the border of Guatemala. We dedicated ourselves to visit as many homes as we could in nine days.

Gordon Magney was my street partner that Christmas. When Gordon had arrived at Wheaton as a freshman that autumn, I invited him to join me at our early morning prayer meeting. He later wrote, "I didn't feel like getting up so early for prayer, but Greg kept encouraging me to come. After listening to one of George Verwer's orientation tapes, I decided to keep coming."

Gordon and another zealot, Dick Dryer, were two of the loveliest Christian brothers one would ever hope to know. They lived in expectation of God demonstrating his power in healing. Unlike other Christians I've met, their hunger for God's interventions increased (rather than diminished) their determination to make disciples of all nations.

Later in life, Dick and his wife Shan pioneered in North Africa and Iran. Gordon led teams to North India before settling into ministry with Dari speakers and Pathans in Pakistan and Afghanistan. In 2008, after more than a quarter of a century in those countries, Gordon was buried in Kabul, having literally laid down his life for Afghans.

But during our 1960 Christmas break, we still had a lot to learn. I smile when I think of how we spent those nine days in Oaxaca.

Our team knocked on door after door to sell New Testaments and give out free literature. Our main goal was to get a New Testament into the hands of people who had never possessed one. Gordon took one side of the street and I took the other. He knew a little German, but no Spanish. I knew more, having been in Honduras. In the evenings, he and I were also the dishwashing team.

Even as students, we understood that distributing Scripture was not enough. Each of us cried out to God in expectant faith that he would give us a faithful Mexican co-worker who would carry on in ministry after we left. Our mission strategy was summed up in 2 Timothy 2:2, where Paul instructs Timothy: "what you have heard from me… entrust to faithful men who will be able to teach others also" (RSV).

Every day, after we spent eight hours going door to door distributing Bibles, we each prayed for our faithful man. One day, a team member would declare, "Hey, I have found José, my faithful man." The next day: "Meet Pedro, my faithful man." By the last day, I still hadn't found anyone. I wasn't quite sure how it was supposed to happen. I imagined that I would knock on a door to sell a New Testament, and a guy would say to me, "Hello, I'm your faithful man!"

Unsurprisingly, that didn't happen. However, on the last night, after supper, Dale Rhoton informed us, "We're going out for one more street meeting. We'll preach the gospel in the plaza and give out literature. Then we'll head back to the United States at about midnight."

While Dale was preaching, interpreted by one of the newly discovered Mexican believers, a young Mexican guy sidled up to me in the crowd and whispered, "*Soy creyente.*" (I'm a believer.) After learning that his name was Evaristo, I excitedly handed him some tracts to distribute. He turned pale at the very notion, not having done anything like that before. Then he disappeared into the crowd.

A few hours later, the street meeting was over and we were walking back to our truck when I spotted Evaristo. He was selling kerosene lanterns door to door at eleven o'clock at night! I watched him complete a transaction with an old man wearing a nightshirt. Then I called him over, "Evaristo, *momentito.*"

In my broken Spanish and his broken English, I challenged him to serve the Lord. He patted the money in his pockets as if to communicate, "There's no money in serving the Lord." He wasn't interested. I told him that I had been praying for a faithful man and he was the only believer I had met, so I was sure he was the right guy and I would keep praying until he surrendered himself to serve the Lord Jesus full time! He shrugged his shoulders with a parting word that I think meant, "You can pray till you turn blue, but it isn't going to happen."

On the way back to the United States, we stopped at a petrol station north of Mexico City. Emboldened by our group's evangelistic efforts, I took the opportunity to ask some Mexican guys to consider the claims of Christ on their lives. I was so engrossed that I didn't notice that our truck had departed! It had no window through which those in the back could communicate with the cab, so I suddenly realized that those in each section would assume I was in the other part. I had been left behind in the middle of nowhere in Mexico!

Running out of the station, I fervently pressured two Mexicans to take up the chase. I sat between them in their cab while, at seventy miles an hour, they slowly caught up with our ancient vehicle. The Mexicans honked at the American truck – to no effect. So the Mexican Good Samaritan drove on the wrong side of the highway until we were parallel to my friend's speeding truck.

As I yelled and reached my arm out to signal them to stop, suddenly my hand was full of gospel tracts! Someone in the truck had interpreted my gestures as a request for literature. It took more yelling and daredevil driving before I heard, to my relief, "Hey, that's Livingston!"

Back at Wheaton College, our prayer group gang had taken possession of the graduate school building's basement boiler room. We taped our prayer requests around an eight-foot-diameter pillar in the middle of the room. Every day at noon, we would march around that pillar like Joshua around Jericho, praying for the needs. Evaristo's name was there. For months, my friends and I prayed for him. I wrote to him several times, but got no response. About six months later, I finally received a letter from him: "Gregorio, I got so sick I almost died. I knew I had to surrender to the Lord Jesus to serve him, and that's what I am going to do."

Evaristo went into full-time ministry with us in the summer of 1962. I was both thrilled and amazed at his gifting. He would sell books and Bibles to every member of a family. He led entire Jehovah's Witness and Mormon families to surrender to the Lord Jesus. He eventually went as a missionary to Spain and Italy, then returned to carry on serving his Master in Mexico.

CHAPTER 9

Men of Influence

Wheaton was not only the place where I discovered my lifetime calling, but also the place where God gave me a second father in the person of Evan Welsh. I had nothing but genes from bio-dad Foss, nothing but a name from Bob Livingston, and nothing but heartache from Carl Fagerstrom. Yet the One who promised never to leave or forsake me knew my needs. I had learned the gospel from the cowboy preacher Dan Raley and how to "avoid the world" from my second pastor, Roy (Christians-Don't-Dance) Tubbs. Verlin Ringle was a superb guardian and mentor. But Evan Welsh, the chaplain at Wheaton College, was the first man who caused me to imagine and appreciate what the Lord Jesus is actually like. For me, Chaplain Welsh was a suited Jesus with a crew cut.

If Evan had a fault, I never saw it. Never before had I sensed that someone cared so totally for my welfare. He nurtured a wide personal parish, including his family, old friends, former church members, and 2,000 Wheaton students, yet he always seemed available to this perplexed kid. My religious fervor shot off in a new direction every week as I learned about new kinds of ministries. Dr. Welsh steadied my pursuit of God.

The love of our heavenly Father seems to be best channeled through the love of human fathers. Chaplain Welsh provided what Paul must have experienced with Barnabas. He fathered me in the way that Paul fathered Timothy, Titus, and Onesimus – each of whom Paul called his "dear son." My heavenly Father was fully mindful that I needed a father with his characteristics to overcome my anger, my fear of abandonment, my blind spots, and my immaturity. I clung to Evan Welsh.

He had three prayers for me: that I would marry Sally, that I would become a missionary, and that I would become an ordained Presbyterian pastor like him. That last goal was quite unlikely. The Baptists had convinced me that infant baptism was heresy. Besides that, the Presbyterians I knew didn't look evangelistic enough.

I was gaining evangelistic experience under Campus Crusade's Pete Gilchrist, pastoral care from Evan Welsh, Reformed theology from Kenneth Kantzer and Walt Kaiser, and vision for unreached peoples from George Verwer and Dale Rhoton. The Lord knew that I needed even more input to prepare me for what lay ahead.

He provided it through John Barrier, a graduate student at Wheaton who was determined to mold me into an Acts 17-style Berean, with the habit of searching the Scriptures to see what is true. The Navigators student group is renowned for setting a high bar for memorizing Scripture. I attended several of their meetings, until the leader expelled me from the group for coming unprepared three times! (To this day, I enjoy reminding Navigator leaders, with a grin, that I am a

Nav reject.) Though he was Navigator-trained himself, John stuck with me after my expulsion from the meetings, teaching me not only how to search the Scriptures but also how to conduct a Bible study.

Dale Rhoton pushed me to memorize and meditate on those Scriptures. He gave me Dawson Trotman's booklet, *Born to Reproduce.* Fifty years later, I still stress spiritual reproduction, as taught in 2 Timothy 2:2, as the number-one missiological principle: We must entrust what we have been given to other people who have a heart to please God.

Before I was expelled from the student group, I was invited to go to a Navigator retreat in Cedar Rapids where the speaker was Leroy Eims. Sitting literally at Leroy's feet in a packed room, I was mesmerized by his message on David and Goliath. He challenged us to become giant-killers for God. I was stirred so deeply that I walked through Iowa corn fields for two hours after the meeting, pleading with God to make me one of his giant-killers.

Sally later told me that God must have smiled at the kid in the cornfield, knowing all along that he had had a plan for me since before I was conceived. He knew that he had already set me apart to help accomplish his purposes in the Muslim world.

Along with about twenty other men from Christian colleges around Chicago, I continued to pray through the night every Friday with Dale Rhoton and George Verwer. The millions of Muslims, who had no idea that God had ever visited the earth, were always weighing on our minds. In addition to praying, we would also listen to George, anointed by God to quote Scripture in a way that drilled right through me: "In Luke 14:33, Jesus says it plainly: 'Those of you who do not give up everything you have cannot be my disciples.'" This passage was the gauntlet the Lord threw down in front of my life. The Lord Jesus was making a distinction between those who were just going along with him and those who would be his genuine disciples. This demand was *the* choice; *the* fork in the road of my life that hugely influenced everything I did or decided not to do.

God was ushering into my life a wonderful cadre of men of influence, but to this day, the one who had the greatest impact was my lifelong friend George Verwer. Only eighteen months my senior, this skinny, large-nosed, Dutch-American from New Jersey picked me up in the same way that the Lord Jesus picked up Matthew the tax collector. I could not help but follow him.

One book that had a great impact on the guys I was hanging out with was Roy Hession's *The Calvary Road*. Outside Scripture itself, no other book had a more profound, lasting influence on my orientation toward God and man. Hession's message was similar to that of Augustine, who said, "In the presence of God I am always wrong." Hession's book taught me a foundational principle that I still find important to practice. Even when the other guy is mainly wrong, and I am perhaps only 10 percent wrong, God calls us *both* to repent. The Holy Spirit showed me that except for Christ's beauty, righteousness, and work in my life, I am rotten to the core. Everything I do has mixed motives. Self is never entirely out of the picture. What a battle I've fought throughout my life to stop seeking the approval of men. No wonder our Lord insisted in John 12 that unless a grain of wheat falls into the ground and dies, it will not produce fruit.

One of the most vital lessons I gleaned from George was to repent with a contrite and broken spirit. He also modeled to me the practice of never giving up on people. When a pastor he knows, or knows of, falls into sin, George is one of the first to be on his doorstep or on his phone. For more than fifty years, George has kept me on his radar. He calls, he writes, he visits, and he prays.

CHAPTER 10

Drafted

In the spring of our senior year, I took Sally to the front of Wheaton's beautiful campus. There under the trees, I proposed marriage to her in a way that, I confess, is very embarrassing for me to admit today.

"Listen Sally, I am willing to marry you, because you are ready to go to the Muslim world. But we need to have an understanding. While we are out there, if you get sick and need to come home, I'm not coming back with you. Will you agree to that?"

Something in both of us said that laying down our lives together for the sake of the gospel was right. Eventually, she told me that she thought I was handsome and funny... and besides that – the Lord had told her to marry me!

That spring, we faced another decision together. Sally and I needed to choose the mission agency with which we would go to the Arab world – and eventually to Libya. We had applied to go to Libya with the Presbyterian Church USA. When we arrived for our interview with their board in New York City, I was stunned to be angrily told by the Egyptian-American chairman that we were arrogant to think that Muslims needed Christ. He certainly didn't want to see any Americans becoming missionaries with the purpose of getting Muslims saved!

So the Presbyterian option was off the table. But before we could consider other agencies, I found myself in the Wheaton College infirmary with such a terrible case of mononucleosis that I could hardly walk. It's embarrassing to admit how I contracted the disease. In my zeal to redeem the time, I considered sleeping every night to be a luxury. I birthed what I thought was a revolutionary idea: I decided to attend classes and evangelize in the day and study all night, every other night. I would sleep Monday night, study Tuesday night, sleep Wednesday night, skip sleep Thursday night, and so on. My clever plan worked – for a while! But rather like driving a car without oil, breakdown was inevitable. I became so ill with mononucleosis that the college physician declared I wouldn't be able to work, study, or do anything for at least a year!

While lying in the hospital bed, rebelling against the doctor's prognosis, I had a visit from Dr. Francis Steele of North Africa Mission (NAM). He came to inquire why Sally and I hadn't followed up on our application. NAM had been the only agency with missionaries in Libya. However, it seemed to me that most of their missionaries had given up expecting much to happen. For a "Verwerized" zealot such as myself, NAM didn't seem to be very compelling. Besides, the last workers in Libya with NAM had just been expelled. NAM was saying that the door to Libya was closed to missionaries.

So, without much interest, I was discussing our options with Dr. Steele. Suddenly, the infirmary door flew open, hiding Dr. Steele from the view of my latest visitor – Bill Bright, the founder of Campus Crusade. Obviously in a hurry, Bright declared with little preamble: "We are ready to take you, Livingston. If you want strategy, it's the university campus." He said a quick prayer and left.

Dr. Steele, probably concluding I was a hopeless case, meekly followed Bright out the door. I wasn't all that bothered. I think I had already made up my mind that we'd team up with Verwer in an unknown mission that barely existed. At the time, he was calling it Send the Light; later, it became Operation Mobilisation (OM).

It was all faintly ridiculous. I was so unwell that I wasn't in a fit condition to go anywhere with anyone! Still, I was determined to lead a team to Mexico after graduation a month later. Then at the end of the summer, I would marry Sally.

With graduation approaching, I received a letter from the President of the United States:

> *Congratulations, you have been chosen from among the citizens of the United States of America to serve your country in the United States Army.*

My student draft deferment had run out. I was ordered to show up for testing and a physical examination in Chicago. During the physical, the agent bumped my head to push it closer to the machine for the eye test. For several seconds, everything was blurry, which resulted in my being rated as having very bad eyesight, although in fact it was outstanding!

Next was the exam. My score on the "tools" section was zero – I couldn't recognize any! I also failed at visualizing what shape of object would be produced by folding diagrams on the dotted lines. On the English section, I got 100 percent. The Army's conclusion was that I should serve my country as a truck driver. They didn't seem to notice that I was so weak with mono, I could hardly walk!

By this point, I felt I was already drafted into the Lord's army, so I phoned Aspen's Selective Service office. Miss Berg, a seventy-five-year-old lady, was the entire draft board for Pitkin County, Colorado. "Miss Berg, I've just been drafted into the Army, but I hope to become a pastor and missionary. I need a ministerial deferment."

"Land sakes!" she exclaimed. "We haven't had a minister from this county in anyone's memory. That makes us look like heathens. You've got it." So I was free to serve my commander, the Lord Jesus, the King of kings.

Yes, I was free. Except that I was facing finals, and I was so weak that the college doctor reiterated that I would not be able to work or do anything for a year. I would certainly not travel to Mexico that summer as a missionary or get married in August!

I was sure that the doctor's prognosis was not God's. I was far from being what would today be called a charismatic (and most would say that I'm still only 49 percent so). I had no experience with healings, but I was bolstered by a note that George Verwer wrote from Spain, simply reminding me: "James 5 is still in the book."

I looked up the passage:

*Is anyone among you sick? Let them call the elders of
the church to pray over them and anoint them with oil
in the name of the Lord. And the prayer offered in faith
will make the sick person well; the Lord will raise them
up.*

James 5:14–15

Well, I wasn't part of a church with elders, so I gathered the
brothers who I thought had the most effective prayer lives. (A
couple of chaps from my theology class thought their lack of
faith might prevent my healing.) Gordon Magney invited the
local Assemblies of God pastor, who told the group, "Don't
worry! I can heal him myself!"

To this day, I don't know who the Lord used, but he
did seem to honor the fact that we agreed in prayer that
I would be healed so that I could press on to Mexico. For
an hour, they prayed for me, laying their hands on me and
anointing me with oil. Then I went home. I was still so weak
I had to climb the stairs to my room on my hands and knees.
However, the next morning, confident in God's promises, I
put on my tennis shoes, went down to the college track, and
ran a mile.

I was so excited about my new energy that I ran straight
from the track to the college infirmary and into the doctor's
office, where I informed him I was healed! Skeptically, he
replied, "Well, we'll see about that." He ordered a blood test,
which showed that I was indeed 80 percent improved.

I wondered why I wasn't completely healed. I scowled at
the Lord, thinking, "God, you really missed your opportunity

to teach this doctor a lesson." But later that day, the Father helped me to understand: "You wanted your energy back so you could serve me in Mexico. You've got it! I didn't heal you 100 percent because I knew you would go on a tangent and think that you should empty out hospitals. That's not my calling for you. Don't forget what I've called you to – laying down your life for Muslim peoples."

If Sally and I were to marry, I realized that I needed to ask for her mother's blessing. During spring break, before I was hospitalized, I had made my way to Pittsburgh, Pennsylvania to meet Mrs. Coltman. Though we both grew up mostly without our fathers, Sally's family life was nothing like mine. She grew up in Mt. Lebanon, a rather posh suburb of Pittsburgh. Her father had suffered a heart attack at work and died when Sally was only seven. Mom Coltman continued to raise their five children, then aged five to sixteen, with grace and wisdom. Their church gave her a job as its bookkeeper so that she could work from home. Life insurance and support from her many friends had also helped.

On my way to Pittsburgh, I prepared myself to answer the classic question: "How do you intend to support my daughter?" I was ready with a sermon about living by faith.

But Mom Coltman didn't ask about money. Her vital question for me as a prospective son-in-law was: "What do you think of Donald Grey Barnhouse?"

I was speechless. I had never heard of Barnhouse, the great preacher at Philadelphia's Tenth Presbyterian Church.

But I promised to read his books, and Margaret Coltman gave her blessing on our marriage. I am still grateful that she saw past all my immaturity to see a young man after God's own heart.

Sally and I had agreed to get married at the end of August, but because of my fears about marrying the wrong woman, I insisted she spend the summer in Mexico to confirm that we were really supposed to be married. She had to demonstrate to me that she was made of what I thought was "the right stuff." Though she had been on a Christmas venture there, I wanted her to spend six more weeks in Mexico with an OM team, selling books and Bibles door to door.

In Vera Cruz, I led a men's team, mainly from Moody Bible Institute, and teamed up once again with my faithful man Evaristo. Sally lived with a local family in Mexico City, serving on a women's team. She passed the test; she was definitely made of "the right stuff."

As OM members (or "OMers," as we came to be known), we earned money by selling our books and Bibles. Trying to live out the model from Acts 2, we "had everything in common" and gave to "anyone who had need." Three weeks before our wedding, Sally needed to get from Mexico City to Pittsburgh. She took a bus from Mexico City to the US border, but there hadn't been enough money to cover her fare all the way home. A relative wired her the money for the rest of the trip. This was only one example of how our "living by faith" failed to impress her family members!

Three days before our wedding date, it was time for me to return to the States. But before I could leave, the guys on the team tackled me, held me down, and shaved one side of my furry chest! During this episode, they made a tape recording, which started with the words, "Now a message by Greg Livingston, on love." The next words on the tape were: "You dirty guys, you crazy guys – I'm going to kill you when I get up. I'm going to take revenge." Other uncharitable words followed. Thankfully, that cassette was never widely distributed!

My zeal for the Lord of hosts and for lost people had developed more quickly than my level of maturity. I can now candidly admit that we early members of OM were unbalanced – and George Verwer would be the first to agree. But everything, including our wedding plans, was viewed through the lens of that zeal. We were determined not to spend any money on our wedding. We invited only a few friends, because we didn't want them to waste the money to travel to Pittsburgh. We had no photographer and no catering. As she walked up the aisle, Sally almost tripped as her high heels punctured the white paper that served as a runner down the middle of the church. Her mother provided some finger food after the wedding, but I didn't want to waste time chit-chatting. So after only an hour at the reception, we left my mother, who had come all the way from Portland; my best man Leo Punt, who had come from Chicago; and my dear foster father Fred Blauvelt, who had come from Virginia.

Even more thoughtlessly, I had failed to make any reservation for our honeymoon. I told Sally that we would "go by faith." That so-called faith meant that we drove for hours before we found a motel with a vacancy. And, as Sally has since said quite bluntly, "It was a dump."

What a trooper she was, and is! Over the ensuing years, I would have been greatly limited in my usefulness for God without the magnificent, faithful, bolstering, serving spirit of Sally Coltman Livingston. Despite all the time and effort she spent to help me pass my courses, she also did well in her own subjects as a zoology major. In 1961, well before it became common for women, Sally earned admission to medical school. She had wrestled with the question: "Should I marry Greg or go to medical school… or both?" I encouraged her to become a doctor, but I must admit that my ego was a little strained at the thought of being introduced as "Mister and Doctor Livingston."

Before we had left Wheaton, Sally took a long walk with her good friend Jackie Thornson to talk it over. Looking back, she says it was nothing particular that Jackie said, but by the end of their walking and talking, she knew that the Lord was telling her to marry me and to give up medical school. She had already begun to doubt that medical school was God's direction. After all, she had wanted to become a doctor as a means of going to the Middle East, but she had come to realize that she could evangelize and make disciples without being a doctor. In those days, we hadn't really developed an evangelical social conscience. We simply saw people leaving the kingdom of Satan and entering the kingdom of God as the clear, unchallengeable, number-one priority.

CHAPTER 11

Making It Up

After a brief honeymoon trip back to Illinois via Niagara Falls, I returned to Wheaton College for further studies to prepare as a missionary. At the time, Wheaton offered no courses in missiology, so I studied for a master's degree in Christian Education.

We rented a studio apartment for $72.50 a month, and Sally landed a job as the door-to-door visitor for the Roselle Evangelical Free Church. She gave a copy of the new Phillips translation of the New Testament to one lady who seemed hungry for God. A week later, Sally was astounded to discover that the woman had read it cover to cover. She asked, "What stood out to you most?" The woman replied, "That fellow Paul didn't like women very much, did he?"

Shortly after I had enrolled in graduate classes, I received in the mail a scrap of paper posted from Spain. It was a summons from George Verwer, commissioning me to bring a chartered plane full of young men from North America to Europe for OM's 1963 summer campaign.

Verwer's vision was to mobilize 2,000 young people to spend their summer vacation visiting every home of every town and village in the five predominantly Roman Catholic countries of Austria, Belgium, France, Italy, and Spain. We would provide New Testaments, evangelistic books, and invitations to a Bible correspondence course. So, while George and others recruited in Europe, it was my assignment to recruit in the USA.

In the early 1960s, church groups might occasionally send a few people to help build a church in Mexico or a school in Central America. But short-term mission efforts like George proposed were rare. Not a few people criticized OM's plan to take students to Europe for the summer as a terrible waste of mission money.

Nevertheless, I went to a travel agency in Wheaton to charter a plane for the coming summer. The agent dutifully phoned around to get the price on a charter from New York to Paris and back. He announced the cost: $27,000! My eyes opened wide in disbelief as I blurted out, "No, no, I don't want to buy the plane. I only want to use it once!" For a student with no supporters or organization, $27,000 may as well have been $27 million.

I gave the agent the $15 I had in my pocket as a down payment, and he gave me a schedule of dates when I must make the next three payments. How was I going to do it? I felt terribly alone and scared.

I wrote to every Bible school and Christian college I knew of, informing them of the day when I expected to be on their campus. I asked, "May I please speak in your chapel to tell your students about this opportunity with Operation Mobilisation?" In retrospect, I am utterly amazed that I – a totally unknown young man with a group no one had ever heard of – was offered the chance to speak in every chapel of every school except one – and they offered me an evening meeting instead.

I found a great deal from the Greyhound Bus Company: I could travel for ninety-nine days for only $99. So I told my new bride to attend my classes and take good notes. I would be back in time for the final exams.

My goal was to fill all 113 seats on that charter plane. Sleeping in buses at night, I spoke to any audience I could corral during the day. Only men were invited. This was "war," and in those days, women didn't go to war!

When students asked how much it would cost, I told them that our OM stance was: "Unless you forsake all that you have, you cannot be my disciple." In integrity before the Lord, each guy was supposed to provide everything he could. One donated $40, another $4,000! We sent the applicants some books and George's orientation tapes; otherwise, the only requirement was to show up at a certain church in New Jersey on the appointed day in June. From there, church buses would take everyone to New York's Idlewild Airport. Applicants were supposed to send in a one-page form, which was really just a notification of their interest. Our application process amounted to this: "Whosoever will, may come."

One day, while I was waiting outside the dean's office at Columbia Bible College, I sat next to a woman I supposed was a student's grandmother. She reached out her arm to shake hands and declared, "Ten Boom."

I thought to myself, "'Tin boon' to you too, lady," and proceeded to ignore her. Sometime later, I realized I had missed a delightful opportunity to converse with Corrie Ten Boom, a woman of God from Holland whose family hid Jewish people during World War II.

When I arrived at Bob Jones University, some students led me to a prayer meeting in progress. Of course, I asked them to pray for people to come to Europe for the OM summer effort. When we pronounced the final "amen" and stood up, two campus policemen politely asked me to accompany them to the dean's office. This reception was rather different to the one I'd received at the other schools. The dean said to me, "Brother Livingston, no one comes here without an invitation. And we don't give invitations to people who sell Billy Graham's books." Needless to say, we had no one on our charter from Bob Jones University.

Once I got back from my ninety-nine-day trip, a man called our studio apartment in Wheaton.

"Do you take divorced people?" he asked me.

"One moment please," I answered him and put my hand over the receiver. I looked at Sally and whispered, "Do we take divorced people?"

She shrugged her shoulders in a bewildered "I don't know" way.

Taking my hand off the receiver, I asked him, "You love Jesus, Dave?"

"I sure do!"

"Yeah, okay. That's fine."

We were making up our policies as we went along.

On the appointed day at Idlewild Airport, 103 recruits piled out of the church buses. Ten of them were unstoppable women! Because the Super Constellation propeller plane held 113 passengers, I was discouraged. Where were the other ten? I walked up and down the airport searching for others I might recruit. I even spoke to one Jewish guy who was interested in getting a cheap flight, but he decided that becoming a Christian and a missionary just to save $50 was probably not worth it.

The propeller plane was parked off the tarmac on the grass. We loaded our luggage onto the plane ourselves, and then we were off. That year, 1963, was the first year that getting from the US to Europe was cheaper by plane than by boat. Our journey over the Atlantic required landing in Newfoundland and Ireland en route to Paris.

The European OM team had recruited about 900 students for July – and another thousand for August. Greater Europe Mission allowed us to use their castle in Lamorlaye, near Paris. Our crew of more than a thousand young people – including the Americans I'd brought plus large numbers of British, German, Dutch, and Spanish folk, and a sprinkling of Belgian, French, Swiss, and Swedish people – sprawled across the grounds of the castle with our tents and sleeping bags and field kitchen. We looked more like a settlement of nomads than respectable missionaries.

My first responsibility was to be in charge of security and discipline. How was I supposed to apply the rule of going to bed by ten o'clock when I stumbled into a vociferous late-night prayer meeting of Spanish students, tearfully crying out for the salvation of their people? They were tossing their watches into a pile in the center of their prayer circle. Selling their possessions was their way of forsaking all that they had in their quest to be Christ's disciples. Though we were only at the beginning of our sixty-day quest to visit every Catholic village, we didn't have much money left in the coffers for essentials like food!

But it was all a great adventure, fuelled by the way we kindled one another's faith and expectancy, fanned into flame by a dash of 1960s *zeitgeist*. In answer to one day's prayers, a farmer brought us a truck-load of cabbages! We had cabbage for nearly every meal. The smell was so bad, we joked that we'd been bombed by gas warfare!

After a week of orientation, we loaded up the old trucks that a team of mostly amateur mechanics had rescued from junk yards. How far these trucks would travel, full of students and literature, no one could predict.

One team had combined members of the German state church with Dutch Pentecostals. As they crossed the Italian Alps, their truck's engine overheated and died. With no help in sight, the Dutch felt led to lay their hands on the engine and exorcise the demons! The conservative Germans were so stunned and shocked that OM's reputation in Germany was summed up as "bizarre" for the next several years. The team did make it to their destination in Italy, though perhaps not before some of the Germans defected.

Verwer asked Sally and me to lead a team of Americans and Brits to the villages of north-east Spain's Costa Brava. The team of twelve men and women somehow crammed into an old Fiat van which managed to crawl from Paris to Barcelona.

Frequently, we had to leave the van in a mechanic's garage while team members walked through the nearby villages offering an invitation to a free correspondence course and selling New Testaments and Billy Graham's *Paz con Dios* (*Peace with God*).

In 1963, Protestants were still illegal in Franco's Spain. We were reported, arrested, and escorted to police stations nearly every day. Whoever on the team had the most proficiency in Spanish would pray out loud in the police station for the souls of the police until the local priest arrived to instruct the constables what to do. Invariably, they called the central government in Madrid. Because we were ten teams spread across Spain, they were getting such calls from all over the country. Possibly to avoid an international incident, the central authorities instructed the police to let us go. Of course, we wouldn't leave until we did our best to evangelize everyone in the police station.

If we didn't sell our books and New Testaments, we didn't have money to eat. Our team sold enough to support ourselves in relatively well-off north-east Spain, but my Wheaton buddy Gordon Magney didn't fare so well. His team was assigned to an area in southern Spain, where people were poorer. After two days without sales, his team had no money for food. They began to rebel. Perplexed, he had them rest beside a country road while he walked off to sit by a small pond, beseeching God to provide for the team.

While he was sitting by the water, a duck landed in the pond and began to swim directly in front of Gordon's feet. Grabbing a stick that was providentially lying beside him,

Gordon whacked the duck and, with a huge smile, brought it back to the team. While he had been gone, a farmer had stopped to chat with the team. They had managed to trade him two New Testaments for some potatoes, carrots, and onions. Amazingly, one of the team members could cook well enough to turn it all into duck stew. *Jehovah Jireh* – the Lord had provided!

Not all events that summer were so encouraging. One of the American students took me into his confidence, whispering that we had a "communist" on the team. Not many Americans had ever met a socialist from Britain before! In those Cold War days, we Americans were so suspicious of anyone whose political views were different from our own.

Now seven years old in the Lord, I had faithfully kept the vow I had made as a new Christian that my lips would never touch alcohol. As a newcomer to Europe, I was unaware that believers there commonly drank wine and beer, so I was not prepared for my first communion at the Brethren assembly in Barcelona. I looked askance at the shared cup, wondering about germs. But following the lead of the others, when the cup was handed to me, I took a swig. In semi-shock, I realized I had broken my vow! In that instant, I thought that I might die – not from a lightning bolt of judgment, but because I could neither spit it out in that holy circumstance nor swallow it, due to my vow. I would need to hold it in my mouth until I starved to death!

Suddenly, I pictured the angels in heaven holding their stomachs in laughter. "Hey, look at this one," I saw them saying, making God himself grin. So I swallowed the wine.

Our culinary cross-cultural lessons continued. The Brethren church members invited our team to join their families who were taking their holidays at Barcelona's beaches. Without considering what the menu might be, I adamantly instructed my team members to behave scripturally and eat and drink "whatever they set before you," without asking questions. Little did I know that the fare would be crabs, scallops, mussels, and *escargot* – all unfamiliar to me. Plus, I hadn't realized that many European Christians not only used wine for communion, but they had no qualms about serving beer, wine, and rum outside of church as well.

We divided the team among four Spanish families. Since Sally and I were separated from the others, I had no opportunity to moderate my command that the team members should eat *all* the food served and drink *all* of the beverages. That night, in the church basement where we were housed, Sally and I stayed up all night carrying buckets, as all the other team members were throwing up!

In one village far from our Barcelona base, we created a scandal when we couldn't find any accommodation one night. Resigned to our only option – a deserted barn – we lay our sleeping bags down in a big "U" formation. Single guys laid down on my right, and the girls slept on Sally's left. It was all quite chaste, yet somehow a rumor spread that the guys and girls on our team were "sleeping together."

At the end of the summer, I helped George decide which of the American participants we would urge to stay on for a one-year program. Clearly lacking discernment, I chipped in that I saw no potential in two of the young guys named Loren

Cunningham and Kevin Dyer. But in fact, each of those brothers later started a dynamic mission agency: Loren founded Youth With A Mission (for the more Pentecostal-oriented young people), and Kevin founded International Teams (for those linked with the Plymouth Brethren). Much to the credit of George Verwer's open-hearted, open-handed outlook, there exist today at least a hundred ministries that were founded by us "nobodies" who got our mission initiation in OM.

The immediate news was less uplifting. At the end of that summer, we owed $70,000 in literature invoices. While I accompanied the Americans back on the charter, Sally drove an ancient Hummer car full of students back to England. I was then stuck at George Verwer's parents' house in New Jersey, because George announced that there would be no more travel until God erased the debt for the literature. After ten days of fasting and crying out to God to provide, the miracle happened. One of the girls, a former Wimbledon tennis player, donated her entire inheritance to OM – just the equivalent of the $70,000 we needed to pay our debt!

The travel ban was lifted, and we were on the road again. Two other OM members and I flew from New York to Manchester, England. There were only fourteen people on the entire 707 jet for that flight – we three, plus nine Mormon missionaries, a priest, and a businessman. We three OMers "took on" the Mormons in rigorous theological debate. The flight attendant was quite disappointed: after she offered free booze to all, only the priest and the businessman took advantage of her generosity.

It was my first time on British soil. The customs agent asked, "How much money do you have, Mr. Livingston?"

"Three dollars, sir."

"Three dollars? How long do you expect to stay?"

"Oh, there is plenty of money at our international headquarters."

"Oh? And where might that be?"

"Atherton."

"Atherton? A most unlikely location for an international headquarters."

I had no idea how correct he was. We were collected by a windowless van, so I saw nothing of England until they opened the doors in the tiny coal-mining village of Atherton, Lancashire. OM had been given the use of a condemned building for our first British headquarters. Gawking at the soot-covered, dilapidated old houses, my first thought was, "I've been lied to! The Germans must have won the war!"

I was delighted, of course, to be reunited with Sally, but not so enamored with our accommodation. We, along with George and his wife Drena, were the only married couples, so we weren't on the floor of the men's or women's dorms. Instead, we had a space in the rafters under the apex of the roof. Our five-by-eight-foot space admitted no light, but that was okay because we didn't actually want to see what might be sleeping with us. We simply slid in on our stomachs, trying to remember not to bump our heads on the roof by sitting up!

We met every day for orientation and prayer with those who had stayed on after the summer for the year-long program.

Some of them would go back to Catholic Europe to follow up people we'd met during the summer; others would head to Asia. We held the meetings in a damp and dark church about half a mile from our condemned house. By this time of year, it was dark when we headed home from our meetings. I was walking back to the house alone when I saw a man lying on the sidewalk. He was obviously sick and maybe dying! A little boy, presumably his son, ran up to me blurting out, "Penny for the guy!"

It was obvious to me that the man didn't need a penny – he needed a hospital! I rushed to his side, only to discover that it was not a man, but a dummy. Deeply offended by the boy's deception to get money, I lectured him with the conviction of a prophet about his likely future in the penitentiary. He must give up this life of trickery and embezzlement!

Wide-eyed and confused, he ran away. Back at the "headquarters," I boasted to the group how I had, hopefully, rescued this boy from a life of degradation and crime. To my surprise, the room rocked with laughter! The Brits explained "Guy Fawkes Day," Britain's celebration of a foiled assassination plot, which is remembered with bonfires to burn the effigy of the offender. Twenty-four hours later, on the same walk, I saw the boy and his dummy again. Wishing to apologize, I hurried toward him, but he tore off down the street.

My next adventure in Britain was to put on a suit on Sunday evening and speak with two others at a church some miles away. Like all OM vehicles, the ancient Austin Gypsy we were loaned had a governor which fixed its speed at nothing faster than forty miles per hour. We got a late start. When we had gone some way down the road, I realized we were almost out of petrol. At the petrol station, the three of us zealously preached to the station owner, Mr. McCoy, that he needed to be saved by the Lord Jesus. Instead of ignoring us, he challenged us: "If you are serious Christians, come into my house and pray for my wife, who is ill." I glanced at my watch; we were already late, but how could we refuse? So we hurried through a prayer and took off again.

Trying to make the meeting on time, I attempted to pass a slow-moving car by pushing the Gypsy as fast as it could go through the pitch-black rainy night. Built for the continental market, the Gypsy's steering wheel was on the left, rather than on the right, as would be normal for a British vehicle. This hindered my ability to see well when passing a car. Seeing two small lights approaching me in the lane of the oncoming traffic, I assumed it was two harmless bicycles which would pull to the side as I passed.

They weren't bicycles. It was a huge truck loaded with copper, driving with only its parking lights turned on. (In those days it was commonly thought in Europe that driving with headlights on drained the battery.)

I slowed to get back into my lane, but the car I had been passing had slowed down too! I tried to dive between the oncoming truck and the car. *Bang!* The truck caught our right fender and whipped us around like a top. We landed on the opposite side of the road in a ditch. The door on the passenger's side was gone. Rudy from Canada realized the sleeve of his suit was gone as well! He checked and rechecked to see if his arm was still there. It was. Beyond a few cuts and scratches from the shattered windshield, we weren't hurt, but the police issued me with three citations, including a court summons for reckless driving.

Some days later, I felt the Lord was telling me to revisit the McCoy family at the petrol station. The parents weren't there, but sixteen-year-old Roderick was. I don't remember exactly what we talked about, but most likely, I walked him through the *Four Spiritual Laws* evangelistic booklet, and he prayed. Would anything come of it? I could hardly think so. The Lord didn't seem to use me to actually usher people into regeneration.

In this case, however, Roderick's was no empty "pray after me" experience. He had met the Lord! He went on to become a representative for Mission Aviation Fellowship, then a pastor, and only recently retired after planting a church among Brits in north-west Spain with his equally zealous wife, Janet.

As the teams were forming for the year-long program, Sally and I naturally assumed that with our calling to Arab Muslims, we would go to Beirut. George Verwer had other plans. "I need you to take the team to India. We don't want to be the 'ugly Americans' who insist on being in charge, so I'm making the East Londoner the official team leader, but I'm counting on *you* to get them there."

I protested, "George, I don't even know where India is!"

"Keep driving east. You can't miss it!" His dismissive reply was the end of the discussion. In those days, one did what the leader ordered! There wasn't much time to debate, in any case, because my court date was coming up. Without money to pay a fine, it was thought that I might go to jail for my reckless driving.

Our OM British base administrator declared, "We'd better get you out of the country." It never crossed my mind that to leave the country with an outstanding warrant would be wrong. (Many years later, I managed to get a British driver's license, so I trust a statute of limitations is in effect on those citations!)

We decided to visit Sally's brother Bill, an Air Force major, at his base in Germany. We would wait for the team headed to India to meet up with us there. We were given just enough money from the common pool to get to Dover and take the ferry to Calais, France. Our only option after that was to hitch-hike. Opening our box of French phrases, we memorized two that we thought should suffice: *Enchanté de faire votre connaissance! Ou allez vous?*" ("We're delighted to make your acquaintance! Where are you going?")

The road seemed to be filled only with freight trucks, which ignored us. After an hour or so, I decided to hide behind a bush and leave Sally out there thumbing for a ride. It worked! As Sally stuttered her *"Enchanté!"* to the crusty French driver, I ran out from behind the bush and jumped in the cab with them. The driver was obviously disappointed.

We managed to explain that our destination was Germany. His was not. At midnight, indicating with sign language that he was driving in a different direction, he dropped us in the middle of nowhere. "Walking by faith" was apparently still the Lord's program for us. We walked toward the only light we could see. Standing in front of a large building, we waited for a car to stop. Finally, to our relief, one did. But as we were about to open the door, it suddenly sped away. A nasty trick, we thought.

About twenty minutes later, the same thing happened. A car slowed as if to pick us up, then suddenly fled. Why? Did we look that bad? Turning around, we deciphered the large sign behind us: "Home for the Mentally Ill." No doubt, those stopping thought we were escapees!

Finally, a police car picked us up and allowed us to sleep in a cell for the rest of the night. The next morning, we caught a ride in a two-seater sports car. I sat very uncomfortably on the gearshift all the way to Saarbrucken!

Because Sally had studied some scientific German in preparation for medical school, we managed to interpret the road signs well enough to navigate to Zweibrucken, near Bill's Air Force base. We called him from a pub. This was the first time I had met my brother-in-law. I can only imagine his first opinion of me – an unshaven, penniless nomad! Sally's first words to him were: "Bill, do you have a Deutschmark to pay for the telephone call?" Livingston, "the spiritual giant," felt rather small. I'm pretty sure that until his death in Vietnam, Bill thought that his sister had married an irresponsible hippy.

The team destined for India eventually arrived to pick us up. As we crossed the border from Germany into Switzerland, we pulled into a petrol station. The attendant was shouting, "*Kennedy ist tot!*" The US president's assassination was another stark reminder that we had been called to God's rescue operation in a world ravaged by the powers of darkness.

All of us driving to India, Turkey, Iran, and the Arab world had agreed to meet up in a *pensione* in Switzerland to touch base, making sure we had all gotten that far. However, before we could continue our journey, several people came down with the mumps and the Swiss government quarantined the entire group for six weeks! As money ran low, blaming started. A self-appointed prophet decided there was a Joshua 7-type "Achan in the camp," who had triggered the Lord's discipline on us. Some Americans decided it must be the Brits, because they had "prayed in" the least money. I'm ashamed to admit that I failed to stand up against that misguided thinking.

Finally, we were on the way to India! By the time we mounted our rust-bucket steeds – two VW vans and two old Ford Bedford trucks – it was December and snowing. For some reason unknown to me, there were no heaters in any of the vehicles. (Perhaps they had been removed during the previous hot summer when they couldn't be prevented from blasting out heated air.)

Sally and I sat in the front seat of our ancient VW van, which had been bought from a junkyard in Holland. In the back, German Helga and British Pauline squeezed between suitcases, boxes of cheese, and huge tins of peanut butter – our staples and sustenance for the entire next two months! We had no money even to stay in cheap student hostels along the way through Yugoslavia, Bulgaria, Turkey, Iran, Afghanistan, and Pakistan. So we drove through the nights. (Two years later, the OM leaders forbade this practice after some OMers died in a nighttime road accident.)

While driving through Bulgaria, I was so cold that I wore a sleeping bag with the bottom loosened enough so that I could work the clutch, brake, and gas pedal. To keep awake, Sally and I made up songs of praise. Our favorite, never published (or sung by anyone besides us) was:

Why should I be called a child of the King? (x 2)
Not that you have chosen me, but I have chosen you,
says the Lord our God.
Not that you have chosen me, but I have chosen you,
And appointed you to go and bear fruit.

Well, at least it kept us awake!

When we arrived in Ankara, Turkey, we enjoyed the luxury of actually sleeping in a horizontal position... on top of packages of Turkish books. We were in the apartment that served as a base for my Wheaton friends and fellow OMers Roger Malstead and Dale Rhoton. They were the first missionaries in almost fifty years to live in Turkey and minister directly to Muslim Turks. The earlier Protestant missionaries were ordered by their leaders only to minister to the members of the ancient Armenian, Assyrian, and Greek churches.

Dale had originally felt God was calling him to join Wycliffe Bible Translators and work among a Bible-less tribe. But back at those Friday all-night prayer meetings at Moody, George had challenged him, "What if I told you about a tribe of 30 million people who have the Bible translated, but almost none of them has a copy. What would you do?"

"I'd go to that tribe!" Dale blurted out.

"Then go to Turkey!" George countered.

Roger teamed up with Dale, and a new mission era in Turkey was birthed in 1961. When we passed through two years later, only one Muslim Turk was known to be walking with Jesus Christ.

Our long-anticipated sleep indoors (even if the "bed" was a stack of gospel literature) was rudely interrupted by the Turkish police. They hauled all of the guys to the police station; we were arrested as anti-Islamic propagandists. My one night in jail did not make me into an instant "apostle Paul," but many gospel workers who entered Turkey in subsequent years were sentenced to many months in prison. How prepared are we to follow them and Paul? How many other missionaries through the centuries have spent time in filthy, rat- and flea-infested Middle Eastern prisons for "his name's sake"?

As we left Ankara, our VW van was followed by twelve of our guys in a Bedford truck. We headed north-east along the Black Sea, continuing until we reached the town of Trabzon, where the body of the guys' truck dislodged from the chassis.

A Turkish army colonel came to our rescue with a welding team. While we waited, we decided to see whether anyone would buy our stock of the first modern Christian book translated into Turkish, *The Peanut Man: The Life Story of George Washington Carver*. A few curious bystanders had walked up. We quickly learned to say "seventy-five cents" in Turkish and starting waving the book. Two people immediately bought copies, which drew a larger crowd. With one person pulling the books out of the box, another placing the books into outstretched hands, and a third collecting the coins, we sold seventy copies in a frenzied fifteen minutes!

After leaving Trabzon, we turned south-east and soon began to climb toward Mount Ararat, where we joked about finding Noah's ark. Foolishly, we continued to drive as night fell and snow drifted down around us. We didn't see the ark, but to our alarm, we did see several trucks that had slid off the road into the snow banks. My experience of driving in Aspen, plus unmerited favor from our heavenly Father, got us over the top and down again to the Iranian border.

We were pleased that the hotel at the border had a roof, but I won't describe the toilets. Given permission to sleep overnight on the floor of the lobby, we were startled when we awakened in the morning to find ourselves surrounded by fifty truck drivers sharing the floor!

I stared at the transit visa form provided by Iranian border guards. "What is your mother?" it asked. Clearly, they were not used to tourists in the winter of 1963. Perhaps very few visitors arrived overland. After all, the Automobile Association in England had warned us: "Motor travel through the Middle East is not yet a reality."

The desert went on and on, and so did the snow. Suddenly, at about 8:00 p.m. on Christmas Eve, I hit a huge pothole, breaking the back axle of the VW van. Sally, the two other women, and I were very grateful that the guys in the truck realized we were no longer following them. They turned back and found us where we'd broken down, with not a soul or building in sight. As they reversed to tie a tow rope to the van, their engine conked out. It wouldn't start again.

By now, the snow storm was so thick that we had to form a human chain to get from the VW into the back of the Bedford truck. Choosing to risk asphyxiation rather than to freeze, we kept a kerosene heater going through the night. Thinking I must have seen a movie about it once, I demanded that no one sleep lest they freeze to death. To stay awake, we shivered through Christmas carols until dawn.

When the sky cleared, the snow on the ground was twenty inches deep. Hearing a freight truck approaching, we ran out to wave it down. It roared past. So did a second and a third, each about half an hour apart. Recalling my tactic in Calais, we sent Sally, Helga, and Pauline out to wave down the next Iranian transport truck. It worked again!

Dick Dryer was the only one of us who knew some Farsi. While he bargained with the driver, the other guys tied the Bedford to the Iranian truck's axle. Sneering at our paltry monetary offer, the Iranian started to drive off, then turned furious when he realized he was pulling a truck *and* a VW van. More money mollified his resistance, but only earned us a lift to the nearest village of mud huts.

There, on Christmas Day, we found a room at the inn – a single big room that we shared with the inn's Iranian guests that night. All thirteen of us huddled under a Persian rug draped over a wooden stand, which covered an iron dish full of hot coals. The "manger" next door was an unbearably reeking toilet for both people and animals. We were stunned at the realization that our Lord had been born in such humble circumstances! Never before had the humiliation of the first Christmas been so real or so meaningful.

A missionary-businessman, Bob Rutz, rescued us. He and his wife Joan had established the first combination hamburger joint/mini-golf course in Iran. His business was popular with the Shah's family, but we were more thrilled by a hot bath in the Rutz's home, which seemed like a palace after a month on "the road less traveled."

The outbreak of the mumps and our automotive breakdowns had cost us much travel time. I was scheduled to meet leading missionaries in Madras at the annual gathering of the Evangelical Fellowship of India to make arrangements for our future teams. Whom might we serve and where? We somehow scraped together enough cash for one plane ticket from Tehran to Delhi, so I left Sally and the others to make their way across eastern Iran, Afghanistan, and Pakistan. More vehicle trouble and illnesses caused them to turn back to Tehran twice. We had no access to phones, texting, email – or even telegrams. For six weeks after I arrived in India, I had no news of my wife or my team.

CHAPTER 12

Continental Challenge

When I arrived in Delhi, my entire wardrobe was a thin pair of khaki trousers, a golf shirt, and sandals without socks. Doesn't everyone know India is hot? To my bitter surprise on that New Year's Day, it was freezing!

When I left England, my orders had been: "Go out to India and start something. Here are three names." One of those was the owner of a Christian bookshop in Delhi. When I tracked him down, I found three others who were planning to travel that day to the same conference in Madras that I had been ordered to attend. Leaving a message at the bookshop for Sally and the other team members who were still en route to Delhi, I joined the group headed south. While they were able to get me onto their train for Madras, the only space available was in the third-class unreserved carriage.

Thankfully, I was supple enough to claim some space on the luggage rack – for thirty-six hours! It was certainly preferable to being squeezed into a seat beside the window through which men continually climbed. I marveled at the patience of two Indian nuns who put up with many people stepping on their backs to enter the overcrowded carriage.

Expatriate missionaries were by far the majority at the Madras conference, but one of the few Indians who had been invited to address the group briefly turned out to be my divine appointment. One evening, all heads turned suddenly to see an entourage of Indians march in. With a clear air of authority, Bakht Singh proceeded directly to the platform, where he led us in non-stop prayer for twenty minutes. Then he stepped down and headed out of the meeting room with his disciples in tow. On his way down the aisle twelve feet from me, he turned and looked directly at me – a stranger, a Western kid of twenty-three – and commanded me with a single word: "Come."

Feeling like Matthew in the New Testament, I rose and followed in his train. I'd never heard of the man before, but I had no other direction, so I obeyed. We walked about a mile to his group's compound, and someone showed me to a small room with a rope bed where I would sleep. Prayers would be at 5:00 a.m., noon, and 10:00 p.m. until midnight. It was not an invitation; it was an expectation.

Bakht Singh, a Sikh, had started to follow Jesus in 1938 while he was studying engineering in Canada. After being discipled in a Plymouth Brethren home, he returned to India and began to preach on the streets of Bombay. One day as he finished preaching, an English missionary invited him for tea at a nearby stall. "Wouldn't you be more effective if after you preached, you gave the people some Scriptures?" the man asked him. Bakht Singh saw the point and immediately used all the money he had to buy Gospels in the different languages of India.

The missionary continued to follow him. The next day, he planted another idea in Bakht Singh's mind: "What if you were to gather together those with whom you've prayed?" Over the ensuing years, across the Indian subcontinent, more than a thousand house churches were birthed as the result of Bakht Singh's indomitable lifetime of labor. But starting in 1964, part of Bakht Singh's mission was to disciple the many OMers, including me, who came to serve those churches.

After six weeks out of contact, I eventually found my team in Lahore, Pakistan. Along the way, one of the trucks had been stuck in the snow in eastern Turkey, dug out by Kurds, and then robbed of everything by their rescuers. Later, they picked up two young British hitch-hikers, who "bowed the knee" to Jesus and immediately joined the team. On the other hand, we lost team members who decided that surviving on bread, peanut butter, and cheese while traveling in a broken-down truck to India – with no clear plan of what they would do once they got there – just wasn't their cup of tea. Others decided that the Lord was leading them to other things, so off they went in a different direction.

With all of those changes, we had fourteen team members left. We divided, and Gordon Magney led one team to work with Bakht Singh's group in Delhi. My team responded to an invitation from the Methodist seminary in Bareilly, Uttar Pradesh to challenge the unmotivated, mostly unregenerate, students to serve the Lord Christ seriously. I found only two people hungry for reality: a seminary student in his late twenties called Samuel Prasad Tyagi, along with his wife Kamala.

A former communist agitator, Tyagi was an activist in whatever he did. The Tyagis had two children, and she was pregnant with number three, but they invited Sally and me to share their one-room home, hanging a blanket across a rope to give each couple a bit of privacy. We began to share our vision with them. Soon, Tyagi was determined to spend the rest of his life making disciples among India's Muslims. He has. Over nearly fifty years, hardly a day has passed without his giving out Gospels in Urdu and speaking winsomely of his Savior in Muslim homes and shops.

The vast majority of Indian evangelists are Tamils or Malayalis from southern India, and most of the Muslims in India live in the north of the country. The two ends of the country are vastly different. When southern evangelists move to North India, it's as culturally challenging as for a Spaniard to become a missionary to Finland. Many years later, I joyfully fulfilled a long-time burden when I assisted Tyagi's son, Sushil, to found Nicodemus Ministries. It is the first Indian mission agency in history, staffed by Urdu-speaking Indian Christians, that focuses on reaching Urdu-speaking Muslims in North India with the gospel.

Meanwhile, family life was about to begin for the Livingston household. We had moved to Pune. The missionary doctor estimated that our first baby was due on 26 September 1964. Determined to be there at the birth of our firstborn, I didn't book any meetings between 15 September and 15 October. But September and October crawled past, and the baby didn't arrive! In early November, I was committed to line up several meetings for George Verwer, who had just arrived in Madras. Leaving Sally behind in Pune, I traveled to meet him. On 4 November, Bakht Singh got through to me by phone. With great dignity, he announced to me, "God has granted you a son."

The train back to Pune traveled at walking speed. Literally. It took a day's train travel for me to get back south to meet our firstborn.

Sally tells the story of the baby's birth:

At the maternity hospital for Muslim ladies, the nurses panicked. The anticipated black hair that indicated that the baby is coming was only white skin. So they panicked – concluding that the baby was coming breech! They had never seen a Western baby with no hair. When the nurses informed the Scottish Presbyterian doctor, she laughed, knowing the baby was fine. Still the nurses commiserated. "Poor baby. Must be ill – so pink and blotchy. Not like an evenly brown-skinned Indian baby."

We named our firstborn Evan Martyn Dale Livingston. Evan is John in Welsh. We liked the disciple John very much, but we felt the name John was too common. So naming him after Evan Welsh, the Wheaton College chaplain who had been a father-figure to me, seemed perfect. We divided my family name, Martindale, into Martyn (one of the earliest missionaries to Muslims in India) and Dale (for Dale Rhoton, my earliest mentor at Wheaton).

One day, when I had taken a colleague to a medical clinic in Mussoorie, the doctor also decided to examine me. When he tapped my side, I almost flew off the examining table. The verdict: amoebic hepatitis. They decided that the old-fashioned treatment, a shot of arsenic, was the fastest way to kill the bugs. A Canadian nurse, new to the mission field, gave me the injection in my derrière. "Don't move," she told me as she pushed in the syringe, "lest you have a heart attack." Then the needle came out of the syringe and stayed buried in my posterior. "Don't move!" she said. "I'll run for some pliers!"

One day, a group of us ventured into Mangalore, home of a fanatical Hindu sect called the Arya Samaj. Before we could distribute any Gospels, we found our team surrounded by angry-looking Hindus. Their hands were cocked back, armed with large rocks that they looked ready to pitch at our heads. The team gave me that you-got-us-into-this-so-you'd-better-get-us-out stare.

I took a step toward the hostile "welcoming" committee. "Good morning," I said, as cheerfully as I could manage. "It's a lovely day. You have a very nice city here. But we were just thinking of leaving – if that's all right with you."

In a loud whisper, I commanded the team to walk slowly backwards toward our truck, then run for it! They piled into the truck which, on this occasion, started immediately. (*Thank you, Lord Jesus!*) I kept my eyes barely above the dashboard as the rocks crashed against the truck, smashing windows.

I cannot remember ever having similar trouble in Muslim communities. I suppose that's because Christians and Muslims are both minority groups in India. The Muslims were mostly friendly because we believed in only one God, as they did. "We Muslims and Christians are not like those idol-worshipping Hindus," they would tell us.

We worked on the hot streets eight hours every day, pushing a banana cart full of Gospels and literature. Our growing number of Indian teammates seemed to decide, "If these foreigners can do it, we can do it." We slept in the same places, ate the same food, prayed together, and got ill together. During our fourteen months in India, I was involved in discipling about thirty Indians who decided to lay down their lives for the peoples of India. But OM later reported that starting with that thirty, several thousand Indians entered full-time ministry to share Christ's claims with Hindus, Buddhists, and Muslims in every corner of their country.

So what did we accomplish during our two years in India? When we arrived in 1964, only three Indian mission agencies existed. Several of our Indian co-workers went on to start their own mission agencies. Today, the India Missions Association has more than 200 member agencies. Roughly 50 percent of them are led by former OM members. That's rather satisfying 2 Timothy 2:2-style reproduction!

However, looking back to those early years, we now realize that our model of preaching to street crowds and selling Gospels in India established a pattern of evangelism that may, in fact, work against seeing communities of redeemed Muslims birthed. We did not take up residence in Muslim neighborhoods. Neither did the Indian evangelists we discipled; nor (with a few wonderful exceptions) do they today. Unless the followers of Jesus live near communities who don't yet know him, trust remains elusive. And without trust, how can a Muslim hear and respond to the claims of Jesus, whom they know only as the dead prophet Isa al-Masih?

Nearly fifty years later, expatriate church planters were still needed among the 160 million Muslims of North India. Indian agencies had still not recruited Indian believers to live among India's Muslims. So in 2006, I took up the task to recruit expats to live in Muslim-majority areas of India's cities. Once again, Westerners and Latinos are demonstrating to our Indian brothers and sisters that God can use them to birth communities of redeemed Muslims obedient to the Lord Jesus. Finally, it's happening. For the first time in history, *jamaats* (or communities) of born-again, Christ-loving Indian Muslims are becoming a reality!

CHAPTER 13

Sheepdog

As we left India, OM provided the airfare for our family of three to fly from India as far as Istanbul. A note from Verwer was waiting there with orders for me to leave Sally and baby Evan in Istanbul and fly to Israel to visit the OM team. Apparently, no one knew much about how – or what – they were doing.

I landed in Tel Aviv and took a bus to Jerusalem, where I asked around for directions to their address. Having located the house on the Jordanian border where I expected to find them, I knocked on the door. Ray and Henry opened the door quite awkwardly, as they were crawling on their stomachs. "Get down! Get down!" they shouted at me. "This is the time of day when Jordan lobs missiles into Israel." In the OM style typical of the time, they had rented this house in the danger zone *very* cheaply!

Ray and Henry were not expecting my visit, and I hadn't been informed that the women's team in Israel had moved to Tel Aviv. In order for us all to meet together, we needed to travel back to Tel Aviv. Ray quickly realized that we had only twenty minutes to catch the last bus before the Sabbath, when bus services would be discontinued for twenty-four hours. I found myself running alongside them to the bus station, glancing left and right in a vain effort to take in some tourist sites.

"What's that?" I asked.

"David's tomb!" was the reply.

We made it to the bus just in time. (I may be the only person in history who has visited Jerusalem, but for less than an hour. And I've never been back!) After spending a day thinking and praying with the team in Tel Aviv, I flew back to Istanbul.

We continued on our way to Europe, where we were assigned to recruit more young pioneers to go where Christ was not yet worshipped and obeyed.

Over the years, I gradually realized that the great Shepherd has chosen to utilize me most often as a sheepdog. Sheepdogs are small, unimpressive-looking dogs who love what they do. They aren't vicious; they don't bite the sheep. They are simply relentless in making sure the sheep are where the master wants them. I've been a recruiter, one who keeps God's sheep moving in the direction of his not-yet-harvested fields.

When I was first "captured" at George Verwer's night of prayer in 1959, I assumed I would take up residence overseas for twenty years to preach the gospel. Sally and I attempted to do that – several times, in several countries! But George kept sending us to new countries to get new teams in place to birth new church planting efforts.

Though I'm wary of committing King David's sin in numbering the people of Israel (as in 2 Samuel 24), I've occasionally wondered just how many cross-cultural disciple makers we've helped to place, especially among Muslims where the church isn't. Of course, it is impossible to know, because many of those I challenged went on to recruit several hundred more to serve in various agencies.

When Sally and I lie down at the end of a day, we feel such satisfaction that our lives are still ministering among Muslims from Tunisia to the Tatars of Siberia. What a joy it is to whisper to the Father name after name of those we've helped to become compassionate disciple makers, from Mauritania, West Africa to the island of Madura, Indonesia.

The prospect of speaking to the Christian Unions on the prestigious campuses of Britain intimidated me to no small degree. After my opening sentence, I was certain that some brilliant scholar would call out, "Rubbish! That's illogical!"

Instead I found myself realizing, "Hey, they're listening!"

To my astonishment, many leaders in the university Christian fellowships declared, "Right, we'll come for the summer." Not a few of them kept going for many years.

Looking back, I see that 1965 was a *kairos* moment in mission history. Not since the Cambridge Seven had left lucrative careers to join Hudson Taylor in China in the 1880s were so many young British Christians willing to throw away their prestigious careers to become missionaries. The *zeitgeist* of those years meant that radical action and revolution were in the air. In that countercultural milieu, I was both excited and deeply humbled to watch as men and women with honors degrees from Oxford, Cambridge, Durham, and the prestigious London School of Oriental and African Studies laid aside promising careers to serve the King of kings as disciple makers in Europe, the Middle East, and India. OM, launched a few years earlier by a handful of mostly American Bible school graduates, was being infused by some of Britain's most gifted leaders-to-be.

One day, while I was seeking the Holy Spirit's guidance for a talk I was to give at Liverpool University, I popped into the men's toilet. There, I found writing on the walls that was much more philosophical than most toilet graffiti:

> *"What is the meaning of life?"*
> *"Is there any point in searching for meaning?"*
> *"Why aren't the anarchists right?"*

I scribbled down the various contributions, then I advertised my talk as "Thoughts from a Men's Bog" ("bog" is British slang for "toilet"). It created a buzz and drew a substantial audience.

George Verwer and I teamed up to challenge the students at Birmingham Bible College. After driving through freezing snow, we arrived at about three in the morning. In spite of the fact that we banged repeatedly on the doors, no one came to receive us. Neither of us will forget attempting to sleep, with a very thin cover, on top of tables in the unheated porch of the college.

On another outing, my co-worker was the normally well-organized Jonathan McRostie. Exhausted, we both fell asleep on a train headed for Manchester, where we would once again challenge students to "give up their small ambitions." The train jostled to a stop, waking me up. Rousing Jonathan in a panic, I threw our boxes of literature onto the platform. We managed to leap out just as the train pulled out of the station. Lying on the ground laughing and congratulating ourselves, we suddenly realized we were at the wrong station. Then we *really* laughed. God's bunglers, at it again!

At times, our recruiting tours found us rubbing shoulders with the well-known Christians of the day. At Liverpool University, my "Men's Bog" talk was part of a series of meetings that featured leading Anglican cleric John R. W. Stott. In 1966, my bud from Turkey, Roger Malstead, managed to register the two of us as volunteers at the Berlin Congress on World Evangelization. While waiting in a corridor, I found myself standing next to the world-traveled evangelist Billy Graham, who was speaking to the evangelistic healer Oral Roberts. Graham was six feet two inches, and Roberts even taller. At five feet seven inches, I was craning my neck to stare into their faces. Roberts reached out, put his hand on my head and said, "God bless you, son." Roger figured I would never be ill for the rest of my life.

On another of our memorable forays, Sally and I, with nine-month-old Evan, crisscrossed Sweden. We were teamed with two hippies who had been recently converted to Jesus. Bertil, my interpreter, spoke broken English. In one meeting, I repeated George Verwer's claim that during the summer of 1963, we had distributed so many pieces of literature that "put end to end, they would have reached to the top of the Empire State Building."

Bertil calmly upgraded the claim: "If you put all the pieces of literature end to end, they would reach to the moon!"

Of course, since we were allergic to spending any money on restaurants or accommodation, we always lodged with believers. People who encountered OM members in those days probably thought "OM" stood for "Operation Mooch." Verwer never tired of pointing out that for the price of a Coke, we could buy twenty-five gospel tracts.

When we stayed in one inviting Swedish home, Mrs. Sunboom apologized that she wouldn't be cooking a meal because they were fasting for Lent. Impressed, I quickly volunteered that we would be delighted to fast with them. While we waited to be called to join them for prayer, we got a call to the table instead. There, Mrs. Sunboom offered us the largest cream puffs and the most delicious coffee I'd ever tasted. Somewhat confused, I exclaimed, "This is my favorite kind of fasting!"

As we trekked through the snow to a marathon of meetings across Sweden, we found that most university students were skeptical of our calling to put God's Word into the hands of every person on the earth who was at least six years old. In one meeting, a communist sympathizer jeered that food, not paper, was what the people in Africa and Asia needed.

I shouted back, "Wow, how wonderful to meet a chap who is living on as little as he can to give all his money to feed the hungry." His mates turned to laugh at their mortified friend. I had guessed correctly that he was actually doing nothing for the poor.

Later that summer in Sweden, we spoke at Umea University at a youth meeting that started at midnight. Because it's inside the Arctic Circle, there was still light outside at that late hour. However, I needed more than light in the sky. Exhausted from driving and from our rigorous schedule of three meetings a day, I fell asleep while I stood preaching! I didn't fall, but I couldn't remember what I had just said. Recovering quickly, I announced, "Well, let's look at the issues from an entirely different approach," then started a new message.

Recruiting in Germany presented different challenges. I was excited to receive an invitation to speak to the Christian student group at Erlangen University. I found the group in the pub where they met. As an American, and at that time still a teetotal Baptist, I needed the Holy Spirit to help me make some instant cultural adjustments. Seated around the long table were about twenty students, each with a Bible in front of them, a cigar in one hand, and a beer in the other! The smoke was so thick, I wasn't sure they could see me.

One day, when I was speaking at the state church in Hamburg, the pastor interpreting me suddenly stopped and began pumping my hand, because I had mentioned that it was my thirtieth birthday. Later, however, he summed up my message, saying, "*Sie haben zu viel Blumensprache*" ("You have too much flower talk").

Despite smoky pubs and flowery talk, Europeans volunteered to become OM missionaries. Swiss, Swedish, and Dutch young people joined the Brits who were leaving their metaphorical nets to obey Christ's command to become "fishers of men," determined to make disciples in the farthest regions of the earth.

Still, I am aware that the fruit of my labors is much more *despite* me than *because of* me. In those days, I often prayed, "Lord, don't waste my time or your time. Lead me to those you are calling."

CHAPTER 14

Church Planter

We had no one to lead OM's work in Germany and Austria, so Verwer asked me to be the interim leader there until we could find an appropriately gifted and motivated German.

Roger and Yvonne Malstead, expelled from Turkey, were now ministering to Turks in Germany. They had been subletting an apartment in Frankfurt, but since they were moving, they invited us to have their apartment. Frankfurt seemed as good as anywhere to set up a temporary recruiting base and prepare for Sally to give birth to our second son.

With very little complaint, Sally set up home in yet another new place. Although she was heavily pregnant there in Frankfurt, an American colleague coerced her to give her testimony to a crowd of astounded Turkish men in the main train station. How's that for cultural sensitivity? Not to mention sensitivity to my wife? I groan now when I think about how often I failed to live with my wife in an understanding manner.

On the day that Sally went to the hospital to give birth, a truckful of OMers had just arrived in Frankfurt from Turkey. A local German missionary pleaded with me to allow him to put the OMers to work distributing 10,000 gospel newspapers to residences throughout the city. Since we only had one day to accomplish the task, I roused the team of twelve from the floor of every room in our apartment and rushed them through a meager breakfast so that we could be on the streets by 7:30 a.m. We were in such a hurry that no one noticed that the one who washed the breakfast dishes failed to turn off the faucet.

After getting the team to their assigned streets for deliveries, I rushed to the maternity hospital for a delivery of a different type! However, the staff told me that no relatives were admitted and there was no waiting room. I rejoined the team until we finished distributing the gospel papers at 9:00 that night!

As soon as we finished, the guys from Turkey drove off towards OM's European headquarters near Brussels. Exhausted, I dragged myself, carrying eighteen-month-old Evan, back to our apartment – where I met an angry, shouting mob! Was I the one occupying the third floor? (It's amazing how effectively body language and tone of voice can communicate.) Our flat had flooded, and the water had poured down onto the floors below while our neighbors were at work. Since we had no rental agreement on paper, their command to me was simply, "*Raus!*" – "Get out!"

At the hospital the next morning, I was informed that David had been born. Sally had bled profusely and been rushed into the operating theater. She wouldn't be able to go home for several days. I had mixed emotions about that news, since there was no longer a place where she *could* go home!

I can't remember where Evan and I slept or what we did while we waited for Sally's release, but I know that we survived by eating *weisswurst* (sausages) and fries from Frankfurt's street vendors. On the day that Sally and David left the hospital, I took them directly to the US embassy, got a passport for David, and put them on a plane to our OM Europe headquarters in Brussels. Evan and I followed by second-class train. I felt like such a *Dummkopf*.

As the summer approached, OM prepared for another influx of short-term workers who would form into teams to distribute gospel literature across Belgium, France, Italy, Spain, and Austria. As the leader in the German-speaking region, it would be my job to lead the team headed to Austria. I sent Johan from Holland to find a place where the summer team could live in Vienna, the city of influence. He did. A helpful prostitute rented us her unoccupied one-bedroom flat (for an exorbitant price). I wish I could draw a sketch of how we squeezed our twenty-two team members into that space, with the girls in the bedroom and the boys in the living room. Sally and I shared a storage room with Evan and David, and we built a loft for the other couple, newly married. Unbelievably, a lot of laughs and a pioneering spirit kept us all sane and 90 percent harmonious!

However a month later, the woman wanted her flat back, so we were literally out on the street. I met some American Mormons who had just moved; they helpfully suggested we contact their former landlady. Frau Aberham's house had

Church Planter

two bedrooms, plus a tiny garden guest room. She assumed I wanted it for my family of four.

"Well, yes. And a few others," I whispered.

"How many more?" she asked.

"Ah… what would you think of… nine?" I asked meekly, quite sure that twenty-two was out of the question.

"Nine!" she exclaimed. "What do you do?"

Quite sure that nine people was a deal-breaker, I decided there was nothing to lose by telling her who we were. I threw in a few mumbled statements about Jesus being the only way to God.

She blinked for a few seconds, then to my amazement she responded, "You are the kind of people we would like to have in the house!"

When she said the rent would be 3,000 schillings for the month, I told her we didn't have much money, hoping she would lower the price.

"Can't your God provide for you?" she retorted.

Now what could I say? Well aware there was no roof at all over the heads of the team that very night, I simply nodded and followed her into the house as she calculated. "Ah, you could put three here and two there…"

Under the cover of darkness that night, we moved in – the whole team of twenty-two adults and two children. We didn't anticipate that Frau Aberham lived two doors away and that she would show up at 6:30 the next morning to see how we were doing! Of course, she was shocked to find twenty-two bodies sprawled everywhere.

At that awful encounter, I recognized what a deceiving, rotten sinner and terrible ambassador for Christ I had become. I told her repeatedly, "I'm sorry. I lied to you. We'll move out within the hour."

Shaking her head in disbelief, Frau Aberham wandered around the house muttering, "Let's see. Four could squeeze in here, and maybe five here ..." To our complete astonishment, she allowed us to stay!

During the previous four years, OM teams had distributed literature to almost every home in Austria, but we had seen little evidence of lasting fruit. So I told our team that instead of massive literature distribution that summer, our goal was to introduce two Austrians to Christ. We wouldn't look for two people who would simply mumble a prayer. We would ask God to call two Austrians who, for the rest of their lives, would care for nothing but the expansion of the kingdom of God in Austria!

God heard us. He gave us not two, but three true disciples of Christ in Vienna.

From the first day, Frau Aberham attended our team's Bible study. At the end of the month, when I asked the team to tell what they had learned that summer, Frau Aberham piped up first. She said, "I've learned how to be born again." I stared at Sally, who was the only person who had spent time with Victoria Aberham. Sally lifted her shoulders in perplexed wonder. She had earlier claimed that she never got a word in edgewise with our landlady, yet obviously the Spirit of God had used her witness. Frau Aberham's son Sandy and a young man called Peter were God's other new gifts to Austria.

Peter and Sandy later went on to establish the first Christian fellowship group at Vienna University. Frau Aberham witnessed to her priest and won to Christ her husband, her other son Ottmar, Ottmar's wife – and even Ottmar's *former* wife!

After that summer, as other OMers came to Vienna, the rent for the Aberhams' house gradually decreased to zero. The Aberham family donated significantly to OM ministries and supported the newly birthed Vienna fellowship. Eventually, with the recruitment of a strong Bible teacher, our little, almost unintentional, church plant became one of the most vibrant Protestant churches in Austria, with 300 members today.

One of our teammates that month was Argentinian Federico Bertuzzi, who had been studying in Germany. He asked me to baptize him in the Danube. Eventually, he became the president of the largest Latino mission to Muslims, PM Internacional.

Another team member was a very serious Finn, Kari Turma. Every day, after I spoke about a Scripture passage, Kari would interject, "I think you are in the flesh." His public declaration was irritating, to say the least. But when I took him aside, I came to understand he simply meant that perhaps I was seeing something from a human perspective. When we work with people of other nationalities, they can help us gain insights into our own culture. Kari seemed more theologically than evangelistically minded, but to our surprise, after that summer he recruited a new generation of Finns to the mission field.

CHAPTER 15

With Our Minds

In the sixties, American and British evangelicals were slowly coming to understand relativism. In the workplace and at universities, we were confronting a generation of scoffers, especially on the European Continent. They assumed that Christianity was *passé* – and definitely not for real thinkers. Sartre, Camus, and the Beatles were definitely more popular than Jesus Christ.

I felt, and Verwer agreed, that it was time to launch Operation University. I recruited a timid dozen from OM's ranks to be trained in a fresh approach to sharing the gospel with intellectuals. In the autumn of 1966, we made our way to L'Abri in Switzerland, a community established by Francis and Edith Schaeffer. They opened their alpine home as a place of ministry to curious travelers and a forum to discuss philosophical and religious beliefs. After each of us had a personal interview, we were assigned to listen to specific taped lectures by Dr. Schaeffer and his colleagues. We attended live lectures as well as debates between Schaeffer and each week's boldest agnostic visitor to the community.

I must confess that when I arrived at L'Abri, I was secretly somewhat ashamed of the gospel. I assumed it couldn't really stand up against the best of the intellectuals. Six weeks later, I left Switzerland as a lion – totally confident that it was the non-Christians who were sticking their heads in the sand. I've never doubted the truth of the Bible since then. (Well, not for more than about sixty seconds.)

Schaeffer helped shore up my conviction that the Bible is truly authentic communication from the Creator. I start with the historicity of Jesus of Nazareth. Secular history agrees he actually lived in Palestine. For centuries, very few people disputed that the New Testament faithfully recorded what he did and taught. Jesus also confirmed the events recorded in the Old Testament as genuine history, specifically mentioning Adam and Eve, Noah and the flood, Sodom and Gomorrah, and the miraculous healings with Moses' brass serpent on a pole. Jesus also commissioned his apostles to make known what he had taught them. Obeying, they produced what became the New Testament. Jesus proved who he is, and his authority to know what is true, by breaking the power of death and appearing after his resurrection, teaching around 500 of his followers for forty days.

When discussing biblical truths, Schaeffer taught me to respond with this helpful sentence: "It depends on your presuppositions." No opening phrase or first response has ever been more helpful.

He also helped me to see that my understanding of God's fullness and purposes was too narrow. As important as it is, fulfilling the Great Commission is not God's only aim, he taught me. One day he stopped me in my mental tracks.

"Greg, if you were God, you would have created the world black and white."

I thought, "Whoa, yes! Why *did* God bother to create colors and beauty? Hmmm…"

Another memorable statement my beloved Dr. Schaeffer made to me is one I recall with mixed emotions: "Greg, you're not an intellectual, but I'm very fond of you." The Father had provided another father figure for me.

When we left L'Abri, the first challenge for the Operation University team was the Netherlands' finest university – Leiden. One of our OM team members in Vienna was about to enter his first year at Leiden, but he knew of no Christians there. "No problem," I declared. "We'll come and help you find some!"

At that time, no evangelical student group existed at Leiden. Two other Dutch universities had groups called Ichthus, so we used the same name to stress our alliance with them. We followed a simple plan: We would knock on the door of every student room, visit every café, and invite students to attend the inaugural meeting of the Christian students' association. For ten days, we distributed hundreds of notices in every corner of the university that stated when and where "all the Bible-believing students will meet to get introduced to each other." At the appointed time and place, twenty-five Christian students showed up! None had ever met any of the others. An instant fellowship was born to bear witness at Leiden. That was the easiest task we ever faced, and as far as I know, the group has kept going ever since.

That year, a leader for Campus Crusade for Christ (CCC) contacted me to let me know that their organization was expanding to Europe. At his request, I arranged for *The Four Spiritual Laws* and some of their other literature to be translated and printed in French, German, and Dutch. Then I arranged for their leaders to meet with a group of pastors in Belgium.

The pioneers for CCC took a very different approach from that of the early OMers. They bought nice cars, stayed in hotels, and wore suits. The Belgian pastors' response to this new American invasion was quite negative. I had a number of conversations like this:

"I don't believe they will be fruitful in Europe, do you?" a pastor would ask.

"Yes, I do," I would answer with confidence.

"Then you agree with the way they are going about things?"

"No, they will need to learn to adapt to Europe."

"Then why do you think they will be used by God?"

"Because they *expect* to be."

My university team, along with four people from CCC, invaded Germany's University of Erlangen, where I had previously taught a few evangelical students. When we tried using CCC's "Four Laws" presentation, we found that at least we got into some sustained conversations.

As the leader of the team, I had a personnel problem to solve. Our brightest team member, a scholar from Cambridge, had devoured the lessons that Francis Schaeffer had taught us, but he was simply too introverted to engage in "cold turkey" evangelism. I was tempted to rebuke Andrew for his failure to be bold, but the Holy Spirit stopped me with a better alternative.

"Andrew, make some coffee and stay here in the church basement while we go find some interested students to bring to you, okay?"

The rest of us spread out across the campus, goading those who smugly thought they could swat away the Bible's claims of Christ with easy arguments. "Do you have the courage to come and talk to a man who can answer every objection you have?" we challenged them.

Some did. Escorting them to the church basement, we opened with: "Andrew, this is Fritz. Fritz thinks Christianity is not credible. I told him you could show him why it is. Sit down, Fritz, and have a cup of coffee."

Andrew was fruitful. The experience taught me to utilize God's ambassadors within the gifting and personality God has granted them. I learned that we are all very good at what we are very good at!

One of our Operation University teammates was Mehdi Dibaj, a Muslim-background believer from Iran. I'm not sure how fruitful he was while on our team, especially without fluency in any European language, but God was shaping a hero for his kingdom.

Some years later, Mehdi was arrested in Iran for apostasy. For nine years, he languished in prison, spending much of the time in solitary confinement. His captors lied to him that his wife had become a prostitute and his children would be taken away if he did not recant. Eventually, Revd. Haik Hosepian, the bishop of the Assemblies of God in Iran, broadcast Mehdi's plight to the international community. It seemed to work. Mehdi was released. Three weeks later, however, an assassin put a bullet in his head on a street in Tehran. Sometime later, I had the magnificent privilege of sitting next to Revd. Hosepian as we were being served communion by another of Christ's treasures from a Muslim family, Khadra from Somalia. Only weeks later, Haik was also murdered.

Was it a waste? Was refusing to submit to the Iranian government a foolish path to take? Didn't five more pastors get killed by Muslims soon after that? Well, some people estimate that a million Muslim Iranians have subsequently "bowed the knee" to Christ! More conservative estimates put the number at "only" 100,000. In either case, it is easy for me to envision Mehdi and Haik leaping and praising God with the angels in heaven that their blood has been counted worthy to become the seed of the Persian church.

Another two of our Operation University colleagues were Jack Roberts and Bob Hall. Both of these men felt as though they left our team as failures. In their own minds, they were not very usable for God's purposes. They both ended up in South Bronx, New York City – a place where few Anglo-Americans live. More than forty years of their exemplary dying-to-self ministry has helped to produce a church that surely puts a smile on God's face: the Bronx Fellowship. It is a joy to behold – full of rescued, happy people from a rainbow of ethnic backgrounds. These two "failures" have a team of their own in a ministry that helps people recover from alcohol and drug addiction. Their two families adopted nearly twenty children; they assisted untold numbers of teenage girls who chose not to abort their babies; and they have performed many other unheralded acts of righteousness.

God loves to use the weak, the struggling, and the unprepared to show what he can do through those who are totally available and have counted the cost.

Not everyone recruited by OM for Christ's service persevered. Some co-workers disappeared, and we never rediscovered them. Some South Asian colleagues found they more greatly desired to move to North America than to follow their Lord wherever he called. I can also remember a smooth-talking man who joined OM immediately after responding to Christ at an open-air service. But his next "conversion" was to convince himself that he was born Jewish – which astonished his Polish mother! He led a lively Jewish debutante to follow Christ as her Messiah, married her, then left her. She has continued to follow her Lord. Whether or not he does, I do not know. Sadly, not a few like him got tired of obeying Christ, and opted for a Christ-denying existence instead.

We managed to recruit Sally's sister Mary to our Operation University team. She then met Colin Crow, a Brit who was raised in France and Belgium. Fluent in French and German, Colin added much to our team, then joined our family. I officiated at Mary and Colin's wedding in Paris. The large

Crow clan (with five brothers and two sisters) became our much beloved "shirt-tail" relatives in England. In addition to supplying me with fathers and mothers, my Father has also given me brothers and sisters, just as he promised.

CHAPTER 16

Nine Wives

We had left India, but three years later I realized that India had not completely left me. That is, the elephantiasis filariasis I had picked up there hadn't left me. By 1968, I realized that I needed to get some help to deal with the microscopic worms wiggling across my eyes. I had grown too weak to do more recruiting, so Verwer agreed that we could return to Wheaton Graduate School so that I could finish my master's degree and get medical help.

It took a renowned missionary doctor to diagnose my condition, but the drug he prescribed seemed worse than the disease. I felt like Dr. Jekyll turning into the mad Hyde! Though the boys were now four and two, Sally suffered more from my temper tantrums, not theirs.

During the five months we spent in Wheaton, I fell into the grip of a powerful obsession. The grand prize of the American Express sweepstakes was a lifetime pass for any IATA airline anywhere in the world. Didn't the Lord promise, "Whatever you ask..."? I became convinced that he was leading me to claim the grand prize. Then I could travel all over the world, every week, and it would cost OM almost nothing! I fasted. I prayed. I tried to get others to agree in Jesus' name. I was more expectant and believing than ever before – or since! I was sure I had met all the biblical conditions. I had not even a tiny doubt in my mind that I would win the airline pass.

I didn't know whether American Express would call or send a telegram, so on the day of the drawing, I sat with the telephone at my side, watching the front door. The phone didn't ring. No one came. I was irate. Someone had stolen my prize! Remembering American Express was required by law to send a list of winners on request, I demanded a copy. When it came, I wasn't anywhere on the list of 5,000 winners. I didn't even win a T-shirt! To add insult to injury, several of the winners lived right there in Wheaton.

I stormed into the King's presence, demanding an explanation. "Have I not fulfilled the requirements for answered prayer? What's the deal?" I've learned over the years that when you truly want to know why our faithful Father does or allows what he does, he will usually grant at least an inkling of what he is doing or preventing. That day, he opened my eyes. It was his gracious loving-kindness and immeasurable wisdom that kept him from giving me that prize.

Non-stop travel would have wrecked my health even further and kept me away from Sally and the boys far too much. I would have become a worldwide errand boy, delivering an engine to India or books to Jordan. Every needed pastoral visit would have put me on a plane. Delays and nights in the wrong places might have led to my falling morally or being mugged. O the wisdom of God!

Hearing that we who had helped to start OM in 1959 were back in the Chicago area in 1968, Lew Williams decided to restart the classic Friday nights of prayer. I can't remember who came to our house on those Friday nights, except for one close friend who, although pushing seventy, is still ministering in an Arab country today. So the sheepdog's gifting was still operating – even in my sickly condition!

While I was recuperating, it took teeth-gritting discipline to work on my master's thesis, and then I had only one more course to finish. I did so poorly on the course that my professor, not wishing to see me fail to graduate because of one failed exam, came to our house and asked me, "You didn't mean to write *such and such*, did you? Of course, you meant to write…" Thus, I managed to graduate.

Eventually, I recovered from the filaria. However, over the years, I've come to realize that the worst disease a missionary can get is not filaria or even malaria. The worst disease one can catch is "dullaria." You know you've got "dullaria" when you are no longer excited about the promises of the Word of God, when you no longer expect God to answer persevering prayer.

Back at headquarters in Brussels, OM's Director for Europe needed someone to shepherd the forty staff members so he could focus on being the field director for the teams ministering across Europe. I was drafted. Could the sheepdog be a shepherd?

We joined a French-speaking Baptist church in Brussels. Although I was an ordained Baptist minister, the elders grilled us doctrinally before we were accepted into membership. Finally, they asked if we had any questions for them. "Just one," I responded. "The Bible says that one of the qualifications for elders is that they are hospitable. We've been coming here for more than a year, yet no one has ever invited us to his home. Have I misunderstood the Bible in this case?" We got two invitations for meals that week, but none after that.

Although the church services were in French, our headquarters was in the Flemish area of Brussels, and five-year-old Evan went to a Flemish kindergarten. At the end of the year, his teacher remarked that although Evan had not learned much Flemish, the level of English in the class had upgraded significantly!

At this point, Sally and I had labored to learn Spanish, Hindi, German, and now French. Occasionally someone will ask me, "How many languages do you speak?" Keeping a straight face, I answer, "Twelve." No one fails to be impressed … until I break into a smile, and add, "Five sentences of each."

After I had studied French for about six weeks, the OM staffer in charge of shopping fell ill one day. I felt I was ready to fill in by making our purchases at the wholesale supplier. Thinking I was ordering five kilos of rice, I said, "*Cent kilos de riz, s'il vous plaît.*" The man nodded and disappeared for quite a while. When I saw him staggering under a bag of 100 kilos of rice, I realized the misunderstanding. I yelled, "No! Not *cent* [100] kilos, *cinq* [five] kilos!"

"*Cinq?*" he screamed in dismay, uttering a few words I fortunately couldn't understand (but got the gist of). I never returned.

In an old paper factory, our European staff of forty lived together under a single roof and ate in the same dining room – administrators, secretaries, mechanics, and a non-stop flow of field teams. It isn't difficult to imagine, I suppose, that forty (sometimes sixty) people living under the same roof might occasionally experience conflict. Over the course of one fortnight, two of the mothers refused to speak to each other. Obviously, this created a rather miserable atmosphere for us all. I pleaded with each woman to reconcile. "No, that wouldn't help." Each was adamant that the other would not listen. After two weeks, our building was becoming a slough of despond. Exasperated, I literally pushed the two ladies together and forced them to talk. Within twenty minutes, they were crying and hugging. Best friends again. I was reminded that when nothing else works, I should try obeying God's instructions!

The women had given each other the silent treatment, but two of the mechanics used the opposite tactic. They started with yelling, then downgraded to a fist-fight! I tried to push apart the two big bruisers, who were each strong enough to pick me up and throw me across the repair garage. Eventually, they too were reconciled.

My two years as captain of the European headquarters crew was an on-the-job course in peacemaking and pastoral care. I considered writing up the lessons from that period of our pilgrimage in a book entitled *I Led Nine Wives*!

If conflict is inevitable, then so is temptation. Single women tend to look more attractive than mothers dominated by the chores of life, surrounded by demanding small children. One of the secretaries had such alluring eyes and was the most feminine woman with whom I had ever had sustained contact. In addition, she was pleasantly eager to assist me.

Today, I am utterly grateful to God for the wooden rules of OM. Unless they were married to each other, two people of the opposite sex were absolutely forbidden to be alone in a room or a vehicle. Ever. This law was most inconvenient at times! However, it meant that my relationship with the secretary never went beyond the fan7tasy that I eventually confessed to Sally. We had a marriage covenant to not hide anything from each other, but my confession was painful for us both. She had always been the scholar, the woman with whom I could discuss any important topic. Being charming had not been one of her priorities. However, when I asked her years later to go to a charm school, she agreed – and even concluded that it was fun! Moreover, it worked; my attentions turned fully to her.

I could probably count on a single hand the number of people who have "bowed the knee" to the Lord Jesus Christ through my personal invitation over the years. Two hands, at best. I've proven to be singularly *un*anointed at evangelism, even though I've always sought to introduce people to Christ. Gifted or not, I feel all Christians ought to take every opportunity to evangelize.

Still, when I have seen people who appear to have little access to a witnessing Christian, I have been drawn to them. Such was the case with the crowd at the University of Brussels. This university required its professors to sign a statement that they did not accept any supernatural revelation such as the Bible. No Christian groups were allowed to function there. No one knew any students who were trying to be salt and light at the university for the Lord Jesus.

The enrollment system at the University of Brussels was simple: Get in the queue on registration day and ask the professor of the course you want to take to sign a card saying that he accepts you in his class. By this time I was twenty-nine, so as inconspicuously as possible, I stood in such a line and got signed up for a course. The professor didn't even look up while signing my card. I found the only empty seat next to a girl who, providentially, spoke English.

"Er, what course is this?" I asked her.

"The history of Egyptian art," she replied, looking surprised that I would ask.

"Perfect," I responded. Since most of the lecture involved viewing slides of Egyptian art, I could almost follow the professor's instruction in French.

Since no Christian activity was allowed inside the university gates, we parked our truck, which could seat a dozen, near the entrance. I showed my fellow Egyptian art student an invitation to an investigative Bible study scheduled for lunchtime in our truck. Her eyebrows lifted, as if I was inviting her to sniff cocaine. "Come if you're courageous enough," I challenged her.

"I'm not afraid of anything," she retorted. She came and returned repeatedly that semester until the Father revealed himself to her. Some of the young women in OM's office became her close friends and discipled her. In gratitude, she gave our sons a huge box of Lego that her brother had outgrown. The last I heard, the University of Brussels had a more or less clandestine Christian student group.

In the summer of 1968, we sent several teams to Paris in the midst of the student protests that eventually toppled the de Gaulle government. As usual, our teams were assigned to distribute gospel literature door to door. It was not unusual for them to climb eight flights of stairs only to find that almost no one was willing to open the door and talk to a stranger. Clearly, the teams needed encouragement, but there was no money for a train journey. So I hitch-hiked to Paris. Giovanni, a kind Italian, offered me a lift, but after a few miles he insisted he would only take me further if I joined him for a glass of red wine. Except for communion in Spain a few years earlier, I had continued to abstain from alcohol. But Giovanni insisted. Desperate to get to Paris, I capitulated. Later, he stopped for a second round. The third time he stopped, we quickly realized that the bar was a front for a brothel, so we ran out before he ordered another two glasses of *vin rouge*.

As we drove on, however, I developed a pretty annoying headache, which worsened as we neared Paris. I managed to visit three of the teams and did my best to exhort them to "press on." But by the time I got to the Paris OM base that evening, my headache was vicious. I concluded that the Lord was punishing me for breaking my vow. After repenting, I went right to bed, but I woke at midnight screaming with pain. After a rush to the hospital, I was diagnosed with spinal meningitis!

After a spinal tap relieved the pressure on my brain, I wanted to kiss the interns on both cheeks, as the French do! But the pain returned. Using my broken French and a pantomime, I got a Haitian assistant nurse to understand I needed something for the pain. She eventually returned with what I thought was a piece of chocolate candy. As I started to swallow it, she yelled, "*Non! Non! Non!*"

So I started to put it in my ear.

"*Non! Non! Non!*"

"*Qu'est-ce qu'on fait avec ça?*" ("What are you supposed to do with it?") I yelled back. She turned around, stuck out her derrière and pointed to the place where a suppository is inserted into the body. Having never seen a suppository, I handed it back to her, turned around and ordered: "You do it!"

I'm quite sure that it's not normal to recover from spinal meningitis in a week, but the Great Physician heard the intercession of my friends and co-workers from literally around the world. I walked out of that hospital seven days later, absolutely fit! I had a family and a Father who cared.

CHAPTER 17

Arab Landing

After two years serving as a shepherd at OM's European headquarters, we finally got the green light to proceed to our original calling – the Arab world. Although I was thirty by this time, I anticipated that I would have the second half of my life to make disciples among Arabic-speaking Muslims. Surely, Libya would open to us in God's timing.

Sally was eight months pregnant, so she flew to Beirut with Evan and David, while I drove there with the rest of the members of the Arab world team. Sally will never forget her first evening in Beirut. Egypt's popular president, Gamal Abdel Nasser, had just died, and the entire region was in an uproar. Her welcome to life in the Arab world was a car journey from the airport that slalomed between burning tires and young men shooting into the air.

On our first visit to Beirut a few years earlier, we had met Mazhar Mallouhi. Mazhar was the first Arab Muslim-background believer I'd ever known, and he's still indisputably one of the most unforgettable people I'll ever know. We were both separated from our extended families. I did not have any siblings, and his had chased him away. We became lifetime brothers, despite events and misunderstandings that would have surely separated most others.

Mazhar had served in the Syrian military on the Golan Heights in 1959. At that time, he had already rejected his family's traditional faith, feeling that Allah was too distant from humanity. He reviewed other religions, and decided against them all, concluding that man had invented religion as a future hope against the pain of this world. But he had refused to read anything about "the Crusaders' religion," even though he shared his tent with a Christian officer.

Having rejected religion, Mazhar turned to politics to save the world. In this cause, he read Gandhi's correspondence with Tolstoy and found that Gandhi quoted Christ, which whetted Mazhar's appetite to know more about Christ's teachings. He borrowed his tent-mate's Bible and read it through several times. In the quiet of that lonely post, Mazhar called on God to give him the new life promised by Christ.

Mazhar, like me, was born running. Never one to hide his views, he began telling Muslims they were following the wrong God. His confrontational manner was no more effective than mine had been as a baby Christian – neither in the Syrian army nor when he returned to his home town. Mazhar's great-uncle had been a highly esteemed religious leader in Syria. His family tried to save their honor by killing Mazhar as a traitor to their faith. A scar on his neck bears witness to their attempt.

Having survived this attack, Mazhar made peace with

his family by leaving Syria for Lebanon, where he studied at a Bible college. His first ministry was as an editor with the Arabic Literature Mission, which developed his writing skills. His first Arabic novel, *The Traveler*, is in its twenty-eighth reprinting. Ten more books followed.

Mazhar struggled to understand why missionaries were so insensitive to Arab culture. His confrontational manner intimidated most Western workers, so OM's Arab world team leader was more than happy to "turn him over" to me. I'm so glad he did. From Mazhar, I learned more about Arab culture than I can recount.

At the same time, Mazhar faced problems of his own. Arab Christian families do not give their daughters in marriage to Muslim families, so Mazhar had trouble finding a spouse. Eventually, after he married, it became evident that his wife was severely mentally disturbed. Her family probably thought that marriage to a convert to Christianity was her only opportunity to marry at all.

As her paranoia deepened, she lodged an official accusation with the Lebanese government that Mazhar and the OM team were working as American spies. This accusation dogged Mazhar for the remainder of his days in Lebanon, where the Christians remained suspicious of him. So we thought it made sense to send him to set up a bookshop in Morocco, where we knew a few other Muslim-background believers. His wife refused to join him, so Mazhar was abandoned by a second family. With little fellowship to strengthen him in Casablanca, he drifted from the Lord, looking for comfort from Muslim friends.

It seemed Mazhar's ministry was over. Sadly, I was too busy forming and sending teams to Yemen, Syria, Iraq, and Libya to keep Mazhar on my radar, but his faithful heavenly Father did not let him go.

Since there were no missionaries in residence in Libya and it remained our personal mandate, I pushed our team in Beirut to dispatch four guys to Libya to provide copies of Luke's Gospel in the summer of 1971. The two Americans, a Belgian, and a Lebanese were soon arrested and sentenced to eight years in prison for distributing "anti-Islamic propaganda." We were stunned, and helpless. As we reiterated the same prayers daily, our faith lost momentum. The embassies were no help. We sent messages to Billy Graham with hopes that he could influence American President Richard Nixon to plead with Libyan leader Muammar Gaddafi on their behalf.

After eight months, for no apparent reason, our four men were released. Not surprisingly, I couldn't convince anyone else to go to Libya until 1980 – eight years later! Who wants to get stuck in a filthy, rat- and mosquito-infested North African prison?

It's curious that Christians around the world crave various kinds of New Testament experiences – power to heal, power in evangelism, or an ecstatic experience with the Holy Spirit. Yet no one wants the other New Testament experiences – prison, beatings, rejection, or expulsion. We get excited about Revelation 5:9 and 7:9, verses in which God tells us that the Lord Jesus wins. There will be disciples from all ethnic groups eventually worshipping the Lamb of God. But few notice that in order to see that become a reality, many must suffer the events of Revelation 6:9–11, in which the Lord reassures believers who were murdered for their loyalty to Christ:

> *I saw underneath the altar the souls of those who had been slain because of the word of God, and because of the testimony which they had maintained; and they cried out with a loud voice, saying, "How long, O Lord, holy and true, will You refrain from judging and avenging our blood on those who dwell on the earth?" And there was given to each of them a white robe; and they were told that they should rest for a little while longer, until the number of their fellow servants and their brethren who were to be killed even as they had been, would be completed also. (NASB)*

Similarly, how many sermons do pastors preach on John 16:2? Our Lord promised his servants: "in fact, the time is coming when anyone who kills you will think they are offering a service to God."

The American University of Beirut was founded by godly, evangelical, evangelistic Presbyterians from the United States. From the late 1800s until World War I, they assumed that what Muslims needed was to learn to think rationally. Surely, they reasoned, if Middle Eastern Muslims became acquainted with Western education and the Bible, they would see the logic of following the One who is the Truth.

But what actually happened at the American University of Beirut, the American University in Cairo, Roberts College of Istanbul, and the many other educational institutions established by missionaries around the world? Education empowered youth to break the bonds of colonialism, while it bred nationalism and autonomy from unwanted rulers – including God! In Europe, we had seen the products of the Enlightenment. The missionary professors had inadvertently prepared the students of the Middle East to do the same as their young European counterparts – to throw off the strictures and traditions of religion. Only in rare instances did those academics lead Muslims to believe in the Savior.

Evangelism is legal in Lebanon. So, bolstered by the success of Operation University in Europe, we decided that 1971 was God's hour to proclaim the good news to disillusioned students in Lebanon. With young Georges Houssney, one of the very few Lebanese Christians who was eager to see Muslims enter Christ's kingdom, and leaders of OM, the Navigators, InterVarsity Christian Fellowship, Campus Crusade for Christ, and a local Lebanese group, we covenanted to declare the claims of Christ boldly among university students in Beirut.

Our goal was to bring in Lebanese-American philosophy professor Mark Hanna as our speaker for a week-long evangelistic mission to the students at the American University. The posters we plastered everywhere had a photo of light coming through the clouds on Beirut's coast, with large letters asking: "Guess Who's Coming Back?"

On room-by-room visits in the dorms, we handed out several thousand invitations to students. Most were from Muslim countries where there were no missionaries: Saudi Arabia, Libya, Iraq, Sudan, Qatar, the UAE, Oman, and the Maldives. Because our leader assumed it would not be safe to use our own names, many of us used pseudonyms in our conversations with Muslims. One day, three of us were graciously invited into the room of a Saudi student whose father sold holy water in Mecca.

"Hi, I'm Luke, and this is Mark and John," I said.

The Saudi grinned, "So where is Matthew?"

Through that multi-agency evangelistic event, the Father blessed a handful of Muslims, and even more students from Maronite and Orthodox families, by opening their eyes to know the reality of the living Lord Jesus. Some people thought an equally encouraging result of the event was the debut of the Christian groups working together. Additionally, some Lebanese and Jordanian Christians learned how to share their faith with Muslims. A few even became missionaries to Jordan, Iraq, and the Arabian Peninsula.

Try as we might, Sally and I could not coax Arabs from the most conservative Muslim countries to come to our home for dinner. However, three Muslim fellows from some islands we'd never heard of took advantage of our hospitality – often uninvited. I guess they adopted us. I had no idea that the Maldive Islands, south-west of India, were 100 percent Islamic – with not even a church for the tourists! Latif, the leader of the Maldive trio, preferred Sartre to any religious writer. Thinking we had nothing to lose, we evangelized those guys mercilessly. Still, they loved hanging out at our home near the university.

Years later, when OM's first ship, *Logos*, docked in the capital of the Maldives, the first local up the gangplank was Latif. "Do you know Luke Livingston?" he asked the ship's leader.

"Well, I know a *Greg* Livingston ..."

Still later, a Frontiers team leader to the Maldives became acquainted with Latif. By that time, he had become a well-known government official. We both continue to pray that Latif and his two colleagues will discover the Lord Jesus and become apostles to the Divehi people.

The gas fixture in our Beirut bathroom was faulty, so one night six-year-old Evan lost consciousness while he was taking a bath. He didn't immediately regain consciousness, so I carried him down the stairs, running as fast as I could to the nearby hospital. By the time we arrived, he was conscious again. Though he seemed not to have suffered any damage, I thought I'd better get him examined in any case.

The receptionist asked me, "Name?... Age?... Address?... Occupation?"

When I answered that last question with "student," the Lebanese lady looked at Evan in my arms.

Avoiding eye contact with me, she said to my son, "Tell your daddy it's time to go to work."

Although it wasn't the kind of employment the receptionist had in mind, work was all I did. All our money went into the ministry as well. When Sally, with newborn

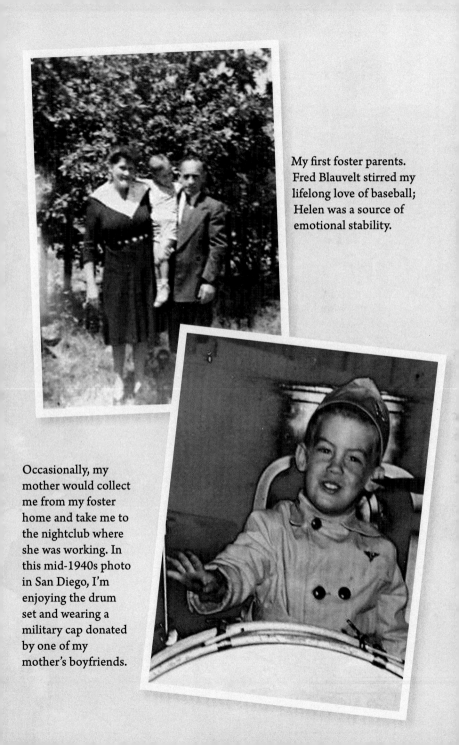

My first foster parents. Fred Blauvelt stirred my lifelong love of baseball; Helen was a source of emotional stability.

Occasionally, my mother would collect me from my foster home and take me to the nightclub where she was working. In this mid-1940s photo in San Diego, I'm enjoying the drum set and wearing a military cap donated by one of my mother's boyfriends.

Mom and Dad Ringle were my spiritual parents as well as my last foster parents. In the early 1960s, I was ordained as a pastor at their Baptist church in Tulsa, Oklahoma.

In the early days of OM, we were not allowed to behave like tourists by having cameras. In this rare photo from that era, I'm telling Swiss OMer Daniel Moser: "Go plant a church in Italy." And he did!

In 1963, I recruited 103 to OM's first charter plane from North America to OM Europe.

Above: Part of our first overland team in 1964. Sally is seated in the middle of the front row; I am second from the left behind her.

Below: An early OM team in India, with Samuel Tyagi kneeling in front.

We didn't realize when we met in Beirut in 1969 that Mazhar Mallouhi would become my lifelong friend. In my estimation, he is arguably the most effective presenter of the claims of Christ to Arabic-speaking Muslims in the world.

This is one of my favourite pictures of Sally, when she was seven months pregnant with Evan, our first son.

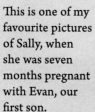

In November 1964, Sally gave birth to our first son, Evan. The Indian nurses were surprised that Evan was bald.

Evan was born in Pune, India. David was born in Frankfurt, Germany. Paul was born in Beirut, Lebanon, where this photo was taken in 1971.

My assignment from George Verwer in 1972: establish OM Canada and recruit 100 Canadians. Nine months later, I had fulfilled my orders and we moved on again.

Our 1975 family Christmas photo in Aspen featured our dog Muzzie, named after our friend Mazhar Mallouhi.

Standing in front of the North Africa Mission offices in Upper Darby, Pennsylvania, I was elated to send off these four recent Penn State graduates to North Africa. They took up my challenge to find a way to take the good news of Jesus to Libya. All four (from left: Greg Fritz, Bob Sjogren, me, Al Stahl, and Harry Gray) continued in full-time Christian ministry for decades to come.

Freshly returned from a year in Libya, Bob Sjogren challenged me to believe God to send thousands more laborers into the Muslim world. Shortly thereafter, we started Frontiers together.

With butterflies in my stomach, I shared the stage at InterVarsity's 1984 Student Mission Convention with missionary statesmen Sam Wilson (left), as well as Ralph Winter and Warren Webster (not pictured).

By the late 1980s, when this photo was taken in Pasadena, Sally and I were well on our way to the twenty-seven homes we would set up over the years.

In Pasadena in the late 1990s, Lady Jessie had replaced Muzzie as part of our family. With (from left) Evan (22), David (20), and Paul (16).

What a joy to meet up again with Tyagi and his wife Kamala in India. When we were newlyweds in India, they and their two children shared their one-room house with us, hanging a blanket across a rope to give each couple a bit of privacy. Over nearly fifty years, hardly a day has passed without his giving out gospels in Urdu and speaking winsomely of his Saviour in Muslim homes and shops.

On a visit to wintry cold Delhi in the early 1990s, Gordon Magney (far right) and I met up again with Tyagi, our first Indian partner in OM. Less than twenty years later, Gordon was buried in Kabul, having literally laid down his life so that Afghans might be introduced to Jesus.

In the early days of Frontiers, we grew so quickly that it was a challenge to keep up with the applications and to read through all our members' newsletters.

Sally and I visiting colleagues in Afghanistan.

Over the years, Sally and I have enjoyed traveling together to coach our Frontiers teams, such as on this trip to north India in the late 1990s.

While we lived in Kuala Lumpur, I joined the Rotary Club, which gave me the opportunity to befriend Malay Muslims.

In 2006, I told Sally, "You've followed me to so many countries, setting up home twenty-six times. I think the next home should be the one from which we'll go to heaven. You should choose where that will be." She was unambivalent: "I want to go back to our home in England."

In 2009, we visited to Aspen, where friends had organized a reunion of First Baptist Church members who had lived in the area while we pastored there. What a joy it was to realize I had had the privilege of baptizing many of these dear people as new believers in Jesus.

In my later years, I have been tasked with coaching Frontiers sending base leaders around the world, such as Marcos Napoli in Brazil, pictured here with his daughter.

In Phuket, Thailand in 2006, Sally and I met with the missionaries sent by our denomination, the Evangelical Presbyterian Church. I was the EPC's coordinator for ministries to Muslims.

After combing through my journals, I wrote the first draft of this autobiography in Arab World Ministry's guest house in Worthing, England in 2010.

When we finally visited Libya in 2011, it felt as though we were entering the Promised Land!

Sally and I celebrated our 50th anniversary in August 2012, honestly more in love than ever.

Paul, asked me to buy her a washing machine, I balked. I didn't want to buy a washing machine, because I was so aware of how many New Testaments I could buy with the money instead! At that point, Sally was uncharacteristically unsubmissive. I sought advice from our Arab pastor, Victor Sadaka, a tough bird himself. "What should I do?" I asked him.

"Well, you've got a choice: either get a washing machine or get a new wife." I bought a washer that day.

I must not omit the event of Paul's birth in the new American Hospital in Beirut. I was so sure that we were going to have a daughter that I'd convinced Sally, too. We chose the name Amy, after Amy Carmichael.

When the time came, I was once again not permitted to be in the delivery room, but at least this time I could be in the waiting room. The only others there were a local family who already had four girls and were desperate to have a son. In those days in Beirut, it was customary that if a baby boy was born, the doctor would emerge to take all the credit as he announced, "I present you with a son." However, in their case, a nurse appeared and revealed in an apologetic tone of voice, "The baby is here." Their fifth girl! To my astonishment, the family began to wail as if the nurse had declared that the mother and baby were dead!

Glued on that scene, I didn't see the doctor approach me to declare, "I present you with a son."

"A son! What?" I couldn't believe it.

Suddenly, the Lebanese family stopped crying, rushed over to me, and started whacking me on the back and shouting their congratulations: "*Allah kareem!* [God is generous!] Three sons!" For just a few moments, I wrestled in my mind about the biblical teachings and implications of trading babies!

Well, if three sons represent a generous God, what about four? A few months after Paul was born, as the girls on our team were visiting door to door, they discovered a two-year-old boy who lived most of the time on his own. He was the son of a Lebanese prostitute and, we supposed, a sailor visiting from somewhere. With the mother's encouragement, the girls brought the boy home for us to adopt! We gulped. Having been abandoned myself, I felt we should probably do it. Sally nodded her assent. That is, until we realized how crazed he had become. Every time we turned our heads he would bite baby Paul's toes until they bled! Though we felt confused and guilty, we returned him to his mother.

Not yet cured of our idealistic goals to be exemplary missionaries, we put Evan into a local school. (This was just a year after he'd been learning Flemish in Belgium!) Soon, we were impressed with his ability to write Arabic script. "What does it say?" I asked. Evan pronounced the Arabic words. "What does it mean in English?" Evan shook his head. He had no idea.

During that school year, Evan suddenly blimped up in weight. We took him to a Western-educated local doctor. "May I speak with your boy alone?" the doctor asked. We shrugged our shoulders at the unusual request, so they went into a private room for twenty minutes.

"You need to help your son get an identity. He doesn't

know who he is." We looked at the doctor wide-eyed. OMers received regular lectures on avoiding nationalism. We were especially sternly warned not to be "the ugly Americans." We were to remember that we were citizens of heaven! But eventually, God opened my eyes to a better understanding of Scripture: You cannot give away something you don't possess. As adults, we could die to our cultural ways, because we had something to forsake. If you have a homeland, you can choose to leave it for the sake of Christ's kingdom. If you don't have a homeland, such sacrifice is meaningless.

By the time he was ten, Evan had spent only a few months in America. So, to help him establish an identity, we encouraged him to pick a hometown. Eventually, we did the same with each of our sons. Evan chose Los Angeles. David chose Pittsburgh, his mother's childhood home. And Paul chose Boston, reflecting my zeal for the Boston Red Sox. We acquired sport hats and pennants from those cities to hang on their bedroom walls.

While we were in Lebanon, I also grew in my understanding of what it meant to lead a team in ministry. It was actually two teams – one of men, one of women. One day, the girls' team leader came to me looking quite disturbed. With anxious embarrassment, she managed to explain that the local men were pinching the girls' derrières.

"That must be terribly annoying," I said, with genuine sympathy.

Looking even more deeply worried, she proceeded to admit that that wasn't the worst thing! I panicked, wondering, "Has one of them been sexually abused?"

"What's worse is…" Her pause increased my anxiety. "They aren't pinching *mine*!"

Some years later, I officiated at her wedding to an Arab Christian, who today leads his own ministry among Muslims in several countries.

We had finally made it to the Arab world, but the truth was, I had no experience helping Muslims understand the gospel as truly good news. I decided to study Islamics at the Near East School of Theology in Beirut, assuming that it existed to bring the truths of Christ to the Near East. I was told I was fortunate to be able to take a class from the great Islamicist, Kenneth Cragg. However, it seemed to me that he didn't think that Muslims needed to be saved through trusting in Christ Jesus. I decided that I simply wasn't on his intellectual plane!

I carried around my 671-page copy of Gibb and Kramers' *Shorter Encyclopaedia of Islam* so that I could figure out questions such as:

- In which respect did the Kharijis differ from the Murjiis?

- What are the five fundamental doctrines of the Mu'tazila?

- What influence did Hellenism have on Muslim theology?

- Summarize the emphases of Montgomery Watt, Duncan MacDonald, Naguib Mahfuz, al-Ghazzali, and Rumi.

I grew inattentive as I realized I was learning much about the different kinds of Muslims, Islamic history, and even some of the content of the Quran and Hadith. But it was the Muslims in the universities and homes all around us whom I wanted to understand and to usher into the family of Isa al-Masih. The Muslim students I met seemed to have even less interest in their Muslim theologians than I did.

As always, our team visited people by knocking on door after door, selling books. One summer, I met a Saudi who was having a holiday in Lebanon's mountains. I put an Arabic version of Billy Graham's book, *Peace with God*, into his hand. The price tag read: "3.00 Lebanese pounds." The young Saudi complained, "This is too expensive."

I frowned. "No, it's not! It's very cheap!"

He took a big breath and disappeared into the apartment, returning with 300 Lebanese pounds (about US $100)! "No!" I exclaimed, "it's only *three* pounds!"

"Oh, then in that case, I'll buy *two* books."

In my diary in those days, I asked myself: "Why am I not introducing Muslims to Christ? At least a few each year? Why does our witness not get past step one? How do I keep expectant in light of so little response?"

We had no Francis Schaeffer of the Arab world who knew how to get through to Muslims. For example, a Muslim might say, "I don't want your *Injil* [gospel]. It has been corrupted. It is no longer the Word of God."

Muslims accept that God has sent four holy books to the world: the *Tawrat* (laws of Moses), the *Zabur* (psalms of David), the *Injil* (the New Testament), and the *Quran* (revelation to Mohammed). However, they typically assert that both Jews and Christians have allowed their books to become corrupted.

We countered with our best argument: "If Allah [God] didn't have the power to keep the first three holy books from being corrupted, how do we know the Quran wasn't also corrupted?" But for some reason, apologetics didn't work among Muslims as it did among Europeans. Someone needed to discover God's answers.

Instead of discovering the needed answers, after only two years in the Middle East, I got fired.

Looking back, I can now see that before I moved to Beirut, the OM leaders should have helped John, the overall leader for Lebanon, and me to think through how we would share leadership responsibilities. I had helped to start OM and had been one of the overall leaders from 1962 until we left for Beirut in 1970. We had a clash of expectations.

Two more totally different personalities we could not have been! John was methodical, and he seemed to want to hold team meetings almost every day. Planning, not implementation, was his delight. I was the opposite. It's no wonder we clashed. We appealed to George Verwer and Dale Rhoton (who was by then OM's Middle East coordinator). They decided I should be the one to leave Lebanon. After all, John knew Arabic; I didn't. Anyway, Verwer preferred to put me back to work recruiting, not planting churches.

We had been in the place of our "calling," the Arab world, for only two years! I was confused and humiliated. I left Beirut with my tail between my legs, a failure. Years later, Verwer referred to the clash between John and me as "Greg attempting a coup!" So much for the godly reputation I had hoped I was developing!

It was one of those critical crossroads: Could I believe that despite my failures and impatience, my heavenly Father was using these circumstances to engineer us *out* of the Arab world? I covenanted with God: "Lord, please make Satan pay such a high price for my feet being on Western soil that the enemy of God will wish I'd stayed in Tripoli or Baghdad planting churches!"

Verwer allowed me no time to feel sorry for myself. Ken Taylor had given OM 100,000 paperback Living Bibles. I was immediately dispatched to visit the major distributors of Christian books in the capitals of every former British colony in Africa. My task was to get orders for 50,000 Bibles from distributors in Africa.

Meanwhile, two Swedish team members drove Sally and the three boys from Lebanon through Syria, Turkey, Bulgaria, Yugoslavia, Italy, and France, back to OM's European headquarters in Belgium. Near the end of the journey, they stopped to visit my foster parents, the Ringles. I had recruited Dad Ringle, formerly the Aspen newspaper editor, to work in a print shop for a mission agency in France. Later, with a twinkle in his eye, he declared to me, "By recruiting us to take early retirement and come to France, you cost us a hundred thousand dollars."

Grinning, I shot back, "Well, by ushering me to Christ, you probably cost me a million dollars!"

While my family was slowly driven overland back to Europe, I bounced from one African capital to the next. Most nights, my plane fare included free accommodation in one of the country's top hotels. Some hotels even provided more than I wanted. As I came out of the dining room one evening, a short African man with a beaming smile pointed to the next "stop" he had chosen for my itinerary – an almost seven-foot-tall "lady" covered with necklaces and not much else. She was absolutely frightening! I thanked the man for his generosity, then tried to witness. I explained to him that I was a Christian and what that was supposed to mean about purity. Looking surprised, he responded, "I don't want you to think *I* am not a Christian!"

CHAPTER 18

In and Out

Never one to look back for long, Verwer had no time to discuss my failure in Lebanon. He focused me on a new goal: establish OM Canada and recruit 100 Canadians.

Yes, sir!

Toronto seemed a logical place to start, since three OM alumni lived there. We were still living under the OM maxim that to pay rent was to lack faith (if not actually to sin!), but one of the alumni responded to our need for an apartment by loaning us his. A month later, when he needed it back, we found another freebie where we could house-sit. When that host returned, we were forced to find a third house. This one demanded rent, but since it was run down, the rent was fairly cheap. During our nine months in Toronto, Sally was forced to set up house three times! (This was yet one more reason why I eventually came to see myself as "God's bungler.") Another local alumnus had connections with a church across the street from the University of Toronto, and they provided space for OM's first Canadian office.

Meanwhile, our sons were becoming quite cosmopolitan: from Germany, to Belgium, to America, back to Belgium, to

Lebanon, and then to Canada. The neighborhood boys in downtown Toronto weren't all that friendly. Once, when they were bullying eight-year-old Evan, younger brother David ran upstairs to grab a souvenir spear I had bought in Ghana. This act of defense of his older brother produced a warning cry among the neighborhood boys: "Watch out! He's got a spear!" The aggressors quickly scattered back to their homes.

One of our sons' fondest memories from Toronto is a trip to a petting zoo. I was encouraging them to stroke the llama without fear. But suddenly, it sneezed a mass of snot all over my face and shirt. The boys couldn't stop laughing.

We enrolled David and Evan into first and second grades at the People's Church School, where they learned to read amazingly well. Our constant moves meant that their schooling was patchwork, but our theory was that if the boys learned to read well, they could always catch up. It worked. Both Evan and David are voracious readers who gained entrance into the University of California, Berkeley. Paul was more interested in doing than studying, and he has become a renowned sitar player, who is also now very well read.

About sixty Canadians joined OM that initial year. One of them, Dave Lundy, became a leader in India, then OM's Canadian director, and eventually the international director of Arab World Ministries.

After nine months, I'd fulfilled George's orders, and we were turning OM Canada over to Canadians when something completely unexpected happened. Mazhar Mallouhi showed up in my office. While he had been in North Africa, some rumors had flown around about him. I had been told some exaggerated stories that he had forsaken his conversion, so I was totally rude – curtly informing him that I had no time for him.

I don't claim this often, but that night the Lord unmistakably spoke to me: "Help that man."

"But, Lord, I hear he's untrustworthy."

"How many times have you needed me to start over with you?" the Merciful One asked. I got the point. I wasn't supposed to worry whether Mazhar would be "strategic." He was the Father's chosen son (prodigal or not), and therefore my brother (faithful or not).

Mazhar had a letter of acceptance from an English language school in Los Angeles, but the US Embassy was suspicious of its authenticity. They accused him of wanting to marry any girl simply to obtain American citizenship. Against my better judgment, I accompanied him to the embassy and I vouched for him. He got the visa, and I figured I'd never see him again.

Having passed on the baton of leadership in Canada, we took a family holiday – our first in about ten years. We spent the summer of 1973 on a transcontinental venture, combining a chance to visit many of our supporters with the opportunity for our boys to see the United States for the first time.

From OM's US office, we borrowed a pickup camper, which allowed the family to lounge in the back during the long hours on the road. There was no window, and therefore no communication between the pickup cab and the living space in the camper. One day, after we had stopped to fill up with gas, Sally waved to me that me she was ready. I heard the back door close, so I drove off.

About twenty minutes later, a police car's siren signaled me to pull over. I knew I hadn't been speeding, so I was puzzled as the policeman came to my window. "Is your wife in the back?"

"Yes, sir."

"Are you sure?"

"Yes, sir."

"Can we look?"

We did. She wasn't.

After informing me that she was ready, Sally had opened the back door, but before climbing in, she decided to visit the ladies' room and closed the door again. Thinking she was inside, I drove off. Ah… the communication challenges in a marriage!

We met George Verwer in Denver to talk about our next ministry assignment. He felt I should become chaplain of OM's new ship ministry on the *Logos*, which was traveling around the world to supply literature, train young people, provide relief, and share the message of hope in Christ. To be honest, being a chaplain didn't feel like the right role for me. But when Sally fell to her knees in front of me and pleaded, "Yes, Greg, let's do it," how could I disagree with them both? I conceded that we would try it for ninety days.

We were to meet the *Logos* in Bandar-Abbas on the southern coast of Iran. Having traveled to Belgium, we packed ourselves into another old Volkswagen van and drove with two newly recruited Canadians from Belgium to Iran. On this, our second overland trip to Iran, we found the journey quite different with three sons. To pass the time, Evan read through *The Lord of the Rings* and David read the Old Testament from Genesis to Psalms.

We made it to Bandar-Abbas on time, but as we watched the ship come into port, we were perplexed when it suddenly turned around and headed back to sea.

Later we learned why. In completing some paperwork for entry to the port, someone on the ship had inadvertently called the body of water from which they were entering "the Arabian Gulf" instead of "the Persian Gulf" – quite a serious political gaffe in Iran. The American naval attaché in Tehran intervened, and eventually the Iranians allowed the *Logos* to dock for twenty-four hours.

While we were waiting for those negotiations to be resolved, I took Sally and the boys to a beach for a swim. We found an idyllic-looking spot with azure water. I got in first to ensure there was no sharp drop-off and no undertow. It was ideal – there weren't even any other people around to disturb our play! I wondered what the sign in Farsi said.

No sooner were all five of us in the water than Sally screamed, "Snakes! We're surrounded by snakes!" This was still some time before I learned the lesson: "Do yourself a favor; listen to your wife."

I authoritatively declared, "They can't be snakes. This is salt water." I insisted we stay in the water. For forty-five minutes, the eel-like creatures swirled around our legs. "They're just playing with us," I reassured my family.

After the ship had finally arrived and we had boarded, Sally asked a crew member, "Is there such a creature as a sea snake?"

"Oh yes," she replied. "They are very, very dangerous."

I still scoffed.

Many years later, while on a visit to a team in Uzbekistan, I happened to be paging through an old issue of *National Geographic* that featured sea snakes. My eyes widened and my heart rate increased as I learned that sea snakes are in fact one of the most poisonous creatures on earth! After a single bite, the victim is paralyzed within ten minutes and dead within twenty. They exist in only two locations – off the Gold Coast of Australia and (you guessed it) southern Iran!

I fell to my knees, half crying in repentance and half worshipping the Lord our protector. Looking back, I can only surmise that we experienced a rerun of Daniel in the lion's den. The Lord simply ordered those snakes: "No bites!"

Well, I was wrong about sea snakes, but I was right about the chaplaincy assignment. Today, pastoral care (sometimes called "member care") is recognized as a vital service within mission agencies. In 1973, especially in OM, no one saw the point. One of the ship's secretaries told me I should get a "real job." So I volunteered to serve meals to the crew from the galley.

The boys loved the ship's school. We dug up mudfish in Bhavnagar, India, and bought a parrot in a Bombay market. They got a kick out of watching it chew up my hands when we gave it food.

On day ninety-one of our stint on the *Logos*, I went into

George Verwer's office on the ship and asked him to allow me to open up new work in Pakistan. He responded that OM was already too spread out and needed to consolidate, not expand. That was not good news for me, because I am fundamentally an expansionist!

Tears filled our eyes as we realized this was the end of the Livingstons' service in OM. That encounter was one of the very few times in Verwer's leadership when he couldn't think of a new job for an entrepreneurial co-worker like me. I believe the Lord blinded him, because otherwise we would not have had the freedom to leave OM.

The organization had become our family, our emotional home. This time, I was the one who was leaving, rather than being left. Yet our departure from OM felt like a replay of all my childhood abandonments.

When I realized our career with OM was over, two very different visions burdened my mind: church planting among Muslims and pastoral care for missionaries. I had observed that some missionaries short-circuited their ministries because they didn't face up to their emotional problems, so I decided to apply to the Rosemead School of Counseling in California. I hurriedly sat for the graduate school entrance exams before leaving Bombay, then we flew to New York. I had no job offer and no ministry, but I was confident that I would be accepted in Rosemead's doctoral program. We boarded a Greyhound bus with our three boys and nine boxes full of everything we owned to make the 3,000-mile journey to Los Angeles.

Shortly after we arrived, guess who found us again: Mazhar. Considering himself my elder brother, he stayed constantly by our side – whether we wanted him to or not. I finally realized that God clearly wanted us to team up – for life! I introduced Mazhar to Charles Kraft and Dudley Woodberry at Fuller Theological Seminary's School of World Mission. He was bolstered in his growing desire to return to the Arab world and to develop fresh ways to share his faith that were more in harmony with his Arab Muslim culture.

Mazhar said later, "Greg picked me up when I was lost and took me to his chest. Through his long-term mentoring and caring, I was restored to God and to many of God's servants who cared for my people." Sadly, it would still take years for Mazhar to become trusted among Arab Christians, as well as in some mission circles.

Meanwhile, I enrolled at California State University that summer to take some prerequisite courses in psychology. Sally became a Cub Scout den mother for David and his new friends. We enrolled the boys in a Christian school, because it was flexible enough to allow the boys to enter in the middle of the year. To pay their tuition, I worked as a substitute teacher, though I had never taught children before. I loved the fourth graders, but I did wonder how a loving God could create junior high kids!

We were so broke that Sally stood in a line for food stamps. The clerk at the counter exclaimed, "Well, it's nice, for a change, to see a white face getting these benefits." Sally wasn't sure it was nice for a person of any color to stand in a food stamp line!

I completed my psychology course, but my graduate school entrance exam results never arrived from the testing agency in Princeton – even after I had been assured over the phone that they were on their way. After discussing my options at Rosemead, a kind professor empathetically explained that even if the test results had arrived, there were only twelve spots available for the doctoral program. He encouraged me that pastoral care of missionaries was a great vision but hastened to add, "You aren't the right person. You're an entrepreneur, not a counselor."

I respect that man and appreciate his insight to this day. But what a difficult wake-up call. How had I made another huge "wrong turn"? I had left OM, dragged my family halfway around the world, even taken some courses in psychology, but then I was not accepted. I had been teaching "How to Discern God's Will for Your Life" for years. Now, I had obviously failed to discern it for our family!

For a week, I stared at the wall, totally perplexed. Then the phone rang. It was the senior deacon from my old church in Aspen. The pastor had just announced that Sunday morning that he was quitting. He walked down from the pulpit, escorted his wife and kids into an already packed car, and drove away! Would I consider coming right away to serve as the interim pastor?

It sounded better than being a substitute teacher at the local Christian school for minimum wage. And besides, didn't we owe them? The Aspen church had supported us every month for eleven years since we left for the mission field in June 1963. Mazhar insisted on helping us move to Aspen.

CHAPTER 19

Shepherd

I knew even less about being a pastor than I did about being a chaplain. I also didn't know much about what was happening in America in those days. Hal Lindsay's apocalyptic vision in his book *The Late Great Planet Earth* had scared a lot of hippies into churches. The Aspen church had a dozen or so.

As I came into the church on the first Sunday, Jim introduced himself and his roommate Susie. "You mean your housemate?"

"No, my roommate."

"Oh."

After my first sermon, I went to the front door to shake hands, as I seemed to remember pastors were supposed to do. The first young lady hugged me, declaring "Heavy, pastor, heavy." Assuming that meant my sermon had made her think, I smiled.

Right behind her was Diane, another rather glamorous young woman, who kissed me on the cheek with the remark, "Far out." Did she mean she couldn't understand my sermon?

Then it was Patti's turn. She shocked me with a kiss on the neck and the exclamation, "No s**t, pastor." My knees buckled. We had entered a new tribe.

Discovering that some of the new converts were living together unmarried, I took one of them (named Archie) aside and asked him not to take communion unless he intended to be obedient to God's commands. When he reared back his fist to bust me one, his buddy Tommy stopped him. "Hey Archie, he's the head scoutmaster. He's right. It's in the Book."

Within a month, I had befriended Tommy and Archie, baptized them and their ladies, and performed their wedding ceremonies.

After his wedding, Archie handed me an envelope, which I assumed would be the standard pastoral honorarium of about twenty bucks. Back at the church, I opened it to discover ten $100 bills. I later learned that Archie was an ex-CIA agent who had been abandoned while he was on a mission. In his disillusionment, he decided never again to do any paperwork for the government – especially not to pay taxes on his profits from selling drugs!

At the church in Aspen, we were quite a mixture of old-school Baptists, former Catholics, and hungry charismatics. One of the latter, whenever asked, "How are you?" would always answer, "Praise the Lord!"

One day, I confronted her. "Cherie, do you realize that it hurts me when I ask how you are, and you tell me to mind my own business?"

"What? When did I ever do that?"

"Every time! Only you hide behind 'Praise the Lord,' divulging nothing."

The First Baptist Church was pretty much boycotted by the rich and famous, who were taking over Aspen. As a missionary who had now spent a number of years traveling around the world, it was natural to me to analyze the culture and presuppositions of the locals. The first thing I did was to stop making altar calls, which I realized scared people away from our church. Then I stopped the visitation program. We found that the people we visited door to door figured they knew what a Baptist was and were quite sure they didn't want to be one. Only the most guilt-prone church members volunteered for visitation, anyway.

As I reflect on those years, I remember my increasing concern that in OM, we had not been leaving behind communities of believers who would demonstrate the difference Christ makes. Perhaps God moved us out of OM to teach me about developing church life as God desires it to be. In Aspen, I had an opportunity to discern what a New Testament church should look like in my own culture.

I told the congregation of forty that our new goal was to become a community that would truly take care of each other and thereby whet the appetite of lonely Aspen folk. Our first step in that direction was a good old-fashioned "house raising" for a family with few dollars and a lot of kids. I recruited the three Christian contractors who lived in the Roaring Fork Valley. By God's amazing grace, they teamed up to plan how we as a church family could build a sizable house in a single Saturday! Having the least talent for tools, the new pastor carried boards. Amish barn raisers had nothing on us that day!

Not long afterwards, a new believer named Pat went bankrupt. Humiliated, he left his wife and children and ran off to Hawaii. The younger men of the church huddled, then decided which of them would fly to Hawaii to bring Pat back. His father, a Roman Catholic, was so impressed that he said, "Now *that* is what Christianity is all about."

Two years later, we realized that God had answered our quest to become a committed, covenanted family when Anna, one of our members, overheard two non-Christian ladies talking: "If you want a ******* friend in this ******* town, you've got to go to the ******* Baptist church!"

One of our new friends was Danny, a Jewish photographer from New York City who had come to Aspen to ski. He was attracted to my church secretary, Cynthia. She refused to go to bed with him, but she did manage to get him to attend "Old Life" (our version of the high-school ministry group "Young Life," for those who were beyond high school). When I sat down next to him, Danny expected me to preach at him. But all I said was, "Boy, I'm tired."

Danny told me later that he had mused, "Maybe these Christians are human after all." He decided to read a book in my library called *What's a Nice Jewish Boy Like You Doing in the First Baptist Church?* After he gave himself to the Lord Jesus, I performed his wedding to Cynthia. To honor his Jewish parents, we had the ceremony in the mountainside home of our richest parishioner – complete with a Jewish canopy and the traditional stomping of a light bulb.

Rosemary was a nominal Catholic who was found by the Lord in those days. She asked for believer's baptism. We held baptisms either at a lake or at a swimming pool rather than in the church building, so that the new Christians would feel comfortable to invite their pagan friends. Ro came out to the swimming pool of her condominium complex in her bikini. "Ah, Ro, do you have any jeans?" I asked her.

"Yeah, sure. Why?"

"Well, ah, baptism is kind of a holy thing, and …"

She went back inside and put on her jeans.

Later, I officiated at her marriage to Marty Martin, who later pastored at Cherry Creek Presbyterian Church near Denver. That church, in turn, became one of our best backers as missionaries to Muslims. Today, Marty is a senior leader of Food for the Hungry.

Obviously, not everyone in Aspen was responsive. On a ski-slope chairlift one day, I found myself sitting with Arkansas Governor Winthrop Rockefeller as a captive audience. I challenged him to follow Christ.

"Another time, maybe."

Ah, what a great soul winner I am … *not!*

As a church, we were not willing to wait until people came through the church door to get acquainted, so we started a softball team and joined the "bar league." The league included teams from seven of Aspen's bars – and the First Baptist Church. "It's booze against God," one of our opponents shouted. During one game, a very large opponent was beating the throw to home, where I was waiting as the catcher. He got there before the ball, and knocked me twelve feet into the dust. The new Christians on our team lost their sanctification, rushing in to "kill the guy." I had to stagger to my feet to separate the brawlers.

I decided to run for mayor of Aspen, thinking that such

a job would be a handy pulpit. The news must have spread quickly. Only a few days later, the church secretary, Cynthia, announced that Senator Mark Hatfield from Oregon (a well-known evangelical) was on the phone.

"Oh, right," I thought. "That'll be one of the church guys being silly."

So I picked up the phone and answered, "Hey, Marky baby, how goes it?"

A voice soberly proclaimed back to me, "This is Senator Mark Hatfield. I have heard that you are thinking of putting your hat into the ring, and I wanted to try to persuade you that having one more Baptist preacher go into politics is not necessarily a great idea."

Still sure it was one of our Aspen fellows, I continued to make jokes.

When the man on the phone started to get angry, I realized it really *was* Senator Hatfield! My face must have been bright pink. How does one back up and sound like a reasonable, mature man after that?

Hatfield's arguments against going into politics were fairly convincing. Then a friend asked me if I really wanted to spend my time planning where to put drainage pipes. I dropped the idea of running for mayor, but the incident also reminded me that I had told the Lord to let us know when we were supposed to get back to "the mission field."

Meanwhile, my Arab friend Mazhar was still in Los Angeles. He realized that God wanted him to go back to the Arab world, but we couldn't find an agency that would accept him as a missionary, since he was divorced. So, along with my old fatherly pastor, Clifford Clark in Oklahoma, I started Caravans of the Middle East – a mission agency for one man. Then, Mazhar could be supported through the Aspen church and Tulsa Baptist Temple.

That same year, a young and very bright Australian woman with a calling to the Arab Muslim world passed through Los Angeles en route to a hospital in the Persian Gulf run by The Evangelical Alliance Mission (TEAM). Christine Hutchins had been praying for an Arab husband so that she might integrate into Arab society to witness for Christ more effectively. In California, she met Mazhar, and he told her to go to Aspen, Colorado to join his mission.

One day soon afterwards, Christine showed up at our house, saying she had come to investigate "Mazhar's mission." Her agreement with TEAM had been mutually terminated at their candidate school, two weeks before she was due to arrive on the field. She was still committed to her calling, but now she had nowhere to go. In fact, Mazhar had decided that Christine was to be his life partner, so it was up to Sally and me to work it out. We did. He soon joined us in Aspen, where they courted under our watchful eye and were married on New Year's Eve at the Aspen church. Together with the church in Tulsa and Christian backers in Australia, we eventually sent them off to Cairo.

I felt that there was no more reason to disqualify divorced people from becoming missionaries than to disqualify people who had failings in other areas of their lives. Our God makes all things new. The Mallouhis have had forty years of absolutely thrilling and fruitful ministry in Egypt, Lebanon, Morocco, Tunisia, Syria, Yemen, and beyond – especially through their books and Muslim-sensitive editions of the Scriptures. Christine writes:

My "candidate school" was Greg, Sally and I with a picnic at Maroon Bells talking about how I wanted to be used in the Arab world even though I was 25 and had no special talents. Greg said, "OK, I can help you accomplish your vision." We ate our picnic lunch and returned to the church office, where he put wheels in motion. Nothing was too hard or too crazy for Greg. His one liner was "you can do it" – or more to the point, "God can do this through you." Greg had great optimism and faith that God could use a person, even when no one else could see it. Greg and Sally remained our close friends and marriage counselors through numerous countries and problems. As Greg moved through various mission involvements, he kept us on his visiting list and had a major part in our life choices. When our baby was born, he flew in with a whole suitcase of baby needs. When we were shriveling under treatment by the Syrian secret service while living in Damascus in 1995, we sent a message to Greg that we needed him. Everyone told him that it was unwise for him to enter Syria. But Greg said, "My brother needs me." Against all advice, he flew in and encouraged us. His visit was Christ's visit to us.

Mazhar went on to become, in my estimation, arguably the most effective presenter of the claims of Christ to Arabic-speaking Muslims in the world. He can begin a conversation with a Muslim who seems diametrically opposed to the claims of Christ. Twenty minutes later, the guy is begging him for a Bible.

Mazhar and Christine accomplished something which was rare in the Arab world by founding an exemplary house fellowship in Cairo. Imagine how much it means to Sally and me to have had a significant role in the lives and ministries of these two great pioneers among Arab Muslims!

Quite late in his journey, Mazhar returned to writing as his main life's work. For more than a century and a half, Arab Christians had been using a Bible translated by a Dutchman (whose mother tongue was obviously not Arabic). Mazhar and Christine began to address this problem by producing commentaries on Genesis, Luke, and John in beautiful coffee-table editions. They arranged for publication through mainstream Muslim publishing houses in nearly every Arab country, so that the Scriptures and commentaries could be sold legally.

Mazhar and Christine have suffered expulsion from Morocco, Egypt, and Syria. Yet they press on, visiting seekers and new disciples in the Persian Gulf, the Middle East, and North Africa, as well as in non-Arab Muslim majority countries.

Meanwhile, during the years in Aspen, Evan, David, and Paul were in Rocky Mountain paradise. They learned to ski, they had friends, and they owned their first dog. When we first arrived in Aspen, the boys had begged for a dog. "Well," I declared, "we aren't going to feed a big dog, and we're not going to pay for a pedigree." Agreed. We went to the grocery store, where a young lady was giving away puppies. They were free, and they were small. (I didn't know that one should examine the size of a puppy's paws to discern its adult size.)

We named the dog Muzzie after Mazhar – well aware what a huge insult that was to an Arab! It turned out that our tiny puppy was a Pyrenees – just a bit smaller than a St. Bernard! As an adult, she could pull all three boys through the snow on a sled. They could wrestle her without ever evoking a growl.

The church folks admired our boys, who were warm and polite. We never heard a complaint about them. When we moved on after three years, I felt that leaving Aspen must have been a huge price for them to pay.

During our time there, the church grew from forty to three hundred. During those years, I felt fruitful and affirmed by the Lord. In fact, it was so satisfying that we were tempted to let returning to the mission field drift from our thoughts. It felt awfully good to be used by God, with visible results in people's lives. I sensed that most people pretty much *liked* Sally and me – both church members and others in town. I liked the sense of belonging. It felt pretty good to be a big fish in a small pond, especially when the young church guys sat around roasting each other – with me, the pastor, being the favorite butt of the jokes. Masculine affection at its best. I've never since enjoyed being with a group of men as much!

But we weren't there in Aspen to coddle the parishioners. I saw that my calling was to be a sheepdog moving them into fruitful ministries. Jill Harris, who started the children's choir, became amazingly fruitful for years, teaching about missions to children around the world. Jim Wurst became a pastor in Denver. John Russell, a tennis and ski photographer, consistently witnessed about Christ among sports professionals. Two or three parishioners were key players in starting new fellowships elsewhere in the Roaring Fork Valley. Some of those who were children during my pastorate are themselves pastors today. It was a very encouraging time of investing our lives into Aspenites, who in turn have provided us with generous financial support ever since we went back to Muslim ministries in 1977.

CHAPTER 20

Turnaround Specialist

George Verwer passed through Aspen and asked if I would staff OM's booth at Urbana '76 during Christmas week. At this massive mission conference for university students, George would be a plenary speaker to 17,000 young people.

"Sure," I thought. "Why not have a go at recruiting some more for OM?"

When I returned to Aspen in the New Year, I took Sally to lunch and told her about a funny thing that had happened. Bill Bell, the North American Director of North Africa Mission (NAM), had confronted me, declaring that God had told him I was to be his replacement!

To my surprise, Sally immediately felt this was God's direction for us. Even more astonishing, Evan and David agreed without hesitation. We were all prepared to leave the cushy, rewarding ministry in gorgeous Aspen for NAM's most dangerous outpost – Philadelphia!

When I arrived at my interview with the NAM board, the men in black pin-striped suits were clearly amused by my corduroys and leather vest. Perhaps Bill Bell had convinced them that it was me or nothing. Whatever the reason, this council of older and much more conservative board members accepted my application.

The following August, we crammed our Chevrolet with all our worldly goods, plus three boys (aged thirteen, eleven, and seven), Muzzie, a cat, a snake, and a box of frogs. The cat abandoned us at the Kansas border. The frogs and the snake died from the heat, because the car had no air conditioner. But the rest of us made it.

However, once we got there, David changed his mind. He wanted to go back to Aspen. "Lord, do something," we prayed, "to win David to Philadelphia." School had not yet started, so we visited a museum. At the McDonald's in the basement, we all filled out sweepstakes cards and dropped them into a jar. A week later, we got a phone call to say that David had won the grand prize. He (and his dad) were invited to the Philadelphia Eagles football camp, where he was photographed with the stars and given a uniform with "LIVINGSTON" on the back and free tickets for the family to an exhibition game against Denver! Suddenly, Philadelphia was A-okay for David. "Thank you, Father," I prayed.

One of the NAM board members provided our family with an interest-free loan as a down payment on a house. The cheaper houses were in the mainly Irish-Catholic neighborhood of Havertown – yet another cultural adjustment for Sally, our sons, and me. I never could relate to my working-class, pugilistic, often drunk neighbors, nor understand their matriarchal culture where the wives were in charge!

The neighbors weren't at all happy that we'd moved onto their turf, either. Taking the boys from door to door on Halloween, we were preceded to one house by an Irish kid who had painted his face black. As we approached, the man at the door cussed and exclaimed, "My God! What's this neighborhood coming to? First blacks, then Protestants!"

During our fourteen years with OM, we literally lived out the organization's name: *Operation Mobilisation*. We had worked side by side ever since we'd married. When we moved to Philadelphia, however, Sally was no longer my teammate pastoring a flock but the housewife who stayed behind while I went off to my office job.

She had always been the serious bookworm of her family – the one who studied Greek for fun. She was the extraordinary woman who overcame the odds to gain acceptance into medical college – in an era when that was somewhat rare for women. I suggested she work toward a master's degree at Villanova University.

After considering the suggestion, Sally asked, "Where will we get the money for tuition?"

"Don't worry," I volleyed, "the Lord will provide."

He did, but not before she took a job. The priests at Villanova University (a Catholic institution) were as helpful as they could be in their efforts to help her find a job there. They gave her a test for secretarial skills. Nope. Then for bookkeeping. Uh, not an option.

Finally, they found something. Since Sally was a missionary, wouldn't she be perfect to supervise the social protesters who hero-worshipped the radical priest Daniel Berrigan? My favorite memory of this is when she accompanied these crusaders on a protest against nuclear proliferation at a General Electric weapons plant!

Sally earned her master's degree in family counseling. When she was hired at a nearby clinic, she quickly ascertained that the staff psychologists considered "born again" Christians to be nutcases. Once, during a group conversation that deprecated evangelicals, one of the staff paused as if in realization and said, "… but Sally is one of those, and she's quite alright."

Dr. Francis Steele had served for many years as the North American director of NAM, then resigned his leadership position but humbly continued to serve on its staff. We had first met when I was in a hospital bed with mononucleosis at Wheaton College. At that time, Sally and I had decided not to join NAM, instead going with the radicals who were birthing OM. In a history of NAM, Steele wrote:

> In 1969, we called Rev. William Bell back from his
> field position in France as Director of Radio School
> of the Bible to give administrative leadership to the
> North American office in Upper Darby, Pennsylvania.
> There had been economic pressures and other problems
> hindering our expected growth. Nevertheless, the decline
> in income and applications continued in spite of all
> efforts to turn the situation around. Goals prayerfully
> set by the Council year by year were not met. So the
> Council was forced to take steps cutting back expenses
> at the home end. A large office building was sold and

we moved into smaller rented quarters. Several staff personnel were let go... A grievous disappointment to us since we were aware of the need for more personnel on the field...

Bill Bell was needed back in France to head up the Missionary Training Centre... in 1976. Now, what about leadership for the North American office? Again, God in His faithfulness provided the man especially qualified... Rev. Gregory M. Livingston.

Greg had known of NAM seventeen years before, but had decided that Operation Mobilisation had more to offer. For twelve years he served as a leader of OM teams in India, Lebanon and Europe, as well as heading up work in Canada. But he never lost his dream of personal involvement in a church-planting mission to Muslims... Greg met Bill Bell at the 1976 Urbana Convention... Eight months later Greg was installed as Director for North America at the NAM and things began to hum; if not roar.

Recruitment has risen in recent years from about two a year to over twenty and is still growing. The Summer Teams are full each year... So we praise God and keep on trusting. (Steele, pp. 90–91.)

This was the kind of job that God created me to do. I'm a turnaround specialist; my favorite challenge is to take something that is stalled or moving backwards and to get it moving. How would we re-create this ninety-six-year-old British mission into the agency of choice for Americans and Canadians?

NAM had experienced tough years of retreat. The staff members who were left were mostly a lovely lot of retired saints with great hearts, but not a great deal of energy. Sam Schlorff and Hobe Dearborn were the only ones with field experience, but their expertise was in teaching and radio ministry, not recruiting.

The board of directors was comprised of several businessmen, a well-known pastor (who was on the board of several mission agencies and sometimes couldn't remember which one he was attending), and a gracious woman who taught at a Bible college. At our first board meeting, I was instructed that I should be in the office from 9:00 to 5:00 Monday through Friday, and speak in churches on Sunday. Expenditures over $25 would need the signature of two board members.

I interrupted the chairman. "I'm sorry, sir, but we may have a misunderstanding. I want you to look at me as you would a football coach. If I win games, be happy. If I lose games, fire me. But I'll decide when and where I'll be at any given time."

The room was deathly silent. The chairman, who saw himself as the real leader of the mission, looked as though he might have a heart attack. I don't remember exactly what happened next or how the meeting ended. But I recall that I got a lift home from Dr. Steele. Before I got out of the car, he looked into my face and commanded me: "Don't back down. It's about time NAM had some real leadership here."

It didn't seem appropriate to me that missionaries in North Africa were forced to live by decisions made by board members who spent a few hours on a committee every three months.

Only weeks into my new job, I received a letter from International Director Abe Wiebe that stunned me. It said, "Maybe we neglected to inform you: NAM is in merger negotiations with Sudan Interior Mission."

"What?" I thought. "They had us leave the pastorate and move from Aspen to Philadelphia without telling us they were likely to close shop to be absorbed by SIM, who have their headquarters in New Jersey?"

It took me a little time to wrestle that out with my heavenly Father. Eventually, I said to him again, "Not my will, but yours. It's okay, sovereign God, if I'm out of a job before I've even gotten started." Besides, SIM's gracious leadership assured me with a grin that they would find *something* for me to do.

Once I got over the shock, I went to work to make the merger succeed. We negotiated for a year until, with the merger almost in place, NAM's international council decided the plan needed a 67 percent approval vote by the field missionaries. We fell just short of it – possibly because the Brits didn't want to be ruled from New Jersey.

In submission to that decision, I saluted the Lord of the harvest again and went back to work, seeking mission entrepreneurs. Over the next five years, the Lord apparently granted me his anointing to find those he had been preparing to pioneer among Arab Muslims in North Africa. My checklist for remodeling a century-old British mission included:

- Revamp the board as quickly as possible.

- Get new backers who are younger than fifty years old.

- Insist that any inquiries get a response within seventy-two hours.

- Buy back the building that was sold before I arrived.

- Recruit an assistant director.

- Increase the salaries to keep staff.

- Recruit a Canadian director to establish a separate Canadian office.

- Replace the candidate committee of laymen with people who had ministered overseas.

- Expand from North Africa to incorporate the entire Arab world.

Until my mother married Bob Livingston when I was nine, my name was Gregory Martindale Foss. When they married, someone must have decided Livingston should replace Foss, and it wasn't until I received my draft board registration card at eighteen that I realized Bob Livingston never formally adopted me. My legal name was still Foss, though I had continued to use Livingston's name.

Normally, when one's name is misspelled, it is slightly irritating. In my case, I felt a bit proud when church bulletins announced that Greg Livingstone (with an "e") was going to speak on behalf of NAM. I suppose that churches subconsciously associated me with Africa's pioneer missionary, David Livingstone. Understandably, I was forever being asked whether I was related to that great Scotsman. I would smile and shake my head. This happened even more frequently after I later earned a doctorate: "Dr. Livingstone, I presume?"

One evening, when the question came for the thousandth time, I paused thoughtfully, as one making a fresh decision. "Yes."

"Really?"

"Yes. By adoption." The inquirer's puzzled look demanded explanation.

"I adopted David Livingstone as my great-grandfather."

For me, it was an announcement that reflected a delightful realization. Our heavenly Father had adopted both of us – me and David Livingstone. We were related – for eternity! Didn't the Lord promise he would give us a "new name"? Didn't the apostle Peter write that all of us in the family of the Lord Jesus are "living stones"? I had envied my Arab friends because all of them knew the meaning of their names. Livingstone *meant* something.

Forrest Foss, my biological dad, had abandoned me. He didn't even admit that I existed! Bob Livingston didn't adopt me and also abandoned me. Carl Fagerstrom, the Norwegian bartender who left Aspen with my mother, never gave it a moment's concern that they were leaving a fourteen-year-old alone – without a relative or a home. I had no reason to be loyal to any of those three unworthy men.

But in that moment, at the age of forty, my heavenly Father bound me with his son and servant David Livingstone.

That unstoppable Scot had the same calling as I. His entire life was also poured out to see communities of Jesus' disciples established where the church didn't yet exist. Livingstone was a name I could be proud of! Eventually, our whole family added the "e" to become Livingstones. In typical fashion, I was fairly sloppy about making it official. Many years later, the computer age forced me to visit a lawyer to make our name change legal, but in a very real sense during that moment of epiphany, I adopted David Livingstone as my ancestral father.

CHAPTER 21

Sea Change

I believe history will record the 1978 North American Conference on Muslim Evangelism as the greatest springboard of mission to the peoples of Islam in history. Don McCurry, a veteran missionary to Pakistan, led the conference, which was held at the Navigators' center, Glen Eyrie, in Colorado Springs.

Only the year before in the journal *Missiology*, Vivienne Stacey, a lifetime missionary to Muslims on the Indian subcontinent, had published a summary of the history of Christians' failure to reach out to the Muslim world. At that time, one-fifth of the world's population were Muslims, yet never in history, anywhere in the world, had there been a breakthrough of Muslims coming to Christ in significant numbers – except among practitioners of folk Islam in Java, Indonesia in the 1960s.

The 1978 Colorado conference may have been the first time nearly every agency and church with significant numbers of missionaries among Muslims had been gathered. I gave a lightly informed paper on the status of the church in North Africa, but the conference ignited a fresh fire in me that has never gone out. In the words of other mission leaders over the centuries: "It *can* be done. It *must* be done. It *will* be done." I found confidence in God's plan: We will see God birth his church among all peoples – including Muslims. *No exceptions!*

The Glen Eyrie conference produced two immediate results. The first was a textbook, *The Gospel and Islam* (McCurry, 1979), that ignited many to look for a better way to make disciples among Muslims. The second was the creation of the Zwemer Institute of Muslim Studies at the US Center for World Mission in Pasadena, California. The members of the consultation rallied behind McCurry to create this training center, which eventually prepared hundreds of enterprising young missionaries to work among Muslims.

McCurry, sensing my fresh ambition to see Christ Jesus be honored as Savior and Lord among the world's Muslims, invited me to serve on the board of the newly established institute. At the time, it was almost the only place where evangelicals were teaching a new crop of missionaries the skills of evangelism, discipleship, and church planting among Muslims. The Zwemer Institute also catalyzed the development of Islamic study courses at Fuller Theological Seminary in California, Columbia International University in South Carolina, Concordia Theological Seminary in Indiana, and probably a dozen other seminaries.

Meanwhile, it was a joy and privilege to ride on the coat-tails of the venerable Dr. Francis Steele. Though thirty-five years my senior, we became a very enjoyable tag team. It was Fran who bolstered me as I cajoled a board of businessmen and pastors (who said they could offer only a few hours a year to the mission) to give up their small ambitions.

Danny and Cynthia Strull joined our staff. The nice Jewish boy who turned to Jesus at the First Baptist Church in Aspen served with a mission to *Arabs* as his first ministry! Eventually, after studying at Columbia International University, they joined the staff of Jews for Jesus. Today, Danny shepherds Messianic Jews in the Olive Tree Congregation in North Chicago. It's quite gratifying to think Sally and I have a ministry among Jewish people through them!

As I hit the recruiting trail for NAM, I remembered my prayer when I left Lebanon. I had covenanted with God, asking him to allow me to team up with him to thrust out workers into his harvest fields. North Africa Mission was losing an average of ten workers a year and gaining only an average of one-and-a-half. This did not bode well for the mission's future.

Yet the candidate committee complained about my methods. "Why," they asked me, "are you recruiting from Harvard, Vassar, Berkeley, Penn State, and other ungodly institutions? Whatever happened to Moody, Columbia Bible College, and Philadelphia College of the Bible?" I realized that, typically, seminary students have one goal after graduation: teaching the Bible to believers. Their training does not prepare them to plant churches – much less to live in Muslim cities that have no gathering of believers at all. I needed to find people who would be pioneer ground-breakers in places where there hadn't been a church in a thousand years!

In those days, NAM sent missionaries to only four countries: Morocco, Algeria, Tunisia, and France. But a year later, a cocky Ivy League student named Joseph challenged me, "What is North Africa Mission going to do about [a specific country in sub-Saharan Africa]?" To be honest, I was ignorant about sub-Saharan Africa – even its Muslim countries.

I found myself in a quandary. I didn't want to admit that NAM had no plans for that country, which mission agencies considered to be "closed." But I didn't want to make Joseph wait for the International Council to decide that we should include a new country in our goals. So I proposed to notify everyone on our mailing list that on a certain Saturday, everyone burdened for that country should come to our offices to pray and strategize.

Fourteen people showed up, and a team was born. I appointed Joseph as the team leader – though he had done no paperwork and we had no references. My philosophy of recruiting has always been: Get the fish in the boat, then decide whether or not it's good eating.

Before Joseph graduated from college, he had gathered a team of friends to find a way into his "closed" country. Their initiative was a catalyst for another team, led by two outstanding veteran NAM couples, to later take up residence in that country also. Together, they became the first missionaries in that desert land after a thousand years of neglect. Today, there are two fellowships of courageous (though persecuted) believers from the ruling tribe in that country, and too many house churches to count among another Muslim tribe!

International Director Abe Wiebe wrote in his autobiography about what happened after my appointment to lead the Philadelphia office:

It turned out to be a major step forward for the Mission.
But Greg's efforts would soon spill over on every side.
I did not know then what a gifted and energetic fellow
leader we had been given.

Greg Livingstone had a combination of great faith,
love for the Lord and unbridled enthusiasm. People
who met him were immediately drawn to him. He made
each feel he had become a special friend. More than one
person has remarked how Greg had deeply impacted his
life. Wherever he entered, Greg hit the ground running.
Before long he was lining up new recruits for North
Africa. I remember reading through some candidate
papers of those days; these prospective newcomers were
outstanding. Greg, through God's Spirit, made each of
them feel that winning Muslims for Christ was easily the
most important use of their abilities. Soon the language
training center was overflowing with these new arrivals…

Having him in a board meeting was like trying
to contain a tiger. He had more ideas than all of us
combined. Of course not all of his ideas were feasible
but many of them were. Greg was such a natural leader
that people tended to get out of the way and let him go.
(Wiebe, p. 107.)

In January 1980, InterVarsity Christian Fellowship, Campus Crusade for Christ, and the Navigators jointly sponsored a mission conference at Pennsylvania State University. They invited me to be the other speaker with some old guy – Ralph Winter of the US Center for World Mission.

Dr. Winter's insights fascinated me. He stressed all the "hidden peoples" of the world – people who still didn't have a church planting movement among them. My hidden secret, at that time, was that I was bored with the never-changing mission discussions I heard every day. It seemed there had not been a fresh thought in Philadelphia since Benjamin Franklin left.

Ralph challenged me to start a new branch of NAM. "How does one put new wine in old wineskins successfully?" he asked. "By creating a plastic inner lining," he answered himself.

Tucking that seed thought away, I realized my calling to Libya was stirring again. Until that day, I had allowed myself to be convinced by the mission establishment that any country not issuing missionary visas was "closed," as in, "Don't even *think* about it!" The other conventional wisdom was, "Go where the people are responsive." That notion turned most candidates away from considering Muslim areas.

With those thoughts bubbling inside, I poured out my heart to the Christian students gathered at Penn State, saying, "Let's go where they're not responsive, because they haven't had any chance to respond! And as for closed countries, I can't find the verse that says, 'Go make disciples of all nations if you can get a missionary visa.' Well actually, I do know where that verse is. It's right next to the verse that says, 'Go make disciples of all nations if it's safe!'"

Still bothered that all the missionaries had been driven out of Libya, I challenged the audience, "Would no one here dare to find a way to get in, stay in, and make disciples in

Libya? In the whole country, there is not even one church for its citizens."

Four young men who were only months from graduation answered my challenge. Al Stahl, Bob Sjogren, Greg Fritz, and Harry Gray came forward to offer themselves to go to Libya as English teachers. None of them had majored in English. None of them had any experience teaching English as a foreign language. In spite of all the obstacles, we booked a strategic planning meeting over breakfast the next morning.

We decided that they would fly to London, where Libya was recruiting English teachers. Once they arrived in London, however, they were informed that the jobs on offer were not for Americans. Undeterred, they flew to Malta, where hundreds of Libyans were studying English. The Libyan Embassy wouldn't let them through the gate. So they made the acquaintance of various Libyan students in Malta, who helped them cobble together a list of the country's tertiary educational institutions. They sent off letters seeking jobs. After six weeks of praying, they received a telegram from the Technical University in Tobruk, inviting all four of them to teach at the university. They would *be* the English department.

They returned to Malta's Libyan Embassy – this time with their letter of invitation and the name of a certain embassy official. They were ushered into a room where he asked them:

"Where are you from?"

"America."

"Where did you study?"

"Penn State University."

"Really? My son is a student there!"

"What's his name?"

"Ahmad Shafir."

"Oh yeah, we met him. We had lunch with him at our university. He's our friend." After forty-five minutes over coffee, they had their visas and were on their way.

When they reached the university in Tobruk, the director apologized that the only accommodation available was in the men's dormitory with 190 students. Did those Americans have the opportunity to witness about the Lord Jesus? They hardly had privacy! Students were in their room asking questions all the time. There were no end of opportunities to explain what the Bible taught about Isa al-Masih. During vacation periods, students invited them to their homes, where the Penn Staters showed the *Jesus* film in Arabic – in Libya, one of the most "closed" countries in the world!

By 1982, we had recruited ninety-five new missionaries. They were quality people who would have been the envy of any mission agency. But then, the unthinkable happened.

"Hold back on the recruiting," the international director ordered. NAM's missionary training base in France was full; they couldn't receive any more new missionaries. I tried to explain to Abe Wiebe that I could not stop calling out for more pioneer church planters. The Lord was raising up a new generation of pioneers to the Arab world and beyond.

"Maybe so," he responded. "But we're still full."

CHAPTER 22

A Faster Gun

Our departure from the NAM family began when Bob Sjogren returned from Libya. Zooming into my office in Upper Darby, Pennsylvania, he gushed out his vision to see 300,000 new missionaries recruited for the unreached peoples around the world.

No cowboy wants to meet a faster gun. I shut the door so no one would overhear this mind-boggling conversation. This kid was deadly serious about his vision. Ridiculous! Did he have any idea what it had taken to recruit ninety-five men and women in five years?

I also realized that Bob could not imagine how such a vision would be heard by NAM's board. I explained that I had to present some goals to the board meeting that very week. Then I suggested, "It might be more prudent if we are a bit more conservative. How would you feel if I use the number three thousand instead of three *hundred* thousand?"

"*Three thousand?*" The two words fell with disdain from Bob's lips as if I had suggested we recruit only *three* new missionaries. Obviously disappointed, he must have seen me as a traitor without faith.

When I announced our new goals to the board later that week, I avoided meeting anyone's eyes. With a wince, I asked meekly, "How would you feel if we made a goal of recruiting seven hundred new missionaries for the Arab countries?"

"*Seven hundred?!*" The room exploded with incredulity. It probably wouldn't have been worse if I'd proposed to support the Radio School of the Bible by selling heroin.

I sensed I had just signed my release papers. From that moment, they no longer perceived me as a visionary. In their eyes, I had become a man unable to live in reality. The chairman quickly changed the subject. I was obviously out of step with their mission's careful, well-laid plans. We were working from different presuppositions. From that day, I was never again able to get on the same page with the decision makers. I walked away from that board meeting thinking that I had let Bob Sjogren ruin my career.

With nowhere else to go, I turned over the US director's job to Revd. Bill Saal, the pastor I'd recruited to be my associate director. Dave Lundy, my colleague in Toronto, would carry on as the Canadian director.

Bob Sjogren and I linked hearts and vision. We managed to get a nod from the leaders to move out to California with the idea to start an auxiliary branch of NAM. We would call it North Africa Mission Associates. I thought that if I could develop some new teams for Arab countries east of Tunisia, surely NAM would be surprised, but thrilled.

At Ralph Winter's invitation, we moved our family to Pasadena, California. NAM Associates was birthed in September 1982 at the US Center for World Mission. The idea behind NAM Associates was to raise up new teams that would try experimental ways of approaching ministry with Muslims, such as going directly into North Africa and learning Arabic first, rather than going to France to learn French.

More than a few other mission leaders considered my ideas to be reckless. Part of our divergence in thinking was regarding how aggressive we ought to be in seeing the gospel penetrate the Arab world. I was focused on all the New Testament decrees that dealt with suffering.

When the Lord Jesus says, "Follow me," what does he mean? He was stripped, mocked, humiliated, slapped around, spit on. He had his beard plucked out and thorns jammed in his face. He was paraded around like the fisherman's big catch!

The Lord Jesus was not forced to go to Jerusalem. His disciples begged him not to go. It seemed stupid – suicidal, even. It was predictably going to be a failure. Our Lord's answer was: "Get behind me, Satan." Man's ways aren't God's ways.

Likewise, Paul's friends pleaded with him not to go to Jerusalem (Acts 21:12). "What are you doing?" they must have asked him.

But remembering Jesus' words in Luke 9:24 ("whoever wants to save their life will lose it"), Paul responded, "I consider my life worth nothing to me; my only aim is to finish the race and complete the task the Lord Jesus has given me –

the task of testifying to the good news of God's grace" (Acts 20:24).

What if we ran out of money? Well, poverty is hardly abnormal in this world, or indeed in the work of God. (In 2 Corinthians 1:8, Paul talks about being "under great pressure" in a pioneering mission situation.)

When I read about young business entrepreneurs, it sets off sparks in my heart. Non-Christians will take huge risks and live on beans for the sake of their vision. Could I do less?

During our first nine months in Pasadena, we either fell off the NAM leaders' radar or no one really thought much would happen in this new venture, NAM Associates. But when they realized that we had already recruited forty new adults to go to Egypt, Bahrain, Morocco, and Mauritania, it was too late to close the barn door. The horses were out and running.

Awakened to the situation, Abe Wiebe upgraded the "problem" of NAM Associates to the issue most urgently in need of his attention. He and I traded our thoughts via cassette tapes, telephone calls, and letters. But eventually, he decided NAM Associates didn't fit within NAM.

Somewhat stunned, I began to ask myself questions: "What do we do with our four new teams? Tell them to find another mission agency? What am I supposed to do? Should I become a generic 'gun for hire,' recruiting for any agencies who want to send new teams into Arab countries?" Abe Wiebe saw no alternative but for me to set up a separate sister mission. But was that what God had in mind?

Dave Lundy wrote an eight-page protest to NAM, saying, "What progressive organization throws out one of its most productive executives?"

When asked for his advice, the missionary statesman David Howard said, "Normally I would not encourage creating a new mission, but we should not miss this day for Islam."

The international evangelist Luis Bush agreed. "We cannot see you pulling back, Greg. If there's no other mission to Muslims for you to join… go for it."

Ed Morgan, the chairman of NAM's US council, declared, "God will be sovereign. Greg must obey God."

Bill Saal said, "The US council feels… ambivalent: they want Greg – their big gun – in the franchise, but they also want peace and unity which Greg does not bring."

In April 1983, I talked by phone with my mentor and predecessor, Fran Steele. He said, "When we were bogged down, God sent the right man to get us going. Now we say 'Thank you,' and let him move on and do it again with a sister mission with whom we can work closely." Fran's non-ambivalence was reassuring.

Was this like the day when I realized there was no longer a place for me in OM? There were no bad guys; it was simply a juncture in mission history. I thought of the rhetorical question from the prophet Amos: "Can two walk together, except they be agreed?" (Amos 3:3 KJV). I definitely had different ideas from the leaders of NAM. I didn't believe an apostolic band should make decisions by majority rule. And I was even more convinced that very part-time players (like board members) should not rule those pioneering a work on the field.

I wrestled with a hundred questions:

- Am I a bad guy, a rebel for no reason, or the Lord's servant with a calling to see a greater breakthrough of Christ's kingdom in the Muslim world?

- The wicked one whispers: "You're a puffed-up megalomaniac, a stubborn idealist." But if I'm supposed to be normal, why do I have such an abnormal vision?

- Am I merely filling the vacuum of a low self-image? Surely not. "Get thee behind me, Satan, father of lies."

- How can I crisscross the West challenging people to go for it and believe in God for new things, to be unstoppables – if I'm going to throttle down to the lowest common denominator?

- Does anyone respect the high-powered speaker who, two minutes after the service, talks like a humanist with no intention of taking any action about what he has just challenged others to do? How could I live with myself – much less keep speaking to others – while living in such a dichotomy?

Not only did I have to challenge my own motives and inner ambitions, but I also fought with myself about the wider strategic benefit of what I was contemplating:

- Do I need to birth a new mission agency? Are there not many good ones already?

- What are my fears? – That I'll be controlled by managers who cannot dream? That I will recruit people who don't fit with the next agency we might join? That if we birth a new mission, my friends will neither endorse it nor rally behind us?

I flew to France to work out a solution with Abe Wiebe and other NAM leaders face to face. Tim Lewis, one of the newly recruited leaders for North Africa, drove up from Morocco to save the union of NAM and NAM Associates. But after reviewing the situation, he concurred with the NAM leadership: The NAM Associates teams didn't fit well within NAM.

Bill Bell, the man who had recruited me for the NAM job, now felt that we would use too much energy trying to keep the different ministry philosophies reconciled. He thought I should peacefully leave NAM.

Confident that reintegration would not work, the decision was made that NAM Associates should dissociate from NAM and become a separate sister mission. I felt as though I had been let loose like a recalcitrant teenager. I needed a charter more compelling than that if I were going to start something new. I needed an honest mandate to birth a mission to the Muslim world. In May 1983, NAM provided it, through this resolution from their ruling council:

> *The International Council of NAM believes that this development will permit greater effectiveness and less confusion as each agency concentrates on its*

own particular contribution to the common goal of establishing churches in the Arab Muslim world. We commend Greg and all his team members to the grace and blessing of our Lord.

In his autobiography, Wiebe describes his organization's decision about me:

It soon became evident that Greg's vision for Muslims far outstripped our own plans and programs. Limiting him to North America was too small a working space. Greg was made to touch the world. I have never worked with anyone like him. From 1982 onward we struggled with how to retain Greg in our organization. The two of us got on well together, but Greg had a capacity that not only surpassed mine, it was wider by far. He both challenged me and overwhelmed me. No surprise, therefore, that by the spring of 1983 a modus vivendi had to be found. We were a hundred-year-old battleship being constantly circled by a clipper with sails all out. It came down to a resolution by the Missions Council stating that we bless Greg and release him to follow his dreams. That was about the hardest thing I have ever done. Imagine telling your regular 20-game winner to find another club or start his own. That is exactly what happened. (Wiebe, p. 107)

Thankfully, I could ride to Marseille Provence Airport and head back to California, still in godly fellowship with my

NAM colleagues, grateful that by God's gifting and grace, I had totally rebuilt an almost dying mission. And I left it not only without alienation, but with mutual blessing.

Yet whether I should start a new organization was still a separate question. When is it the time to start a new mission agency? There must be an appropriate time, if we approve of Hudson Taylor, William Carey, Cameron Townsend, and the founders of Africa Inland Mission, Sudan Interior Mission, OM, YWAM, and others. New missions are born when God raises up a servant with a specific new vision.

When we started Operation Mobilisation with George Verwer, we were led to pray together for areas without significant witness: Spain, Russia, Turkey, the Arab world, and India. Why were we all not led, as our friend Phil Parshall was, to join conventional agencies instead of birthing OM?

In a personal letter to me, John Kyle of InterVarsity advised me:

> I disagree with those who say we should not start new missions. I think it is time for a new organization to the Muslim world. Count on me for endorsements. I might even be able to raise some money. You'll be surprised how many will stand with you. I have never believed that existing missions could do it in the Muslim world. However, I think a new mission must go beyond the Arab world to the entire Muslim world.

During the days of indecision, Paul McKaughan of the Presbyterian Mission to the World invited me to join them, saying, "We want to test soils in the whole Muslim world." I knew that if I were truly kingdom-minded, I needed to be willing to join them, or the Southern Baptists, or even the Assemblies of God. I told the Father I was willing to serve anyone who was determined to accelerate a breakthrough across the Muslim world, even if they weren't entirely my theological preference.

On 3 May 1983, my forty-third birthday, I wrote in my journal:

> *I'm full of gratitude that I am appointed by the King,*
> *endowed and gifted to accomplish his purposes.*
> *However, I fully realize and mourn that I'm not an easy*
> *person to work with. I have been pushing for six years*
> *in my own heart for the NAM mission and evidently, I*
> *pushed too far. I have said too much. I have damaged*
> *my relationship with [the leadership]. I'm feeling all*
> *the trauma of a divorce but it seems clear that both*
> *[parties] will be able to minister more effectively without*
> *the threat of a mutual censor.*

Despite the gracious, godly attitudes and actions that my NAM colleagues had shown me, this was personally a very difficult transition for me. I fought fresh feelings of being abandoned and unwanted. Again.

I never had any intention of leaving OM in 1974 or NAM in 1983. What was God engineering each time? Neither organization could find a place for me – both because they were at a juncture where they felt a need not for expansion, but for consolidation. I made a mental note not to allow any of the "starter types" to become redundant in any mission I might start.

My journals reveal a significant level of inner questioning regarding my possible motives for everything I did or failed to do. Was I simply doing this out of some misguided ambition? Why wasn't I "more normal"? Did I waste too much time in introspection?

During this time of searching, I set aside three weeks for prayer. On a walk with my Savior along a beach in Ventura, California, I finally sensed the Lord say, "Okay, it's time." At that moment on 28 May 1983, Frontiers was born. With a smile, the Lord promoted Livingstone, at forty-three, to captain his own ship. What was the ship to be? We didn't really know and, to be honest, the forty former NAM Associates that I'd recruited weren't terribly concerned about putting everything down on paper. Frontiers' official establishment was still ahead, but from that day, I accepted that the Lord was calling me to birth something new.

Doug and Patti Norrison left the United States as members of NAM Associates. By the time they arrived in France, en route to Tunis, NAM Associates had been dissolved. They were suddenly without a sending agency. Doug later wrote me about this time, illustrating well the chaos of life at the genesis of a new movement:

> *We left the US with NAM, and suddenly we were*
> *only with Greg – and he was without a mission! On*

*a walk in France, he told me that we were welcome
to stay with NAM (but he wasn't sure they wanted
us). Or he would of course welcome us with him in
whatever NAM Associates would become. It was
never a question for us – we were drawn to Greg
and his vision, and not concerned about structure,
organization, or security.*

*So we landed on 31 May 1983 in Tunisia, with
a newly forming mission led by Greg. And I was
appointed the "team leader" for Tunisia. Right! What's
a team leader? And what's a team?! We knew nothing in
those days!*

To my surprise, George Verwer phoned from England to say
he was extremely upset that we were birthing a new mission
agency. For forty-five minutes, he warned me of the inevitable
discouragements I could expect:

- "Frontiers will have bodies strewn all over the Muslim
  world."

- "You actually know very little about the Middle East."

- "You have made hurtful remarks about other mission
  leaders."

- "You work too fast."

- "Your workers will rebel and scatter; it's vicious warfare
  out there."

- "You've been sick in the past; you'll really get sick now."

- "This makes a PR problem for OM."

- "Where's the money going to come from?"

But he ended with this: "Still, you know we will stand with you." Verwer did continue to stand by us, not only during the transition stage, but even to this day.

More than anyone else in my life, he had always demonstrated how much he believed in me. Giving me assignments that were way over my head, he had simply expected that, by God's grace, I would manage to carry out the plan. It was an operating principle I would take with me into Frontiers, as I released team leaders to carry out the impossible.

Though he had sounded negative and upset in that phone call, I could see right through it. Verwer was telling me, "I love you, and I don't want to see you suffer."

CHAPTER 23

New Wineskins

Talk about mixed emotions! I was free, but so is a sailor who falls overboard and ends up on a desert island! We had our own ship, but it was a little sailboat compared to the freighter we'd been sailing on. I had the freedom to try it my own way, thereby merging the conflicting emotions of exhilaration and panic.

The first dilemma was how to tell the ninety-five people I'd invited to join NAM that I had, in effect, just gotten a divorce from their mother. Predictably, not a few felt deserted. "Hey! You got us into this, and now you're abandoning us?"

Sally and I had grown close to most of those we'd recruited, and I was sorely tempted to invite them to defect to the new mission. But I felt the Lord commanding me, "Don't do it." To be honest, I was a little surprised that only one couple inquired about transferring to… but then I realized, "… transfer to *what*?" Frontiers was a vision – not yet a reality for anyone to evaluate.

Tim Lewis, who had come from Morocco to France determined *not* to allow the split to occur, stood with me to birth Frontiers, then led his large team in Morocco to join the newly forming organization. The Norrisons, who left US soil as part of NAM Associates and arrived in France without a mission, went on to land in Tunis affiliated with Frontiers. I invited Mazhar and Christine Mallouhi to join us, inviting Caravans of the Middle East to be absorbed into Frontiers. We quickly formed other new teams to go to Muslims in Bahrain, Egypt, and Mali.

Our ragtag gang back in Pasadena huddled. Wonderfully, there was nothing but relief as the NAM Associates team raised their glasses to welcome the new start. We probably looked like a high school football team running onto the field, about to play against the National Football League. Would we simply be another mom and pop outfit? Or would we even survive at all, since we had almost no donors or start-up money?

We took stock of our not-so-tangible assets. We had an office in Pasadena, California. Our landlord, the US Center for World Mission (affectionately known as "the Center"), was established on a former Nazarene college campus, so our humble headquarters consisted of a converted college dorm suite of three rooms and a walk-in shower. It was furnished in "early Salvation Army" decor. Our filing cabinets, made from orange crates, reminded me of my 1962 OM office.

Dr. Ralph Winter had dreamt of enabling world mission synergy at the Center. On the same campus, he established William Carey International University as a place to train people for cross-cultural service. He had also recruited several dozen mission study groups, mobilization and training institutes, and mission agencies to set up shop. This brought a steady stream of visitors to that mission mecca. It certainly all worked in our favor. At the Center, we had advocates, encouragement, and at least some credibility by association. It also provided campus housing, guest rooms, meeting rooms, and the cutting-edge insights of mission thinking. In addition, it provided us with visibility.

Recruiting new candidates at the Center was like fishing in a stocked pond. Where else would we have such a quantity of "drop-in trade"? Our presence there meant we met Great Commission-minded leaders. Zwemer Institute of Muslim Studies provided hands-on equippers as well as academic training for workers among Muslims. Other new entities at the Center, led by pioneers like Greg Fritz and Steve Hawthorne, acted as sister organizations for us. Since I served on the boards of the Zwemer Institute of Muslim Studies, the William Carey International University, and the Center, we were all scratching each other's backs.

But we weren't yet legally established as a mission agency. NAM had graciously agreed to allow our funds to stay on their books for six months to give us time to apply for non-profit status with the government, so that we could offer tax-deductible receipts to donors.

Soon after my retreat on the beach in Ventura, when I had sensed God's go-ahead, I bumped into Steve Holloway, a member of a newly forming team headed to the Maldive Islands. He approached me with an offer. They had established the Maldive Islands Outreach (with the necessary non-profit status), but they had lost their US-based director. So their team was headed for the islands without an office to handle their US affairs. He wondered whether Frontiers would be interested in taking over the Maldive Islands Outreach. We agreed, but the State of California insisted that our legal name should incorporate the earlier organization. So we officially became MIO Frontiers.

I had assumed our agency would only work in the Arab world. After all, that was *my* calling. But by including the Maldives, an archipelago south-west of India, we were stretching well beyond the Arab world.

A short time later, John Jewell came into our offices, declaring his vision for China. "Ah, the China office is down the street," I told him, gesturing across the campus. "We are a mission to Muslims."

"I know," John countered. "We're going to the Muslims in China."

"There are Muslims in China?" I asked incredulously.

While I was still trying to work out the implications of having a mission beyond the Arab countries, I met Rick Love, a surf-boarding, Jesus-movement hippy who was not long off California's "Jesus People" beaches. "I want to take a team to the Sundanese," he told me.

"Great!" I responded. "I have a deep burden for Sudan."

"Not *Sudan!*" Rick protested, with wrinkled brow. "Haven't you heard of the 30 million *Sundanese* – the most unreached people in the world?!" I got an earful about the Sundanese Muslims of West Java, Indonesia that day.

Then came Bruce Graham and Rich Slimbach, asking, "What is Frontiers going to do about the Muslims in India – the third largest Muslim population in the world?" Well,

I'd been there, I knew that. Was God calling us back to do something significant among the Muslims where we'd started in OM twenty years earlier?

It seemed that every week we were adding a new field to the agency before we had even figured out who should be making such decisions!

One day, while washing the dishes and listening to the radio, I heard a US Army ad: "Join the Army and bring three friends." The Army was enticing recruits by guaranteeing that up to four friends could live in the same barracks, march in the same company, go to the same classes, and serve together. What did the Army understand about American youth culture that I didn't? I also noticed that our youngest son Paul always went on group dates – several boys and girls would hang out together. Sometime after that, I seized on the notion that I could challenge a minimally experienced visionary to be a team leader, and to recruit his own friends to be his team members.

Two primary fears seemed to hinder men from joining mission agencies:

- What if I go to a foreign country as a missionary and fail? I'll be totally embarrassed! And how will I get a job again if I've left my career path?

- Who will the mission leaders force me to work with or under? What if they are old-fashioned, legalistic, or just plain uninspiring?

We could deal with the second fear. Instead of coaxing young people to adopt *our* way of doing ministry, we decided to be a Burger King-style mission: "Have it *your* way." We would go wherever the applicants felt God was leading them. We would facilitate the visions of a new generation of pioneer missionaries to the Muslim world. As long as they wanted to plant churches among unreached Muslims, we would encourage them to discover ways to do it more effectively than ever before.

But how could we be a credible agency without an adequate home staff? Bob Sjogren, who had created the "problem" of our outrageous aspirations, now provided some answers by recruiting a number of young women to serve as our home staff. Donna, Beth, Diane, Betsy, Cathi, Aleta, and Debra, plus Ted and Denise, and Bob's own brother Jack became a close team as we shared our passion for the impossible. I feel so grateful to these "founders."

I have no idea how they managed to survive financially. We offered no salaries and no payment to cover the cost of dorm rooms. Bob slept in the shower room of our offices.

In fact, we were all rather stretched financially. Sally and I had used the $10,000 profit from the sale of our house near Philadelphia to launch Frontiers. We were renting a one-and-a-half-bedroom house. The boys (now seventeen, sixteen, and twelve) took the bedrooms; Sally and I slept on the screened porch. It was not at all adequate – and it certainly fell far short of my boast to Sally that we would find a house with which she'd be happy.

About this time, Paul got interested in baseball. I had told him about my failure to make it onto a team, but I reassured him that in his day, no one rejected kids from Little League teams. So he tried out. But to my horror, they didn't put him on one of the teams in the league. I was incensed! Like a mother bear, I dropped what I was doing and tore after those coaches. Fueled by the agony of my own childhood memory, I screamed at them that they couldn't let this happen to my son. The coaches raised their hands as if to say, "Don't shoot the innocent." Explaining that there were not enough coaches to put all the boys onto teams, they said that if I was willing to coach, then the rejected boys could play.

Although I was working night and day to keep Frontiers from going "belly up," I declared without hesitation that I would do it! They turned over to me all the boys who had been cut from the other teams. That was the beginning of our own personal version of "The Bad News Bears."

Knowing I couldn't be in town long enough to actually run the team every week, I recruited Evan and David – and even Evan's girlfriend Christine. The team became a family affair. Unfortunately, there was a reason those boys hadn't been chosen by the other teams. They didn't know how to play baseball!

I remember trying to get left-fielder Gomez to stand up. He retorted, "Nobody ever hits the ball out here." A catcher who joined the league late was assigned to our team. He actually had ability but was so disgusted with the other boys on our team that he quickly resigned. We had to forfeit two or three games when not enough players showed up. On one of those days, we were happy to recruit two kids who were visiting their grandmother. At the end of the game, they disappeared without returning their uniforms.

After zero wins and fifteen losses, it actually appeared that we were going to win our last game, against one of the better teams, because we had eventually developed a pitcher who could deliver the ball over the plate. However, with one inning to go, an opponent hit a hard line drive right to the head of our pitcher. Though I initially tried to get him to stand up and finish the game, it was obvious he needed to go to a clinic and get examined. Our back-up pitcher kept walking the other team's batters until they won the game. Oh well.

I fared better at recruiting for our Frontiers home office staff. I went after Gary Taylor, my fellow bench warmer from the Wheaton College football team. He was in the middle of a successful career in the Navy. Gary tells the story in his own inimitable manner:

> It started with Greg's call to a phone in the Pentagon Senior Officers' strategy room. My friend rang in on what was once a "red alert phone." I knew it was either him or my wife – or an admiral upset by a misplaced colon in a congressional letter I had ghostwritten for him.
>
> "Taylor," he said. (In O'Reilly Pennsylvania style, best friends are called by last names.) "I'm calling our fellowship into red alert."

Did he know this was an erstwhile red alert phone?! Spooky. Maybe significant.

"How soon can you be up here in Philadelphia? Have to talk to you." Few words – like most orders issued in wartime crises.

"Gimme four hours. I'll have to come in uniform." Four fast, wintery cold hours full of wondering had me at a table at a greasy cheesesteak diner. (I knew Greg, the OMer, was hardly a flagrant spender.)

Still unaware of the set up, I heard Greg moan about his frustrations. Maybe he should start fresh with a nontraditional agency to the Muslims, the most neglected (human) creatures on earth. I was poised to give advice.

But out of the tall grass leapt a question as surprising and riveting as a belly dancer in Philly. I was prepared for neither. The next 30 seconds changed my life.

"Taylor, you've been successful at many things."

I acknowledged his insight. How well he knew me, and I scrolled quickly through the list of successes, including the bright gold Navy captain's sleeve I was flashing at an early age.

"Now," he continued, "join me and become significant. Join me in seeing tens of thousands in the Muslim world follow the Lord Jesus."

The next pause was mine. We were in the middle of the Iranian hostage crisis!

"Saving Arabs?!" (It was one of the stupidest of the multitudes of words that have left my lips in haste and

error. Like many at the time, I thought every Muslim was an Arab.)

The story did not stop there. It began there. Within ten minutes, I was transformed from blanching at the unexpected challenge to flushing with excitement.

A fast sixteen months later, Carolyn and I were jammed into a donated van with two young children and a dog heading to Pasadena, California, and the US Center for World Mission, our home for the next nine years.

He had gotten me with "significance." In all of my quintessential American success, no one – never, no how – had challenged me to be significant. Success is an outward frame of reference for inward satisfaction. Not a bad thing. But alone, it is a lonely, empty, short-lived thing. Success will not be a marker on anyone's yardstick past heaven's gates. My bet is that the successes of a life of walking with God and serving those he assigns you to will fall somewhere on heaven's significance scale.

No mission ever had a more fascinating jet pilot for its first field director. What Gary didn't know about mission to Muslims, he made up for with his willingness to be a "donkey for Jesus," hauling goodies to field workers. The wilder the assignment, the more he reveled in it.

Of course, US law required that we have a board of directors. Quite incredibly, we found board members who agreed to our terms, which were – and still are – unlike what most board members anticipate. We made it clear that the board would exist for the missionaries – not to control them, but to serve them. The missionaries (not the board) would make their own decisions on the field, since they are closest to the action. It would be a staff-run mission. Of course, we also sought the board members' counsel, prayers, and expertise. Tim Lewis' father, Norm, our first chairman, exhorted his fellow board members to sacrifice as much as the field workers.

The board would exist only to keep the US law regarding finances, morals, and ethics – and to ensure our public that our theology was biblical. That would be it. It's still that way to this day. Only rare persons qualify as the board members of the twenty-two Frontiers sending bases, which now stretch from Buenos Aires to the Philippines.

Steve, one of my earliest colleagues in Frontiers, calls me a "holy skeptic." Sometimes I feel as though I have two fighting dogs within me: one is the gift of faith and the other is critical faculties which demand verification. (For example, I find myself suspicious of claims that lack quantifiable data, such as "tens of thousands got saved" in Iran or Bangladesh.)

In the early days of Frontiers, this holy skepticism was clearly on display during a talk to a group of candidates. When I opened up the floor for questions, one of them blurted, "I think you gave Frontiers the wrong name."

"Really? What should we have called ourselves?"

"Well, from the orientation you've just given, I would have thought it should be called, 'Cut-the-Crap Mission'!"

I complimented him for grasping our ethos, but we agreed that such a name wouldn't be all that marketable.

Nevertheless, as I recruited I sought people who would love God with all their *minds*, as well as with their hearts and strength. It was our desire to learn from history, building on what God had taught those who went before us.

I learned from Wycliffe Bible Translators founder Cam Townsend to keep the vision simple, to avoid disputes on doctrinal issues, to breed champions smarter than myself, to be generous toward other agencies, and never to stop opening the work among new people groups just in order to consolidate.

I also looked for wisdom from the secular environment, reading books by astute observers of Western society such as *Future Shock*, *The Third Wave* (both by Alvin Toffler), *In Search of Excellence* (by Tom Peters and Robert H. Waterman, Jr.), and *Megatrends* (by John Naisbitt). They woke me up to realize I was not the ugly duckling of missions (out of step with the way things should properly be done), but a swan who had, in God's providence, lived among ducks. I began to think of workers in Muslim countries as either "swans" or "ducks." In my vocabulary, "ducks" work only with the existing Christians. "Swans" focus exclusively on either discipling Muslim peoples or equipping those who are learning how to make disciples among Muslims.

A year after the birth of Frontiers, I gathered our eight charter team leaders in the Netherlands to take stock. We hashed out how we felt we should function as a company of church planting ground-breakers.

We determined to have the world's thinnest book of rules. We wanted to be able to adapt to changing opportunities and to facilitate experimentation, so we needed to be nimble. When I had walked the beach in Ventura where the Lord gave me the nod to start a new organization, I felt he had given me the conviction that Frontiers must have only six non-negotiables. The others agreed to these, which formed the backbone of our ethos:

1. We would work only among Muslims. The church had neglected Muslim peoples. Our teams would go where others didn't. By concentrating on that single religious bloc, we hoped we would gain some expertise over time.

2. We would focus on church planting. Everything we did needed to contribute toward leaving behind a community of obedient believers – who would, hopefully, produce yet other churches (though not necessarily ones with a church building). Social work is vital, but biblically, who is supposed to do it? In the first three centuries of the church, it was not the missionaries, but the people in the churches they planted who served their neighbors.

3. We would work in teams. Our teams would need multiple members to accomplish the goal of planting churches. Usually it takes a mixture of gifting – not only evangelists, but also disciple makers who will help establish new believers in their faith in Jesus. Teams usually also need facilitators who help

them stay on task and find ways to sustain their residence for sufficient years to live productively in the country.

4. We would be field-governed. The missionaries would be closest to the action, so they should make decisions about their work. Team leaders would have the final word on who would join (or need to leave) their teams. Pioneer work demands entrepreneurs, and entrepreneurs need freedom to try new ways. Our semi-autonomous teams would have the flexibility to respond to an open door, unhampered by mission bureaucracy. Our highest ruling body would be comprised of the leaders of church planting teams that had at least six members. (We were making it up as we went, but our conviction was that the mission agency should exist for the church planting teams, not the other way around.)

5. We would be eager for coaching and upgrading. (I'd been around long enough to realize that most missionaries are held accountable mainly to keep their agency's rules. Few are well monitored as to whether they are actually making disciples who reproduce other disciples!) We decided to reverse the emphasis of the accountability – focusing less on lifestyle choices and more on fruitful practices. Business has no patience for tradition, because tradition does not get them to their goal. Why should we? It's no good to try the same methods year after year if they aren't working. In addition, it can be a temptation for overseas workers simply to raise our families overseas and fail to work as hard at our jobs as those

who financially support us work at theirs. We would need to be willing to open up our lives and practices to our colleagues for honest evaluation and accountability.

6. We would be as grace-oriented toward each other as the Lord is to us. Within biblical parameters, we would honor different convictions toward lifestyle choices and theology. In other words, we would happily accept both a Hudson Taylor and a Bill Bright. A Wesley and a Whitfield. Folks with PhDs and self-taught blue-collar workers. Wine-bibbers and teetotalers. The hyperactive and the phlegmatic. We would accept them all, so long as they were endorsed and commissioned by a biblically based church.

Back in Pasadena, I sought out mission statesmen who could help me give our new mission visibility, credibility, and desirability. I am grateful to leaders of Mission to the World, Wycliffe, World Vision, the US Center for World Mission, and the many others who helped us with practical tasks. Open Doors loaned us the use of their powerful computer to send out our communications to our meager number of prayer partners and donors. George Carey (later to become my overseer as the Director of World Outreach of the Evangelical Presbyterian Church) created radio spots to help us get exposure on Christian broadcasts.

It was one thing to get new recruits into place where the church didn't yet exist among Muslims. But as veteran mission leaders had warned me, keeping them in place and out of trouble was another matter. "How can you send out teams with all new people?" they asked. After all, we had no country leaders and no field councils of veterans. In some places, such as Mali, Mauritania, or Tajikistan, there was no one nearby to help them. Since those were pre-Internet days, no one was available over Skype, either. Faxes and aerograms came into our Pasadena office, revealing our young workers' struggles. One day, after reading yet another report of a team leader's visit from the secret police or a visa being denied, Sally asked me with a pained grimace on her face, "Why are we spending our lives getting people in trouble?"

I paused. It was true. We were urging people to take huge risks.

"Maybe because we really believe this is God's idea," I told her. That thought steadied my own doubts.

Still, I realized that we needed coaches and pastoral care for our rookies. As I sought for God's answer, I realized that he actually has only one Great Commission army. Why not call on my friends in other agencies to serve as coaches to our "freshmen" until they gained sufficient experience to coach one another? I'm sure that one or two of them wanted to say, "I told you so." But overall, the response from God's senior servants was gratifying and, I'm sure, most pleasing to the Lord.

It's no exaggeration to say that Frontiers ran on a shoestring in those days. Yet whenever the "widow's oil" was drained, the Lord rescued us – once with $10,000 from Campus Crusade for Christ, other times with substantial donations from friends. George Verwer had started a chain of bookstores in England that supported OM in India. I prayed for some business people to start a business to underwrite Frontiers. It didn't happen.

We had hoped to have a hundred adults on the field by the end of our second year of operations. About seventy made it onto Muslim soil. So Bob Sjogren revved up our recruiting effort. He pulled together two teams of young people who were ready to go overseas with several different agencies. Providing a van for each team, he sent them to universities around the USA to tell students, "Come with us to reach the unreached peoples of the world." It was brilliant strategy to use recent graduates to pull other young people into our ranks. Then after a couple of years, Frontiers turned its two recruiting vans over to Caleb Project, which formed student mobilization teams made up of candidates from five different missions in each of five vans.

We wanted churches and would-be missionaries to put us on their shortlist of agencies to consider. The message we wanted to project was: "If you're thinking Muslims, think Frontiers." We even highlighted Nehemiah 9:22, shamelessly adding the emphasis on the last word: "You gave them kingdoms and nations, allotting to them even the remotest *frontiers.*"

Being based in California had its pros and cons. California is creative (for good or for evil), but it didn't necessarily project the image of "solid, responsible, and trustworthy." With Bob Sjogren and a few others, we opened a second base in Columbus, Ohio – the heart of America. From both Pasadena and Columbus, we continued our strong campaign of challenging the American church to focus on God's promise that the good news is for *all* peoples. An early poster proclaimed: "Muslims – It's *their* turn." The message got through. In thirty years, Frontiers grew from 40 adults to 1,300.

Not long ago, a distraught Bible college student gushed to me, "I don't know whether God is calling me to the Muslim world or whether I'm just responding to peer pressure."

Another young woman wondered if her interest in Muslims was only because "it's trendy."

Muslims? Trendy? Peer pressure to go to the Muslim world? Their remarks stunned me and opened my eyes to how the Lord of the harvest was thrusting out laborers. When we first started Frontiers, God's people seemed almost entirely unaware of the existence of Muslims. They didn't realize that nearly a quarter of the men, women, and children on earth are taught that Jesus did not die on the cross and that the Bible isn't the Word of God. But times have changed, and the surging interest of the church to evangelize Muslims continues to astonish me.

At Urbana 1984 (InterVarsity's student mission conference), twenty-nine seminars and workshops focused on taking the gospel to Muslims. Nearly all of them were packed to overflowing. Mission organizations that did not work among Muslims felt increasing pressure to get on board. One mission exec complained that as soon as inquirers learned that their agency did not work among Muslims, they lost interest in talking!

Was it possible that in the next two decades God intended to open the eyes of tens of thousands of Muslims to Jesus Christ as the way, the truth, and the life? Was he preparing his church for a harvest never before imagined? Would the church be well prepared to assist a whole new generation of pioneers that God was now calling? Unless we restructured our agencies, I was sure that neglected peoples would continue to be unreached because we would not be able to place (and keep in place) those who would be willing to go and serve among them.

CHAPTER 24

Panic Attack

When Frontiers was five years old, I was in Canada as the missions week speaker at Prairie Bible Institute in Alberta, with a repeat performance scheduled for the following week at Briercrest College in Saskatchewan. Our teams were multiplying so quickly that I couldn't keep them all on my radar. I had left Sally in Pasadena caring for my mother, who had just moved in with us because she was dying of lung and bone cancer. Evan, David, and Paul all seemed to be struggling in different ways, but it wasn't clear to me how I could "be there" for them. To top it all, Paul was pushing us to adopt his African-American friend, Shadow X, who had been expelled from his home.

Suddenly, in the middle of the week at Prairie, I was overcome with a panic attack! I wanted to run away. How could I get from rural Alberta to Tahiti without seeing or talking to anyone? As soon as I finished each session, I disappeared into the guest room. Maybe I could finish my last two days at Prairie, but there was no way I could go on to Briercrest. I asked someone to call them with the excuse that my mother was dying.

From Prairie Bible Institute in Canada, I crawled back to Pasadena with my tail between my legs. Greg Livingstone was paralyzed; I was in a walking coma. I couldn't bear to see a letter or take a phone call. I felt as though I'd been running a marathon from Spain to India to Europe to Lebanon to Toronto to the OM *Logos* to Aspen to Philadelphia to Pasadena – twenty-six years without stopping. I couldn't run any farther. Every day I pondered, "How little can I get away with today?"

When I spoke at meetings, it was like a campaigning politician robotically rattling off his message. I had an overwhelming desire for privacy. I didn't even want to see friends. I was fearful, angry, easily agitated, blue. I blamed others and positioned myself to look good enough not to be embarrassed. I worried that I was becoming just another "good old boy," staying busy but having little impact. I became conscious of how little I actually accomplished in a given week. Lack of productivity is a fate worse than death for me.

Sally, my ailing mother, and all those co-workers across the globe and in our office were looking to me. The weight broke me. I cried out to God in agony.

I sent a message to Tim Lewis in Morocco: "You've got to come back. I can't handle the whole mission. I need to take a break. Maybe I'm already having a breakdown!"

Keith Butler, our new business director, agreed with my decision to call Tim home. Then a cadre of men began to surround me with their care. Bill Thrall dropped his pastoral responsibilities in Phoenix and came to sit with me. Former college president Harry Evans could relate to what I was going through, so he organized a support group of men from Pasadena Covenant Church. Gary Taylor and Bob Sjogren stood nearby like the president's guards – baffled, but ready to take the bullet. Tim and Becky Lewis had just had their fourth child, but when I asked them to return, they quickly packed up their home in Morocco, putting things in storage for an expected three-month assignment. Tim traveled to the US with their three oldest children, leaving Becky to get a passport for their newly born son and join us all in Pasadena. Once it became clear that Tim would have to take on the role of field director long term, they divided their very large team into five smaller teams, focusing on different tribal groups, and joined the international leadership team.

Imagine my embarrassment. Retrenchment wasn't in my vocabulary. My rampart had disintegrated. I had always resisted retreat, consolidation, and in-looking, but this time I couldn't whistle in the dark.

As I look back, I realize our wise God was engineering a chain of events that would lead to a restructuring, which in turn provided better shepherding across Frontiers. It felt something like the story of God giving to Moses a group of elders who would respond to first-level complaints.

Sally needed me at her side during her own journey through the dark night of recurring depression. I had little capacity to help her, but being relieved from my crushing (albeit self-inflicted) load enabled me to at least be near her, giving her whatever I had left to give.

The Lord spoke to me through a number of passages of Scripture:

Come to me, all you who are weary and burdened [who work to exhaustion and are striving (swinging and missing the ball), struggling, toiling – maybe I wasn't the first of the Great Physician's patients!], *and I will give you rest.*

Matthew 11:28

In repentance and rest is your salvation, in quietness and trust is your strength.

Isaiah 30:15

I love the Lord, for he heard my voice; he heard my cry for mercy. Because he turned his ear to me, I will call on him as long as I live.

Psalm 116:1–2

The Lord is gracious and righteous; our God is full of compassion. The Lord protects the unwary; when I was brought low, he saved me. Return to your rest, my soul, for the Lord has been good to you.

Psalm 116:5–7

Pastor Thrall helped me think through our next steps, to avoid the wrong kind of rumors and to come up with a plan. He advised me to beware of overreacting, thereby painting myself into a corner. Sally and I should join a small group, he said, which could monitor our condition as our key advisors. Further, he suggested that after a quiet break, we needed to make a plan to live differently and think through how to rewire the machine so that the batteries wouldn't run down again.

With 200 adults, more than 100 kids, and an operational budget of more than $2 million, Frontiers needed to reorganize. In consultation with others, Thrall suggested that I needed to let the Frontiers family know that there was a need for change, and how each task would be handled.

Tim and Becky's arrival was no disappointment. A gifted administrator, Tim implemented Thrall's recommendations. His sterling leadership led to him taking over as field director, then deputy general director.

Assured that Tim and the others were going to keep Frontiers on course, I retreated to Ventura, my "Bethel," where I scribbled my thoughts into a journal:

May 10, 1986

I must learn the art of taking minute vacations – of slowing down to look at a flower, to chat with a friend, to pat a dog, to smile at a child, to read a few pages from a good book.

I need to take more time to reflect, ponder, and enjoy companionship with God. Seven minutes in the bathtub to get my Commander's orders for the week is not regenerating worship. I crave a more simple life without a house and yard to maintain or being confronted by someone in whose schedule I must fit every hour I'm awake.

I spend 90 hours (maybe 100 including mental activity) of my 112 hours awake each week adapting to others, trying to meet their needs or my perception of their needs and expectations. Like my very occasional golf game, I consistently fall far short of my aspirations.

If I graded myself with what I think the team leaders would grade me, it would be a C+ or maybe a D+. Tournier calls this "a deprived child syndrome." He either becomes bitter or the Junior Assistant Savior. I went from the first to the second!

What shoulds and oughts am I living with?

I must be the pacesetter for all Frontiers personnel.

Frontiers' people must be the pacesetters for other "swans," showing how to do it better.

We must show those who think we're wasting time and money with Muslims that it can be done.

I must keep the team leaders happy, feeling good about their team.

I must keep our mission efficiently and effectively productive.

We will enact a new chapter in church history! We will believe for something that has never yet happened among Muslims.

We must see 200+ viable Muslim convert congregations birthed where none exist today – exclusively where it is not permitted.

We have announced that we will build this tower (Luke 14:28). What if we don't?

Cognitively, I could explain failure with minimum embarrassment. But deep within, there's no way that I will accept failure, dropped balls, or lack of productivity by colleagues. Giving up is an intolerable thought.

Along with that impossible to-do list, I fought the fear that time was running out for me to get the job done. I pictured the days arriving when my mental faculties would lose their sharpness. I fixated on the day when I would be sixty – which meant I had only twelve more years to make a lasting, historically significant contribution. I felt it was my task to get us far enough toward the goal so that we'd have the momentum to accomplish it. I feared we might settle for just respectable activity, leaving little lasting fruit behind. The possibility of playing at mission haunted me.

Despite others exclaiming the opposite, I felt I accomplished very little in any given week or month. I feared that Sally's needs ought to be my top priority, but that giving her preference would prevent me from being where I thought I should be when I felt I should be there.

I was, of course, well aware that it was not God's idea that I had been emulating Jimmy Carter running for president: eight campaign stops a day, desperate for votes, brushing hands but not really connecting with people. At other times, I felt as though I was already elected but was now under pressure to carry out my campaign promises.

More from my Ventura journal:

Chuck Colson says beware of the quest to be number one; it's corrupting. Don't spend your life getting votes and checking the polls daily to gauge your popularity as a leader. But honestly, I am hungry for recognition. I'm still the little kid in La Jolla trying to get someone to notice me – to affirm me, to approve me. That's why I need Sally to say "I love you" over and over again.

That's what OM did for me. I became somebody to my peers and I worked around the clock to avoid getting crossed off the Little League roster. I boasted because I had no one else to do it – to be proud of me out loud.

As I write this now, I realize that many do appreciate me; some even highly esteem me and look up to me. Wheaton College and Missio Nexus have given me awards of recognition, calling me one of the major leaders of mission of our era. Yet I had to give myself permission to stop trying to "win an election" and focus on simply pleasing an audience of *One*.

I've lived most of my years feeling guilty both ways: for not accomplishing more and for not slowing down to smell the roses. I can identify a bit with Paul's writing in 2 Corinthians. On the one hand, he needed to set the record straight, but on the other, he was embarrassed that he was boasting.

With the fellowship of the band of brothers who surrounded me, my panic eventually subsided. Periodically over the years, it would creep back into my heart again. But it never again dominated me as completely as it did in 1986. I would get fearful that team members would reject our financial policies, or that some teams would decide they didn't need Frontiers. But eventually I would find the place where I could say, "So what if they don't wear the Frontiers badge?"

I had many fears: of not meeting the expectations of others, of rejection, of abandonment, of being devalued by my colleagues, of not getting the appropriately gifted persons into the right positions, and of failing my sons. But over the years, I have gotten into the good habit of bringing my fears to my Master, the Lord Jesus. And he always gives me, his toddler, an understanding smile and hug.

I'm not sure why I thought I ought to get a doctorate. After all, I had just faced up to the fact that I was overwhelmed. So overwhelmed that I needed to bring Tim and Becky Lewis back from Morocco and recruit someone to be a US director to manage the home team. In addition, teams were complaining that I hadn't visited them. Do over-busy, overwhelmed directors of fast-growing agencies start a doctoral program? (The fact that I didn't see the ridiculousness of this notion proves once again the truth of my foster mother Ruth Ringle's statement: "If God can use Greg, he can use anybody!")

I did at least wrestle with myself: "Is this an ego thing? Is it because so many other leaders I know are getting doctorates?" Biola University, a forty-five-minute drive from our home and office, so keenly wanted someone in the field of missions "with name recognition" to launch their doctor of missiology program that they were offering a full scholarship. Was that reason enough for me to do it?

In spite of my doubts, I told myself that I needed to be aware of the best thinking and practices out there. I wanted to set the pace in upgrading my understanding of what it would take to see 200 church planting teams have lasting fruit among unengaged Muslims. A doctoral course would force me to read and reflect on what I felt I should be wrestling with as an exemplary leader in our area of pursuit. It's peculiar that we pay universities to force us to study what we ought to study anyway, but we don't get around to it unless we have professors pushing us with deadlines.

In order to qualify for their program, Biola's rule keepers normally required a Master of Divinity degree rather than the Master of Arts degree I had from their older, more highly esteemed sister, Wheaton College. They also normally required that cross-cultural doctoral students be able to work in a language besides English. I appealed that my twenty-five years of exposure to other cultures (and my attempts to learn French, German, Spanish, Flemish, Arabic, Hindi, and Urdu) ought to count for something! The Biola faculty was more impressed that I had studied Islamics for three semesters at Beirut's Near East School of Theology with well-known scholars including Kenneth Cragg. (I didn't reveal that I had hardly understood a sentence of Cragg's lectures.) Despite my shortcomings, Biola's doctoral program committee voted to let me into their program, by a margin of five to four.

My first hurdle was anthropology. Why had we OMers ignored such a vital subject? My professors were extremely patient with this full-time mission director who had to force himself to sort out the difference between matrilineal and patrilineal cultures.

Many of my doctoral program's requirements seemed to me to be irrelevant, busy work. One day, I was loudly fussing about what I was sure was silly minutiae. A fellow student who was a member of the Navigators looked me in the face and whispered, "Greg, it's *their* playground."

Stopped in my tracks, I stared at Jack. I suddenly realized that if one wants what a program offers, one must accept what it requires. With appreciation I said, "Thanks, Jack. I needed that. Okay, what is the straightest line from here to graduation?" I never fussed over their hoops again. (It helped that I had an empathetic doctoral committee.)

My assistant Ginny Williamson, in her sixties, tirelessly typed out my dictation and deciphered my notebooks, usually scrawled while I was on airplanes. When I received my doctoral degree in 1990, I insisted that she join me in my graduation photograph.

As I developed my dissertation, I used my seniority as Chairman of the Board of William Carey International University to temporarily claim a large unused classroom. I filled it with boxes, each of which held my research on a different topic. After I graduated, not eager to see all that work staying on a shelf in a library, I was gratified to see it published in 1993 in a popular version as *Planting Churches in Muslim Cities: A Team Approach*. To my amazement, it was reprinted thirteen times over the next twenty years.

CHAPTER 25

Twenty Bucks

My experiences with OM and NAM taught me that agencies that recruit personnel from different countries experience both depth and tensions. Every nationality brings its advantages and disadvantages. The important question was to ask, "From where is the Lord of the harvest calling new pioneers to do church planting in Muslim regions?" The answer was certainly not solely from America or Britain. In fact, South Koreans recently surpassed Britons in the number of overseas missionaries. Per capita, South Korea now has more missionaries outside its own borders than any other country in the world!

Wondering how we could find an apostolically gifted person with a burden for the Muslims in Europe, I tried to recruit the most dynamic Swiss couple I'd known from OM days, Heinz and Anneliese Strupler. They didn't feel led to join Frontiers, but Heinz insisted that I recruit one of his young Bible school students who had been reaching out to Muslims.

Anthony looked even younger than his twenty-three years. At our first meeting, I could not discern anything apostolic about him. I went back to Heinz to ask for someone else. He sent me back to Anthony. I gave Anthony a test I was sure he'd fail. "Come to our International Council meetings in California," I told him, "and we'll talk further."

Tim Lewis, who was organizing that year's council meeting, loathed to spend money unnecessarily. So he and the other organizers chose rustic Camp Colby in a forest near Los Angeles for our third International Council meetings. It was the worst, most primitive venue we've ever used for our annual meetings, but Anthony showed up. My next test was to give him a $20 bill to start our European sending base. He didn't protest – didn't even blink. He and his dear wife, Karin, just did it. Before he handed over our Swiss and German sending bases for others to run, nearly 200 Swiss and Germans had joined Frontiers to proclaim the riches of Christ among Muslims in Africa and Asia.

Our next sending base was in Canada. A Canadian friend pointed out to me that most interdenominational mission agencies based their Canadian offices in Toronto. Each one had to wait in the queue to get the opportunity to speak in the local churches, and some Toronto churches decided not to let any missions representatives speak in their services, lest they show favoritism. The message was clear enough. We moved to Vancouver.

Bob Granholm had been dramatically converted as a hippy who ran into an OM ship crew's street meeting. Starting a Frontiers base with no money didn't seem any more overwhelming to Bob than it had to Anthony. He set up shop in two rooms of the Vancouver branch of OM.

What about Latin America? It seemed that everyone was saying the time had come for the Global South to heed the Great Commission. A number of former OM colleagues were motivating Latinos to go to the Muslim world. We prayed we could establish sending bases in Central and South America.

Andrés, a graduate of the prestigious Johns Hopkins Medical School, could have been a king in Costa Rica, his home country. Instead, he and his wife chose to leave it all. After recruiting thirteen Latinos to take up residence in a Muslim country in the midst of civil war, they were used by God to birth nine house churches of redeemed Muslims.

Meanwhile, I had met the Dutchman Jan Zwart, who had been a pilot for Missionary Aviation Fellowship in South America. "Why not use your life to see the Dutch pioneer once more in Muslim countries?" I challenged him. His first recruit was his brother Theo, and the Dutch started joining our ranks.

Clearly, Frontiers was becoming an international community, but we wouldn't flourish as one if we kept our headquarters in California. Furthermore, housing in California was too expensive for our under-supported home staff members, who were living on a shoestring. Deciding we needed to establish a US sending base and a separate international office, we sought the Lord's direction regarding the cities where we should locate.

Personally, I wanted to move our international headquarters to Bahrain – the exact center of the world between North America and New Zealand. "Why not establish our staging center right under their noses?" I reasoned. In a show of their subservience to me, the other leaders voted nineteen to one against the Bahrain option! We eventually agreed that London was the hub of the world for an agency focused on North Africa, the Middle East, and Asia.

I was adamant that we should not move our US operations to a city where other agencies were based. What city did *not* have a major sending agency? We whittled down our options to Minneapolis or Phoenix.

Meg Crossman, a veteran mission activist in Phoenix, mobilized a contingent of mission pastors to visit us. The group invited us to set up our US office in Phoenix. Wouldn't a desert city be appropriate for a mission to Muslims? I hesitated. Our colleagues would need to fly around the world, and at the time the Phoenix airport offered international flights only to Mexico.

"How long does it take you to get from Pasadena to the Los Angeles airport?" they asked.

"Forty-five minutes," I replied.

"Same as us," they countered triumphantly. Flights between the two cities barely take off before they land again. They had a point. It would be no worse than commuting from Pasadena.

Keith Butler had become our US director just in time for the move. He found a dilapidated bank building for sale for only $250,000. Volunteers from Phoenix churches helped with the renovations; more importantly, they opened their churches to undertake financial support of the home staff.

In England, the welcome was not as warm for a new mission from California. Americans were strange enough, but the British seemed to think that Californians were from "the land of the fruit and nuts." As we contemplated establishing an international office near London, I was strongly advised that to be acceptable to the Christians of England, I should first find a proper Englishman to be our British sending base director. The Lord brought to mind someone whom I had met while he was involved in the Oxford University Christian Union. I had recruited him to join OM, and he had served for many years in the Middle East. I found him again – this time in the basement of the European Christian Mission, developing literature for Albania. "No, I'm sorry, there is no salary, nor start-up funds for a British sending base," I admitted to him. "But would you please come anyway?" Along with his visionary wife, he agreed to birth the Frontiers British sending base, which started in their living room.

Back in Pasadena, I received a new assignment: raise $150,000 to move the international office to England and to set up the US sending base in Phoenix. To me, a rather feeble fund raiser, that sum felt like $150 million!

A friend in Memphis tried to introduce us to donors with substantial means. He was probably embarrassed after he introduced me to the leaders of a potential funding foundation. When I stressed prison, expulsion, and dying as standard operating procedure in the rescue operation among Muslims, they rejected us as reckless.

In OM, George Verwer had taught us simply to pray for the funds we needed. Asking outright made me feel uncomfortably awkward. But two faithful brothers held a metaphorical gun to my head until I started making phone calls to potential donors. Our gracious God honored our plea. The money started to come in from our small list of Great Commission friends – even from the US Center for World Mission staff members, whom we would be leaving.

Where in Britain should we locate our international office? I liked a horse farm for sale in Guildford; it had a great train service nearby, and it was near the major airports and London. Our new British director said the area was too posh – potential donors would be put off. Besides, Guildford's planning commission told us, "You can raise horses on that property, but not missionaries."

Then we found the ideal property! The children's charity Barnardo's was selling an inner-city London orphanage that had offices, kitchens, and apartments. It was even next door to a train station. Perfect! We rushed to London with a deposit check. The sellers told us to come back the next day. When we did, they told us that they preferred to sell (for less money) to fellow Brits. I was angry and disappointed.

Next we learned that the British mission WEC wanted to sell two three-story buildings in London that they were no longer using for their radio ministries. We agreed to buy. They changed their minds.

Word of our plight began to spread among Britain's evangelical mission agencies. John Bendor-Samuel, the international director of Wycliffe Bible Translators, phoned me to make an offer. After the British government built the M25 motorway through Wycliffe's south-east London property, they compensated the organization's loss with a World War II-era school for disabled children evacuated from London during the Blitz. It was in a little hamlet called Horsleys Green, halfway between London and Oxford. If Frontiers wanted to renovate some of the old buildings into offices and flats, Wycliffe would apply what we spent toward rent.

I was not thrilled. I'm an urbanite. I'm wary of cows. They never smile. (In my experience, there is no such animal as *la vache qui rit*.) My book was titled *Planting Churches in Muslim Cities*. The Wycliffe Centre was in the boondocks.

Still, it seemed we had no choice. Besides, the old wooden buildings, which looked like barracks, fit the wartime lifestyle promoted by Tim Lewis, who was the deputy general director. Becky Lewis designed three flats – one for their family, one for Darrel and Linda Dorr, and a cozy two-bedroom for Sally and me, who would be leaving our now-adult sons in the US.

Of course, God knew it would turn out to our advantage. Our association with Wycliffe influenced British churches to assume the new Americans were acceptable. It was evident from our rustic offices that we certainly were not Americans who could afford to throw a lot of money around. The ensuing twenty years at the Wycliffe Centre provided us with meeting rooms for conferences and training events as well as a dining hall for our staff and visiting missionaries – without having to worry about repair and maintenance of buildings. It meant we were able to support a sister mission working among the unreached and develop a relationship that enhanced Wycliffe's production of Scripture in the languages of Muslims.

What I didn't realize, at first, was that the Wycliffe Centre is only an eleven-minute drive from High Wycombe, which has one of the highest concentrations of Pakistani Muslims in the UK. (My colleagues on High Wycombe's Council for Christian–Muslim Relations estimate that by 2020, the population of our town may increase to 25 percent Muslim.)

After enjoying the convenience of living for four years at the Wycliffe Centre, a two-minute walk from our office, Sally and I felt we should move into town. Why would we live on a mission compound when, not far away, were more than 20,000 Muslims – none of whom were known to be followers of our Redeemer? We decided that God wanted us to set the pace and find a way to make disciples among the Pakistanis in High Wycombe. We sold our home in California, realizing exactly enough money to meet the required down payment on a house fifty yards from a street the Brits labeled "Khyber Pass."

Purchasing a home in High Wycombe conjured an old inner struggle: being a responsible household leader versus being a disciple who forsakes all for Christ. Over the years, my lack of financial acumen has made me feel less than adequate as a husband. In fact, I can't seem to do many of the things a "real man" is supposed to know how to do. I never did get a man in my life who taught me how to use tools or fix anything. Although I had bought a broken-down 1940 Ford coupe as soon as I earned my driver's license at sixteen, I never got it running. Still today, I hardly know which end of a hammer to hold. I can't figure out the three TV remotes. I always need help with simple household repairs. To this day, I usually end up resorting to Tom Sawyer's tactics: "Hey, wanna have some fun helping me assemble my new tool shed?" That doesn't fool my co-workers, but they come to do it out of love for the old man anyway.

Of all my "real man" failings, my shortcomings in the area of finances bothered me most. A few years ago, jealous of another brother's wise dealing with investments, I "yelled" at the Lord, "Why didn't you make me a better businessman?"

In one of those rare, almost-audible responses, I heard from my heavenly Father: "Have I provided for you?"

"Yes, sir."

"Are there any more questions?"

"No, sir," I whispered meekly.

CHAPTER 26

Where Others Don't

Sometimes, we were scared the Frontiers ship might hit the rocks. I remembered that some years earlier the crew of OM's *Logos* had to abandon ship when they ran aground on the rocks at the tip of Argentina. That was the end of the MV *Logos*. Similarly, churches and mission agencies must be alert to Satan's schemes to knock their leaders out of service and sink the entire organization into oblivion. We'd had our close calls in both OM and NAM. And we weren't immune in Frontiers, either. In 1993 we had one such close call.

Keith Butler's arrival in our Pasadena office had been a clear answer to prayer. It was because he was ready to become the US director that I felt I could move with the international office to England. Our board chairman objected to my leaving the country, discerning that the recruitment of new personnel would diminish. I thought not, but he was right. It did. It was no fault of Keith's that he was not a recruiter, but the numbers in our candidate schools were dwindling.

The leaders of our International Council were concerned. As we met in Singapore, we felt that the Lord was designating Rick Love to leave his team in Indonesia and to take over as the US director of Frontiers. It was obvious that Rick, with his field experience and motivational gifts, would be used to increase our ranks. Keith had earlier told me that whenever I wanted to replace him with someone who could do his job better, he would be ready to move over. However, the field leaders at that council meeting in Singapore failed to process the decision with Keith and the US board. Understandably, the US board didn't want to accept a decision by others for an area of authority they felt was their purview.

When I finally realized what an awkward situation we had, I flew to the US to discuss the International Council's decision with Keith, the board, and the staff. Despite attempts to reconcile our views, Keith and the entire US board resigned.

Even in this serious scenario, the Lord had a laugh on me. My early ambition had been to be featured on the cover of *Time* magazine. When I started to follow Christ, I "Christianized" my ambition slightly. Well, now I finally made it into *Christianity Today* magazine – though not on the cover and certainly not for the reasons I would have hoped. Conflating two incidents, a *Christianity Today* article noted that a Frontiers team in Cairo had been arrested and imprisoned for "impersonating" Muslims (because the women were wearing headscarves), and that the entire US board of Frontiers had resigned! I was mortified. Humiliated. Deeply embarrassed. I surmised that the magazine's readers would assume that the missionaries were badly led and that the general director of Frontiers must have sinned in one of the three major areas (embezzlement, womanizing, or heretical doctrine). In fact, the board members had resigned because I had failed to process an important personnel decision.

The board members' resignations meant that Sally and I needed to return to the States again. While retaining the general director's hat, I filled in as the interim US director until Rick could take over the job. It was no fun to oversee a staff of unhappy campers. After a few months, we left the US sending base and the staff in Rick's capable hands.

Eventually, I was fully reconciled with the former board members, all but one of whom became full advocates of Frontiers afresh. Keith and his delightful wife Dolores remain very close and supportive to the Frontiers family as well as to Sally and me personally. What a great God we have who rescues people like me – no matter how many times we make a mess of things.

Some years later, Keith wrote to me:

First Greg, I assure you that you need not ask for any forgiveness, as long ago I came to the realization that God had me at Frontiers for a season. I look at Frontiers today and thank God for kicking me out of there…
[The current US director] is certainly more gifted for the job than I was. God knows what he is doing.

Proverbs 29:18 reads: "Where there is no vision the people perish." Greg, God gave you a vision to reach Muslims and in doing so to create Frontiers. However, in my experience, high visionary people need the support of good administrative people. That is where my gifting came in. God had a role for me at Frontiers. I am glad I

> *accepted it and was given a chance to be a part of what*
> *God was and is doing among Muslims.*

Clearly, God had rescued our ship from hitting the rocks.

There was nothing routine or boring about being the general director of Frontiers. One day, it was a financial crisis in Germany. Another day, a leader had lost perspective – feeling left out, or overruled, or that God had left the universe. My problem was that I was a lousy Calvinist. I don't mean that being a Calvinist is lousy, but that claiming to be one, then living in fear and anxiety, is a denial of what I know to be true about God's great, overruling, long-range plans. Too often I would feel I must be the Junior Assistant Savior of every situation, which is totally inconsistent with what I teach others about our God's marvelous, comprehensive sovereignty. It is actually true that all things work out for the good of those who love God and do their darnedest to do his will (Romans 8:28, my rough paraphrase!).

I also failed to be an adequate leader of the women in Frontiers. I often failed to perceive the concerns they expressed to be important. Through my own experience, I should have been empathetic. I know what it's like to fear that someone will hold me back from what I sense God wants to do through me. So, I have made a commitment not to hold back any of my sisters from fulfilling their full potential or to limit anyone's opportunity to wholly follow the Lord in the way they understand him to be leading them.

After our 1996 International Council meetings, I headed

to Central and South America. It was time to recruit from the Caribbean and for the general director to show up at our first Latin world sending base in San José, Costa Rica. My journals reveal that I vowed countless times to "cut back," in order to spend more time in reflection or to intercede for longer periods, but I failed. There was simply no end of people to write to, stalled situations to reactivate, sheep and shepherds needing encouragement, or prayer letters to read and pray over. I can only hope my Lord smiled like a daddy does when his toddler fiercely tries to move an impossibly heavy object.

The tragedies and difficulties never stopped. A team leader in Pakistan fell ill with cerebral malaria and died within three days. Another brother drowned off the coast of North Africa. The Swiss sending base team rebelled against their leader. The first three sending base leaders in Singapore faded away one by one. The accountant in the Philippines ran off with nearly the entire bank account. In one rather positive, but still difficult, problem, three consecutive Mexican sending base leaders left their post to go to minister among Muslim people groups in Asia and Africa.

I realized that we needed more staff at the international office. What kind of coaching, oversight, member care, and leadership would enable our family of missionaries to realize our goal of reproducing churches for every Muslim people? No matter how many talented leaders joined us, I wanted to see even more teams among unengaged Muslim peoples. But growing in numbers without growing in godly character, I realized, would be ultimately counterproductive – not to mention the fact that to do so would fall short of the goal of pleasing the Lord. Our fellowship of pioneers was able to press on because God provided gifted leaders who surrounded me. It would take pages to give them all due credit. Allow me to mention only one example.

Tim Lewis has been a Jonathan to me since we first linked up in 1980, the same year I began to be tutored by his father-in-law Ralph Winter. For more than thirty years, Tim has been the man who was *there* for me.

Together, we designed NAM Associates, then Frontiers. I was a sounding board to him when he had major leadership responsibility at the US Center for World Mission. Tim eventually agreed to become Frontiers' third international director. No one was happier than I. In that role, Tim still turns to me as a sounding board. He's rarely persuaded that I have the right answers, but I help him think through the issues until he gets to what often seem to be the Lord's answers!

We both walk with God in a similar way. While we may not sound as holy as some, we are both allergic to the notion of being anything more than struggling sinners who have apostolic, whatever-it-takes determination. We are also of one mind regarding leaders. Leaders are people others want to follow into a venture that is over their heads. Leaders are people who make things happen toward a goal that is so important that it's worth failing in the attempt.

CHAPTER 27

Stepping Down

As the turn of the millennium approached, many around me worried about the Y2K bug, a potential worldwide meltdown due to a design flaw in computer systems. Meanwhile, as I was turning sixty that year, I was convinced that I should step down from my post as general director of Frontiers. Both strategically and emotionally, the issue of who would lead "my baby" weighed on me far more heavily than whether or not, at midnight on 31 December, all the computers in the world would go haywire!

In drafting our Frontiers policies, we had failed to provide a policy for succession. No one was hinting that I needed to move on. Still, I felt the new generation of missionaries needed a younger leader who could better track with their ways of thinking and expression.

Rick and Fran Love, charter members of Frontiers, were exemplary models. By agreeing for Rick to take over the US director role, they had demonstrated vision and their willingness to be team players. More impressive, they didn't quit in the face of the US board's opposition. Rick was able to mollify the offended loyal staff members, who were more focused on their love for the incumbents, Keith and Dolores Butler, than the need to accelerate growth. In the ensuing years under Rick's leadership, the staff grew in numbers, depth, and wisdom. Rick had also served well as a fund raiser. Frontiers' family of backers grew significantly during his period as US sending base director.

My study of the history of mission agencies convinced me that one thing was most important in this leadership transition. My replacement needed to be a visionary with motivational gifts, not an administrator.

Rick and I became a mini version of Moses and Joshua. Rick recruited a Christian leadership expert and other mission leaders to coach us through the passing of the baton. Fellow mission executives marveled at our transition from founder to second general director, seeing this as an exemplary model of how such a change should be managed.

Darrell Dorr, as faithful and accurate a scribe as any fellowship could desire, wrote a careful analytical summary of our changing of the guard:

> Frontiers continued to grow throughout the 1990s,
> becoming a pacesetter for other mission agencies in its
> sense of expectancy, its willingness to encourage team
> experimentation, and its ready accommodation of
> risky models of contextualized witness among Muslim
> peoples. On more than one occasion, Livingstone
> remarked, "I've needed to recruit to my weaknesses, and
> that's why Frontiers is so big." Livingstone's willingness
> to acknowledge his weaknesses and to confess his sins –

*a willingness nurtured, in part, by his experience in OM,
where a tender heart and the broken spirit of Calvary
Road were prized virtues – was part of what endeared
him to many who joined Frontiers and who came to
work with him (including this writer)…*

*In a "Changing of the Guard" internal memo
written around this time [1998], Livingstone noted,
"Frontiers is moving from a founder, General Director,
to a Shepherds' Group providing overall leadership
to Frontiers." He noted a variety of criteria (largely
character qualities and professional competence)
expected of the variety of "shepherds" that had emerged
under his encouragement and nurture: Team Leader
Overseers coaching one another in small "collegia,"
"master builders," and other senior leaders in the society.
He also noted the pattern of growth that had stretched
Frontiers:*

*"Frontiers has grown to over 600 adults plus
children spread across 38 countries. For the last ten
years, Frontiers has averaged an annual net growth
of between 13–17%. In the last four years, many of
the new pioneer missionaries are coming from Latin
America, Africa and Asia."*

*By now a number of notable leaders had emerged
among Frontiers team leaders, at Frontiers sending
bases, and at the Frontiers international headquarters.
In considering options for his successor as General
Director, Livingstone had a range of viable possibilities.
But his preference was clearly Rick Love, who had*

distinguished himself as a pioneering team leader (from Frontiers' earliest days)…

Love was the Frontiers leader most similar to Livingstone in temperament (outgoing, jovial) and gift-mix (teaching, exhorting, encouraging). What Livingstone occasionally said (only half in jest) to others was especially applicable to Love: "What I like about you is that you remind me of me." Steffen (2002) has noted that it is common for founders to select successors similar to themselves…

During the summer of 2000, in the countdown to the August international conference, the Frontiers U.S. sending base published an issue of its FrontLines newsletter featuring a cover story on "Dr. Greg Livingstone: A Legacy of Humility." In this story Livingstone had another opportunity to pull out a favorite quote and embellish it:

"The leader is somebody who recruits to [make up for] his weaknesses. That's why Frontiers is so big… I've got so many. What puts me in awe is that such quality people would join me in this magnificent obsession… God has held us together, despite the fact that we come from a huge diversity of theological and cultural backgrounds. This is what has thrilled me the most, and we're still going and becoming more godly."

In a sidebar article in this same newsletter, Love, writing as "International Director Elect," gave his own tribute to Livingstone. An excerpt reveals the widespread affection for the founder as well as his readiness to acknowledge his weaknesses. Biography was not yet morphing into hagiography:

"Because of Greg Livingstone, I will never be the same. Greg is more than my former boss and predecessor. He is my mentor, close friend, and fellow soldier of the cross. He is uncle to my children and lover of my Lord.

"Weaknesses – yes. Failures – sure. But when Greg sinned, he swiftly repented. During Frontiers' International Council in 1994, Greg realized that his decade-long attitude – 'We can make it happen in the Muslim world' – had unwittingly fostered pride and arrogance. He quickly confessed his sin and led our team leaders in a time of corporate repentance.

"Greg's great sense of humor makes it hard for people to stay mad at him. His love for the Frontiers family and his passionate singleness of purpose to make disciples among Muslims far surpass any of his faux pas. I rejoice that Greg will continue to serve with Frontiers – as a coach and catalyst.

"As he told me right after I was elected as the new International Director, 'Rick, I want you to be like Joshua leading Frontiers, and I want to be your Caleb.'

"This leads me to my last point – Greg's humility. Few men can birth a movement and then change roles in a leadership transition. It isn't easy shifting from the role of Moses to Caleb, so Greg needs your prayers. Pray also that Joshua will be wise in his deployment of Caleb!"

… By August 2000, when Livingstone passed the baton to Love, Frontiers was home to almost 600

*missionaries on 109 field teams working in 39 countries
and nurturing fellowships of Muslim-background
believers among 79 peoples. Some 78 churches or
fellowships had resulted...*

*Meanwhile, following a year of sabbatical teaching
and writing in 2000–2001, Greg and Sally Livingstone
relocated to Malaysia, a base from which Greg has
not only served as "coach and catalyst" in a variety of
cultural basins (as the 1998–2000 game plan originally
envisioned), but where he has also become team leader
of a Frontiers church planting team. The former General
Director now reports to his successor via the Field
Director he helped to recruit in 1994...*

*And since August 2000 has Livingstone managed
to avoid meddling in the domain of the new General
Director? Love was quick to praise the founder: "Greg
has done a magnificent job of not interfering. Greg
continues to mentor me, but it is mentoree-directed –
when I ask. Greg is one of my best friends! I think it was
very wise for Greg to go to Pasadena for the first year."
(Dorr, 2004, pp. 50–62)*

I wasn't sitting around worrying about what my successor
was doing, so it was right to get me busy on a big challenge
(the Malay world). It was a good antidote to my interference.
However, it did surprise me how much I personally missed
being included in Muslim worldwide issues.

As Rick and I prepared to pass the baton, our first task
together was to enlist Rick's replacement as US sending base

director. We felt it to be God's confirmation that we both thought of the same man – Bob Blincoe.

Bob and his wife Jan were proven veterans of ministry among the Muslim Kurds of Northern Iraq. Jan was the first missionary mother to take up residence there. She only insisted they find some method to be in contact with the outside world. The Southern Baptists provided what was then a $5,000 satellite phone. I can remember visiting them, watching Bob hang over the balcony to get a call through to Europe.

Bob, by then resettling Kurdish refugees in Seattle, turned us down. Rick and I pleaded to the Lord, and called him back. He said "no" a second time. While we wrinkled our brows and wondered what to do next, fully confident that we had heard correctly from the Lord, Jan Blincoe challenged her husband to "come out from the luggage" and take on the task!

Bob and his team in Phoenix have been so fruitful that they have made it difficult to maintain our goal of keeping the Americans at less than 50 percent of our ranks.

The International Council of Frontiers voted almost unanimously for Rick Love to be my replacement. The Frontiers family, meeting in England that year, came in from forty-three countries and showered Sally and me with praise – plus oriental rugs and other gifts.

Two of our sons joined in the farewells at that conference. Although they haven't followed in our footsteps in every way, I appreciate that each of our sons shares our values; they are concerned for the poor and disenfranchised. They are professionals in their chosen areas. I'm proud of Evan, who as an attorney takes on *pro bono* cases. As a professor in Central Europe, David teaches that racial hatred against Gypsies isn't a Christ-like attitude. Paul, who makes his living as a musician, has compassion on the weak and struggling people of the world as well – once even getting arrested in Wall Street protests. Though I struggle with feelings that I failed my sons, Sally and I are proud of all three of them.

At the conference, our son Paul honored us by playing the sitar, which Frontiers co-workers from South Asia especially appreciated. But the highlight of the conference for me was our son David's speech, titled "Rebels with a Cause":

It's not easy being a missionary kid. No matter how hard you work at being a rebel, it's impossible to outdo your own parents. I'm often asked by people in the Czech Republic, where I've lived for the last ten years, "What do your parents think about you choosing to live over here in Central Europe?" (Czechs are deeply offended if you refer to them as being from Eastern Europe.) I can tell by their tone of voice and look on their faces that they expect to hear of bitter parents unable to understand how their son could be capable of leaving behind his own beloved land.

Imagine their surprise when I answer, "Oh, they think I'm rather boring."

"Boring!" they say to themselves in disbelief.

"Yes, boring! They would rather I lived somewhere more exotic, not merely have settled down in the middle of Europe."

My wife Ladislava and I have two kids and a third on its way. One of my favorite things about a pregnancy is the opportunity it gives to annoy my wife by thinking up absurd names. My personal favorite is Julius Erving (or Dr. J, for short – great Philadelphia 76er basketball player), which she can't seem to appreciate for some reason, partially because Julius was the first name of the most obnoxious Czech communist writer. Once again, however, my own attempts seem feeble in comparison with my folks. My older brother Evan didn't do too badly; he received two middle names, Martyn (after Henry Martyn, of course) and Dale (after Dale Rhoton, I believe). I received a larger mouthful: Verwer (after, the minor league shortstop for the Baltimore Bullets, Jack Verwer... no not really, I think you know who). And Coltman, my mother's maiden name. David Verwer Coltman Livingstone. Try to fit that onto a job application form. My younger brother Paul received the prize winner: Zwemer (after Samuel Zwemer) and Schaeffer (after the theologian/philosopher Francis Schaeffer). Paul Zwemer Schaeffer Livingstone – sitar player.

My father is fond of saying that he's very proud of the fact that none of his sons are materialists. That's just another way of saying that none of us make any money. I have always thought of myself as a radical of sorts, rejecting the American rat race of mass consumption. In comparison with my folks, however, at times I feel like Donald Trump. I mean, these are people who sold their wedding presents to help buy their plane tickets over to Europe in order to evangelize the world. According to legend, my father used to dunk his tea bag in his cup only once in order to reuse it as many times as possible. These are people who slept twenty people in one apartment and drove VW buses in sleeping bags.

Over the years, my brothers and I worked hard at trying to shock our parents. I would bring home snakes, frogs, and spiders – only to have my mother enthusiastically examine my terrifying specimen; I always forgot she studied zoology at Wheaton. Long hair, mohawks, bald heads, and ear-rings failed to do the trick. Outrageous behavior? Who can beat my mother going shopping with our dog and wearing dark glasses – pretending she's blind, so she can receive a discount? How can we get a rise out of people who have traveled to almost every country on the globe and met with people of all shapes and sizes?

One would think the easiest way to offend missionaries would be to show disrespect to the church. But how can you top a father who has been escorted at gun point off of Bob Jones University campus, offended Jerry Falwell and his whole congregation, and insulted former US Senator and prominent evangelical leader Mark Hatfield, and even forbade his own children to attend a Christian college?

Of course, the difficulties were not only on our side. At times, my parents could not understand what was happening to their sons. My father could never understand why I might have posters of famous football players on my wall when instead I could have Hudson Taylor or C. T. Studd glaring at me over my bed. He never appreciated my interest in collecting baseball cards: "Nolan Ryan," he would scoff, "big deal. I would like a card of Jim Elliot or David Livingstone. Now that would be something!"

I doubt they were initially able to understand how their son Paul became such a devoted musician. I have a personal theory that neither one of them is able to sing one whole song to the end. Not that my parents lack musical ability; my mother has a good singing voice and played the recorder, I believe; my father flirted with the ukulele. They had a decent record collection when we were kids: the complete repertoire of the Slightly Fabulous Limelighters, for example. If you are not familiar with their work, I am sure my father will be happy to give his best rendition. I must admit, however, that they did have a copy of the Beatles' Sgt. Pepper's at home.

Actually, my father is always in best singing voice in the morning. Every morning I can remember as a child (when my father wasn't out of town, of course) began as follows. First a bugle call: do, do, do. Then, the philosophical statement, "If you're man enough to stay up all night, you're man enough to get up in the morning." Followed by the famous Czech folk song, "Roll out the barrel, we'll have a barrel of fun." Finally, he ended with the mysterious profundity, perhaps his own translation from Arabic, "If you put a bullet in the furnace, it's gonna explode."

I must admit, however, that I have a great deal to be thankful for. Having had such radicals for parents has helped me a great deal as a husband and father. Whenever my wife gets worried about, for example, traveling long distances with the kids, I can just respond with, "Don't worry, my mother took three kids on a Greyhound across the USA on her own, a three-day ride, and loved every minute of it." (I'm not sure about that last bit.) If she is hesitant about taking the kids swimming in the sea: "Don't be silly, my dad took my brother and me swimming in the sea off the coast of Iran in water infested with deadly poisonous sea snakes and nothing happened to us." When my daughter doesn't want to eat her food, I have at my disposal: "Hah, you're lucky! When I was a kid, we had to eat all sorts of disgusting things. We were only allowed to choose three horribly nasty foods which we didn't have to eat, everything else went down the throat: monkey brains, caterpillars, horse heart, etc." A little exaggeration never hurts; I only remember eating the last delicacy on the list.

So when people talk about pastors' kids and missionary kids turning into rebels, I have to disagree, in the latter case at least. If you follow in your parents' footsteps, you may at worst be accused of lack of originality, but if you don't, you will, at least in my case, be forever, unsuccessfully, trying to equal the radicalness of your own parents.

All hope is not lost, however. They are finally retiring from their work with Frontiers. Now, they can settle down to a nice suburban middle-class lifestyle… in Malaysia!

CHAPTER 28

New Start

Convinced that I needed to get out of the way to help our community re-gear under the new international director, I accepted an invitation to be an adjunct professor at Fuller Seminary's School of World Mission. I will simply summarize that experience in one sentence: During those fifteen months, my Father verified that formal teaching is neither my gift nor my calling! Teaching and recruiting are not the same gifts.

We were gratified for the opportunity to be near our sons Evan and Paul and their families, who were living in southern California. But my other major goal for the year was to write a textbook about the history of Christian mission among Muslims since Mohammed. Teaching left little time for research, so the history book is a project I'm still working to complete.

As a sheepdog, I could never let go of my passion to see the Lord of the harvest thrust out more workers, so we got back into the people business. Finally, after my retirement as a mission exec and a seminary professor, Sally and I became resident workers in Malaysia, a predominantly Muslim country.

A team leader in Malaysia had sent us a request during the year I taught at Fuller. Would we sheepdog more disciple makers to create church planting teams for the 24 million Malay Muslims? If we were to raise up twenty-seven teams, he reckoned, that would allow us to make disciples within each Malay-majority province in Malaysia, Brunei, and Indonesia.

Sadly, Malaysia provides a prime example of the church's historical avoidance of ministry to Muslims. Though Muslims are by far the majority in Malaysia, its population includes a significant minority of Chinese, many of whom are Christians. The difference in Christian outreach to the Chinese in the region compared with outreach among Muslims draws the picture clearly. Robert Morrison pioneered among the Chinese in the nineteenth century. In the 200 years since he arrived in Macau, perhaps more than 2,000 Westerners have obeyed God's call to make disciples among the Chinese. Yet there had been no sustained efforts to plant churches among Muslim Malays nearly 200 years after Morrison! Ironically, when it was difficult to get visas for China, Malaysia became a staging area for missionaries to learn Chinese in preparation for the day when the door would open to China. But only about five of the Lord's servants had sought to share the good news with Muslim Malays before the 1980s.

The Malays are not the only Muslim peoples whom the church has avoided. After an abortive communist coup in 1965, about 900,000 Javanese Muslims were baptized, yet few of them were willing to cross cultures to birth biblically alive fellowships on other islands among their neighboring

Muslim peoples – the Aceh, the Madurese, the Minang, the Bugis, and the Banjar. Still today in Sumatra, large populations of Muslims do not have their first gathering of believers. The church worldwide has overlooked Muslim peoples in other parts of the world, as well. By contrast, in Latin America and sub-Saharan Africa, translators had made the admirable effort to provide the New Testament in their heart language to tribes with as few as 500 souls. Yet Muslim peoples numbering in the millions in Uzbekistan, China, Tajikistan, and Malaysia had to wait until the 1990s to get the New Testament in their language.

Sally and I felt it was right to move to Malaysia and have a go at what we'd been telling everyone else to do for forty-nine years! While I was serving as general director, we were also what Frontiers calls "team leader overseers" for two teams in western Malaysia. The Malay had already become our number-one burden after Libya. Our team in Kuala Lumpur had yet to disciple a single new believer in Jesus after twelve years of continuous presence. Glenn, the current team leader in the city, was happy to turn his team over to me.

Only later did I discover that I had misunderstood the Malaysian team leader's original request. He only wanted us to recruit new workers from afar, not actually move to Malaysia ourselves. He thought my profile as a missionary to Muslims was too high. Other workers in the country would surely be expelled if they associated with us! Another leader protested that face-to-face disciple making did not seem to be good stewardship of someone he described as "the world's greatest recruiter."

I can't recall that we had any other specific offers! So we turned our faces toward Malaysia. Though we had been missionaries since 1963, I realized at the last moment that we knew almost nothing about how to learn a language adequately. Just forty-eight hours before our departure, I called Betty Brewster. This Fuller Seminary prof specialized in teaching missionaries how to learn language and culture. With no time to teach us in a proper class, she loaded us with books, tapes, two recorders, and a prayer.

Of course, Malaysia didn't offer missionary visas – at least not to persons focused on seeing Malay Muslims adhere to the Lord Jesus as their Savior. What they did offer was a program called "Malaysia, My Second Home." We were granted a ten-year visa. (At that time, such a visa did not stipulate that one was not allowed to evangelize Muslims.)

Our next step was to find a place to live. Friends recommended their old neighborhood; they knew a woman who led the local ladies in *t'ai chi* exercises in the local park at 7:30 every morning – before it got too hot. Sally was so enamored by the idea that she claimed we'd find a house to rent within walking distance of that park. I didn't have quite such faith, but Sally insisted on driving round and round the neighborhood. Just before giving up, we noticed a tiny sign with a phone number on the gate of 155 Persiaran Zaaba. The owner, called Sheikh, was a jovial retired Shell Oil executive. Like most upper-class Malay, he had attended mission schools and spoke English almost flawlessly.

Still, we determined to learn Malay. Thinking we might find university students open to discuss the claims of Christ,

Sally and I drove forty-five minutes each morning to Malaysia State University. We were the only students in the beginner class. The teacher couldn't comprehend why we couldn't move along as quickly as his previous foreign students. How could we explain that we were sixty years old, and they were only twenty-six – and also Wycliffe missionaries with degrees in linguistics!

After nine months at the university, it was time to take the exam. To save face (his and ours), our teacher awarded me an A and Sally (to her chagrin) an A-minus. Apparently it was culturally inappropriate to allow the woman to match her husband's prowess! We carried on at a language school in Kuala Lumpur, but we still tended to learn ninety words, forget eighty, and mispronounce the other ten. Once, when a doorman in a high-rise apartment building guided me to a colleague's door, I thanked him not with the Malay phrase "*terima kasih*" but with the Swedish "thank you" – "*tack så mycket*"!

In order to fathom people's possible interest in pleasing Allah, I tried to drop redemptive elements into every conversation. However, we discovered that (unlike the Arab Muslims we had known) Malay Muslims avoid talking about religion or politics – even with each other. It simply isn't done in polite society. I was frustrated, to say the least.

My relational highlight in Kuala Lumpur was two Malay men in our neighborhood. I met Nasir at a party in the home of our mutual neighbor. The host, who thought much of his own uninformed opinion, announced to the rest of the men having coffee that there were fourteen women in the world for every man! I saw Nasir roll his eyes and sensed, "Ah, that man is probably a better thinker."

He was. A retired former chief financial officer for a power company, Nasir had gone to university in Perth, Australia. He was totally relaxed with me, his senior by three years. He invited me to his patio for coffee. Discovering that he methodically walked three miles every morning (except Sunday) at 7:20 precisely, I decided to join him.

Over the next five years, we chatted about every world problem and a spectrum of views from various religions. Of course, I provided some sort of biblical exposition at least twice a week.

It was clear that he was a Muslim only in the sense that Islam provided his community identity. He didn't pray – except to recite a memorized prayer in Arabic at his mother's grave once a year. When I asked him if this action provided some merit for him or for her, he replied almost with impatience, "C'mon, Greg, I'm the eldest brother. It's a family obligation." So was being married by the imam in the mosque. Otherwise, he seldom went there.

In every culture, one must learn how to define a real friend. In Malaysia, a friend is one who is there when you need him or her – no matter how inconvenient it is. Nasir is the only Malay I felt I could call when my car wouldn't start in the underground parking lot at the mall.

Though we've now moved back to England, I still phone him occasionally, and it's always a pleasure to chat with him. When I passed through Kuala Lumpur in 2009 and again in 2012, we took our traditional walk together. To my surprise, he opened the conversation with, "You're going to heaven, Greg. And so am I. The Buddhists have got it right. Peace and compassion. That pretty much sums it up." In all of those walks and talks, I had managed to convert a Muslim – into becoming a Buddhist!

My mission training had taught me not to put all my evangelistic eggs in one basket. But where else could I find a thinking man with whom I could discuss the claims of Christ? I had wondered whether there was a Malay Rotary Club, but before I could ask about it, a Malaysian Indian Christian told me that he was moving to the United States. His one regret was that his departure would leave his Rotary Club without a witness of Christ. Would I like for him to sponsor me for membership?

In the providence of God, I had joined the Rotary Club many years earlier when I pastored in Aspen, so it was a transfer membership. My Frontiers co-workers insisted that I present myself with a secular identity – as a history professor whose doctoral work was on the history of Christian–Muslim relations, which was technically correct. However, as I look back, I wish I had identified myself as a professor of history *and* the Bible! If I had, I might have been able to host a course on the Bible in our home. Those who had any inclination to know what the *Injil* teaches could have studied with us. They could have avoided potential embarrassment by telling their families, "It's a course. Aren't we supposed to honor the prophet Isa al-Masih? How can we honor him if we don't know what he taught?"

Relationships grew friendly at Rotary, although again, conversations about the Creator were always short-lived. Then, for a banquet, the Chinese Rotarians hired male

transvestites as strippers! Sally and I walked out. We made
a bit of a fuss at the next club meeting. Taking it as personal
criticism, the president searched for me on the Internet and
discovered that I'd written *Planting Churches in Muslim Cities*.
The executive committee called me in. They liked me. (In fact,
I got the feeling that they liked me better than they liked the
club president.) But they asked me, "Do you realize that it's
very difficult to get Malay Muslims to join the Rotary Club?
It's generally perceived as a drinking club. If people realize
there is a Christian missionary in the club, we'll really have
trouble recruiting Muslims. Would you consider switching to
a Chinese club for the good of our club?"

"Of course. For the good of the club, I'll resign," I told
them.

I had sponsored another missionary to join the club. They
asked me whether he was with Frontiers. Since he was sent by
the mission board of the Evangelical Presbyterian Church, I
assured them that he was not with Frontiers. They asked no
further questions. A few weeks later, they asked John to bring
me to the club's annual golf tournament. All but the president
welcomed me warmly.

Malay Muslims are avid golfers. I had known that before
we left California, so I had asked my Father God to lead me
to a yard sale where some divorcee would be selling off her
husband's $500 set of golf clubs. The very next day, I found
exactly that and walked away with a great set, plus accessories,
for only $30.

The hazards on Kuala Lumpur's twenty-five golf courses
include more than just water features and sand pits – there,

you'll also find monkeys who drop out of the trees and steal your ball, and monitor lizards who waddle in front of you as you're about to swing the club!

At the tournament banquet that evening, the club held a drawing for various prizes. At the end of the evening, I was surprised to see one of my former club members look at me and smile as he announced, "The grand prize goes to... Greg Livingstone!"

I knew the prize draw had been fixed. This was their way of saying, "We like you and are very sorry you had to leave the club." We gave the prize, a washing machine, to a Malay believer who had been washing her family's clothes by hand.

By the time we had lived in Malaysia for five years, I realized that I had failed to be the disciple maker I had hoped to be. Sally had discipled one Malay woman, who had found the Lord while studying in New Zealand before we met her. But I hadn't helped even one man decide to follow Christ. On the other hand, during those five years, the number of other disciple makers among Malay Muslims increased from fewer than twenty to nearly ninety – just as some friends had predicted. I realized again that I'm just a sheepdog for Jesus.

CHAPTER 29

Home

As much as it disappointed me, my evangelistic score of zero was not the reason we left Malaysia.

Sally and I had been visiting Frontiers teams in India when suddenly she became emotionally paralyzed. She dropped into a deep depression. By the time we returned to Kuala Lumpur, Sally didn't want to leave the house, or cook, or do anything. She did not speak more than absolutely necessary – only one to three words at a time. The doctors were stumped. So was I. So were our team members.

Our overseers pointed out that there were two good reasons for us to leave Malaysia. Although the number of Frontiers teams working among Malays had grown from two to nine, several of the team leaders were afraid to meet together. My being asked to leave the Rotary Club made some of them feel that the police knew who I was, so some of the other team leaders feared my presence might get them expelled.

But the primary reason to leave Malaysia was that Sally simply could not function. I realized that my dear wife had loyally followed me around the world for forty-three years.

Perhaps it was time to allow her to retire. "Sally," I told her, "you've followed me to so many countries, setting up home twenty-six times. I think the next home should be the one from which we'll go to heaven. You should choose where that will be. I'll trust that I can do whatever I'm supposed to do from wherever you want to live."

She was unambivalent: "I want to go back to our home in England."

Providentially, the colleagues who had been renting our English home were preparing to move back to the United States at the same time. Co-workers in High Wycombe took care of everything to prepare the house so that Sally didn't need to do anything. We still had a family in Frontiers.

While we lived in Malaysia, I had begun to modify my round-the-clock work life. Feeling the need to make the most of every opportunity, I usually worked every day until 10:00 p.m. My overseers exhorted me to put a 6:00 p.m. quitting time firmly in place and to remember that I had a wife whose main love language was "presence." Now, I curbed my work life even more in order to focus on taking care of Sally. She still couldn't cook, clean, or converse. She only slept, did jigsaw puzzles, and read Victorian novels. When her younger sister Mary died of cancer, Sally felt nothing. I attended the funeral in France without her. It was as if all of Sally's emotions were unplugged. She had no fears, no joys, no interest in anything. So I learned a bit about how to clean house, do the shopping, and heat up frozen dinners. Taking care of Sally was a refresher course in servanthood and patience.

When I wasn't busy running our household, I worked a bit on the history textbook that had lain dormant for six years. I found it difficult to have no role within the organization I had founded, yet by this time in life I had come to understand that it is God himself who orders our steps. Any argument I had would need to be with him.

We sought solutions for Sally's condition from all over. Her brother, Dr. Charles Coltman, made appointments for her at the renowned Mayo Clinic in Minnesota. After a week's battery of tests, they shrugged their shoulders. Oxford University's neurological specialists called it bipolar depression, saying, "This is the worst kind. It's the there's-no-point-in-anything kind of depression that does not respond to medicines." I deeply appreciated the ladies on the office team, as well as Hilary from our church in Hazlemere, who took turns visiting and praying for Sally.

Well-meaning friends of all theological stripes advocated their favorite therapies or special kind of prayer. Various ones advised everything from getting an affectionate dog, to using a sun lamp, or even flying to a particular church in Florida for healing prayer. The local psychiatrist advocated electric shock treatment. Eventually, I sensed that the Lord directed us to stop searching for a silver-bullet solution and simply to wait until our Father was ready to say the word.

In his time, two years and eight months after it had descended during our trip in India, the Lord lifted Sally's darkness. Her happy, affectionate, and creative self re-emerged. Yet the Lord, in his mysterious wisdom, continues to allow us to alternate between "rainy" months and "sunny" ones. We don't know why, but we accept what happens and adjust to it. We've learned simply to press on in obedience to our lifetime calling, whether she's up or down. Evangelicals in years past had too many pat answers, taking the mystery out of the Christian life. Sally and I have come to realize that God's people suffer in the same way as non-Christians. Some have diabetes or multiple sclerosis or migraines or cancer, and still others are in wheelchairs. That's just how it is in a fallen world. Now in our seventies, we are both fully aware that the mind and body will lose ground sooner or later. Still we are at peace, knowing without doubt that God our Father does all things well.

Sally grants me much affirmation for taking care of her. And in the periods when she has more energy, we're dancing; our marriage is a delight. We're like two new lovers. I'm mindful of the poem *Rabbi Ben Ezra* by Robert Browning, which starts with these lines:

> *Grow old along with me!*
> *The best is yet to be,*
> *The last of life, for which the first was made:*
> *Our times are in His hand.*

CHAPTER 30

You've Got Libya

After we returned from Malaysia to England, the make-it-happen activist that God created in me found it difficult to stay off the recruiting trail for very long. When Sally improved, the Lord gradually added responsibilities back into my commission. Locally, I set to work rebuilding a team of people committed to planting a church among Pakistani Muslims in High Wycombe.

My denomination (the Evangelical Presbyterian Church) asked me to help form and send out new church planting teams. While we lived in Pasadena in the early days of Frontiers, we had discovered this fledgling denomination that immediately felt like home to us. Before long, I was re-ordained as a pastor/teaching elder within the EPC. After Malaysia, I sensed that I ought to make myself available to build up the denomination's mission agency, World Outreach. Digging into history, I wrote a paper to demonstrate that it was Presbyterians who were the first pioneer church planters among Muslims in Turkey, the Middle East, Egypt, Iran, Afghanistan, Pakistan, North India, and Indonesia. As that paper circulated, the denomination decided that the Muslim world was our mandate; they resolved to pick up the dropped baton. George Carey, the director of World Outreach, appointed me as their coordinator for ministries to Muslims. In that capacity, I launched a project to place eighty new pioneering missionaries from EPC churches on teams. The goal is to birth churches among Muslims where the church isn't. By the time I left the job six years later, seven of EPC's eleven presbyteries had committed to raising up, underwriting, and providing member care to pioneering EPC teams. The other four presbyteries had plans in the works.

The EPC assignment occupied some of my energies, but not all. So I had a huddle with my King, the Lord Jesus. "What else, Lord?"

"Have you forgotten? You've got Libya."

I had showed up at the Friday night prayer meeting at Moody Bible Institute in 1959 hoping to drink a cup of coffee, eat a few doughnuts, and meet some girls. Instead, I met George Verwer, who gave me an assignment for prayer. Over the years, while we worked in Europe, India, and the Middle East, mobilizing others to live among Muslim peoples, Libya remained a special, unrevoked assignment. In 1971, when I was in Beirut, I sent four OM guys into Libya to distribute Gospels of Luke. They were jailed for eight months. In 1980, when I was with North Africa Mission, I challenged the four Penn State graduates to teach English in Libya for a year. But

I'd never been there myself. More importantly, there was still no church among the 6 million Libyans.

I heard about an annual meeting of people from many agencies at work in North Africa. I sensed I ought to attend in order to find out what was happening in Libya. While there, I learned that the entire missionary force in Libya was only three Canadian couples.

Because Gaddafi had blown up a Pan American plane over Scotland in 1988, American President Ronald Reagan had dropped a bomb on Gaddafi's house. Americans and Brits were both forbidden and unwelcome in Libya. Mission agency leaders could see no way to place missionaries there.

In my years as a sheepdog, I had realized that Americans tend to be initiators. We're not so strong on following through. We're not necessarily deep. But Americans love to hear the challenge: "This isn't being done. Roll up your sleeves. We're gonna try it." I felt that one of the reasons there were no missionaries in Libya was because American passports weren't allowed.

A small group of folk in Europe and North America had been praying for Libya for years. This old sheepdog began to nip at the heels of these mission leaders: "Isn't it time to take the next step? Let's find God's answer for placing long-term disciple makers and church planters in Libyan cities."

With fresh energy, we renewed our prayers to find ways for disciple makers to reside in the country. While some veterans rolled their eyes, we asked the Lord of the harvest to send seventy new workers who would be hired by Libyans into local jobs by Christmas 2012.

In February 2011, the people's revolutionary movement, which quickly came to be called the Arab Spring, burst into Libya. Their civil war brought to an end Gaddafi's forty-two-year dictatorship. Suddenly, this "closed" country was open to all nationalities – even Americans!

Since the new government was still in flux, getting a visa was no mean feat, but with the help of others, Sally and I managed to get the coveted stamps in our passports in May 2012. Fifty-two years and five months after that prayer-meeting commission back at Moody, Sally and I landed in Libya. It felt as though we were entering the Promised Land. "Thank you, Father!" I exclaimed. "You let us visit here before we came home to you!"

The revolution was still fresh for the Libyan people. They were basking in their new freedom, eager to get acquainted with the rest of the world on fresh new terms. Beginning with our fellow travelers on the flight, almost every Libyan we met greeted us warmly. On the streets, in shops and homes, the Libyans we met repeatedly said to us: "Welcome! Welcome! Welcome!"

Not long after, the national exuberance tempered, as extremists prevented a new government from forming and low-level chaos became the new norm. Some Christians who entered the country to assist with its development were jailed; one died in prison.

In spite of setbacks, two things have kept me going all of these years. One is that I keep focused on "that day" – that day when I'm going to meet the Lord Jesus face to face. As he was able to say to his Father, I want to be able to say to him: "I've accomplished what you sent me to do." That's what keeps me focused. I feel like a marathon runner who just wants to fall into the coach's arms at the finish line and see his big smile. I want to hear the Lord Jesus say those most wonderful words: "You've run the race to win. Well done, good and faithful servant."

The other thing that has kept my life focused is an image from Jesus' parable about the steward of a rich ruler in Luke 16:9. Jesus tells his disciples to make "friends… who will welcome you into eternal dwellings" (my paraphrase). Here's how I picture it. I think that when we reach heaven, we'll all get a print-out. (It's the one place where all of the computers will work well!) On my print-out will be a list of all of the people whom God used in my life – Judith who lured me into the Baptist church, her parents who took me home for a chicken dinner, the pastor who steered me toward a Christian college, the father-figures at Wheaton and elsewhere, George Verwer and my other fellow OMers – all of the people who nurtured me to follow the Lord Jesus with all my heart.

Why? So I can welcome them into eternal dwellings. Imagine everyone in heaven – a number that no one can count – and we've all got our print-outs. I want my name on thousands of those print-outs!

Those two pictures of being welcomed into heaven – by Jesus and by those whose lives we've touched – are what keep Sally and me going.

An Afterword

by Sally Livingstone

I married a whirlwind.

I went to many places with that whirlwind, and I am glad of that! Many people have asked why I married Greg. I tell them, "He's handsome. He's got a sense of humor. And God told me to do it!" There were times when I had to remember that God told me to marry him. But I know that I was called to him, and I was called to the ministry God gave us. Having celebrated our fiftieth wedding anniversary, I can honestly say that Greg and I are more in love than ever.

It's true that some of the places we ended up living in were real dumps! Memorable among them were the house with bed bugs in Toronto, the small house in Pasadena where Greg and I slept on the porch, and the shared community house where I, as an introvert, had to stretch to make conversation with others all of the time.

Some people may think that it's no wonder I'm depressed, considering our nomadic life. But I don't think there's any connection between my depression and the lifestyle we've lived. I didn't start to experience depression until after we came back to the United States, and we had already been living in a lot of exotic places before that!

I especially enjoyed our time in Lebanon. Paul was born there, and we rented an apartment for the family. Other couples on our team had young children, so that was helpful. Evan liked the British school he attended, and we had fun taking the kids into the mountains in the summer.

Our years in Aspen were also a very good experience for me. It felt good to lead a Bible study with young women in the church. And of course, Aspen is a beautiful place to live, and the boys loved it.

I love to study, so it was a real joy to go back to university in Philadelphia to earn my master's degree in counseling. But the low-grade depression continued. Therapy helped substantially, but then the move to Pasadena was very hard for me. I had thrived as a counselor in a clinic in Philadelphia, but in Pasadena I ended up working in a counseling relationship that dragged me down. Greg's mother and her husband Carl lived with us, so those relational demands were also on top of me at a time when I was struggling with my own depression. When I ended up in the hospital, I was so thankful that Greg made the effort to visit me – every day – even though he had to drive ninety minutes each way. When I have told him what I need, he has been very supportive. To this day, he has never been ashamed that I have been depressed. He just sees it as an illness for which one needs medication – like diabetes. That has been very affirming.

We found a psychiatrist who sent me home from the hospital with some new medication that helped to stabilize my mood. Not long after that, we moved to England. Since then, I've had ups and downs, including a very long time down that started when my Malaysian doctor changed my medication to a less effective one.

So yes, there were difficult times. But I never had a time when I thought I should never have married Greg. I had such a strong communication from God that I was supposed to marry him! I think that my confidence that God had spoken to me about the matter has helped to keep that commitment strong.

In 2000, at the Frontiers conference when Greg stepped down as international director, it brought me such joy to see all the teams that came up on stage to honor us. It was a wonderful experience to see all those people who were living out the gospel in different areas around the world – especially the women who are on the field with children. I know the sacrifice they're making to do the work that God's called them to do.

I'll admit that I have asked the Lord, "Why didn't you make me different?" I thought, "It would have been helpful if I were more gifted in hospitality." I've never been able to have people in our home easily. God's answer to me was, "I made you the way you are because I want you to be who you are!"

One time when I visited my sister, I told her, "I don't think I could ever manage to take care of a house like you do. I would be too overwhelmed by it."

She responded, "But you're very good at what you're doing – moving here, moving there. That's such a gift!" The truth is that Greg didn't drag me around the world. Missions was my calling even before I met him, and I'm glad we are on this journey together.

At our fiftieth wedding anniversary celebration, I asked our friends to sing this song with me. It captures how I feel as I look back over our life together:

"Never Once" by Matt Redman

Standing on this mountaintop
Looking just how far we've come
Knowing that for every step
You were with us

Kneeling on this battle ground
Seeing just how much you've done
Knowing every victory
Was your power in us

Scars and struggles on the way
But with joy our hearts can say
Yes, our hearts can say

Never once did we ever walk alone
Never once did you leave us on our own
You are faithful, God, you are faithful

Epilogue

Snapshot of an Itinerant Life

- 6 months in **Boston** – birth.
- 6.5 years in **San Diego** with three sets of foster parents.
- 6 years in **La Jolla** with my mother and Aunt Charlotte, then mother and Bob Livingston.
- 6 months in **New Jersey** with my Berge grandparents.
- 5 years in **Aspen** in middle school and high school.
- 5 years at **Wheaton** in college and birthing OM.
- 6 months in **France, Spain, and England** with OM.
- 1.5 years in **India** with OM.
- 3 years in **Austria, UK, Germany, Switzerland, and Holland** leading evangelistic university missions, and recruiting and coaching workers.
- 6 months back in **Wheaton** to finish a master's degree.
- 2 years in **Belgium** leading the team at OM's European headquarters.

- 2 years based in **Lebanon** to catalyse outreach throughout the Middle East and North Africa.

- 1 year in **Toronto** to birth OM Canada, then traveling in a camper around the USA.

- 6 months in **Iran and India** as a chaplain on the *Logos*.

- 6 months in **Rosemead** studying at California State University.

- 3 years in **Aspen** as senior pastor of my home church.

- 5 years in **Philadelphia** with North Africa Mission.

- 9 years in **Pasadena** birthing Frontiers and the Zwemer Institute of Muslim Studies, and earning a doctorate at Biola University.

- 9 years in **Horsleys Green and High Wycombe** developing Frontiers internationally.

- 1.5 years in **Pasadena** teaching at Fuller Theological Seminary.

- 5 years in **Kuala Lumpur** on a church planting team and recruiting new missionaries.

- Since 2006 in **High Wycombe**, church planting among Pakistanis, recruiting for the Evangelical Presbyterian Church, mobilizing workers for Libya, and working on a history of Christian mission among Muslims.

- 2 weeks (finally... 52+ years after God called me) in **Libya** in 2012.

When Sally's post-Malaysia darkness lifted, she told me she wanted to travel with me. So we have visited Argentina, Brazil, Switzerland, and Norway, recruiting God's people to die to their careers at home in order to reside in cities where the prince of darkness still holds sway over Muslim men, women, and children. Inviting our grandchildren along, we also took time to see the sights in each of these countries. (See how I've changed!)

I was sorely tempted to throw myself into a new Frontiers effort to recruit 500 Indian workers and 100 expats to form church planting teams among India's 170 million Muslims. My merciful heavenly Father used several circumstances to show me that India, this time, was a bridge too far.

But why would I even be tempted? Because 86 percent of the 1.7 billion Muslim men, women, and children on the planet are unaware that the Creator has ever visited the earth and sacrificed himself as their redeemer. At the moment, they are unlikely to meet anyone who speaks their language who will tell them the Christmas and Easter stories.

As far as I'm aware, the Lord has only ever given me two dreams. I mean, the biblical kind of dream with spiritual meaning that you have while you're asleep. I'll close with the one that disturbs my waking thoughts.

Two Muslim men died. They had been decent men – good family men. They didn't beat their wives. They worked hard to get their kids through school. They sought to be faithful in their prayers, though they didn't always manage to perform the prescribed five prayers a day because their jobs kept them working long hours.

Suddenly, they were in darkness. They weren't screaming, but they were in shock. It was the moment of truth. They realized Mohammed was not the way, the truth, or the one who was the door to paradise. They had been deceived. They were stunned, speechless.

Eventually, one of them found his voice and whispered to the other:

"Did you… did you… ever have a Christian friend?"

The other man was deeply thoughtful. Then he replied sadly, "No. No, I never did. Did you?"

The first man, looking down into the darkness in agony, gnashing his teeth, paused for what seemed to be a full minute. "No… I didn't either."

Bibliography

Dorr, D. (June 2004). "Transitions to Second-Generation Leadership in Mission Societies: a Medley of Insights and Comparative Profiles of Three Notable Societies." Unpublished essay submitted in fulfillment of course work, William Carey International University.

Gillquist, P. (1970). *Love is Now*. Grand Rapids: Zondervan.

Hession, R. (1950). *The Calvary Road*. Retrieved 25 September 2013 from christianissues.biz: http://www.christianissues.biz/pdf-bin/sanctification/thecalvaryroad.pdf

Livingstone, G. (1993). *Planting Churches in Muslim Cities: A Team Approach*. Grand Rapids: Baker Book House.

McCurry, D. M. (ed.) (1979). *The Gospel and Islam*. Monrovia, CA: MARC.

Piper, J. (2002). *Brothers, We Are NOT Professionals: A Plea to Pastors for Radical Ministry*. Nashville: Broadman & Holman Publishers.

Randall, I. (2008). *Spiritual Revolution: The Story of OM*. Milton Keynes: Authentic Publishing.

Steele, F. R. (1981). *Not in Vain: The Story of North Africa Mission*. Pasadena: William Carey Library.

Trotman, D. (n.d.). *Born to Reproduce*. Retrieved 23 September 2013 from NavPress.com: http://www.navpress.com/product/9781615216574/Born-to-Reproduce-Dawson-Trotman

Wiebe, A. (2006). *How Wide is my Valley*.

Other Publications by Greg Livingstone

Planting Churches in Muslim Cities: A Team Approach. Grand Rapids: Baker Books, 1993.

The Visit to Earth by Our Lord Jesus Christ, According to Matthew. Sevenoaks, Kent: Firm Foundation Trust, 2000.

The Book of Acts. Secunderbad, India: OM Books, 2005.

Links of Interest

Frontiers: **www.frontiers.org**

OM International: **www.om.org**

Arab World Ministries (formerly North Africa Mission, now a part of Pioneers): **www.awm-pioneers.org**

Greg Livingstone: **www.greglivingstone.com**